Virtual Private Networks

Making the Right Connection

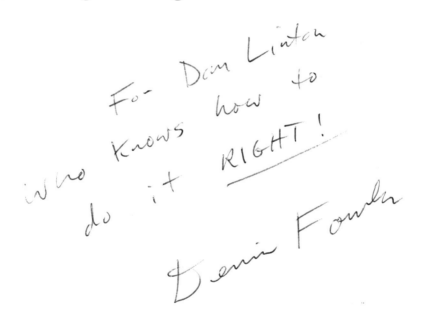

For Dan Linton
who knows how to
do it RIGHT!

Denis Fowler

Virtual Private Networks

Making the Right Connection

Dennis Fowler

netWorker Magazine,
Association for Computing Machinery

MORGAN KAUFMANN PUBLISHERS, INC.
San Francisco, California

Senior Editor	Jennifer Mann
Director of Production and Manufacturing	Yonie Overton
Production Editor	Cheri Palmer
Editorial Assistant	Karyn Johnson
Cover Design	Ross Carron Design
Cover Image	© Patrick Ingrand/Tony Stone Images
Text Design	Side by Side Studios
Copyeditor	Jeff Van Bueren
Proofreader	Jennifer McClain
Composition and Illustration	Technologies 'n Typography
Indexer	Ty Koontz
Printer	Courier Corporation

Designations used by companies to distinguish their products are often claimed as trademarks or registered trademarks. In all instances where Morgan Kaufmann Publishers, Inc. is aware of a claim, the product names appear in initial capital or all capital letters. Readers, however, should contact the appropriate companies for more complete information regarding trademarks and registration.

Morgan Kaufmann Publishers, Inc.
Editorial and Sales Office
340 Pine Street, Sixth Floor
San Francisco, CA 94104-3205
USA

Telephone	415 / 392-2665
Facsimile	415 / 982-2665
Email	*mkp@mkp.com*
WWW	*http://www.mkp.com*
Order toll free	800 / 745-7323

Library of Congress Cataloging-in-Publication Data

Fowler, Dennis.
    Virtual private networks : making the right connection / Dennis
Fowler.
      p.   cm.
    Includes bibliographical references.
    ISBN 1-55860-575-4
    1. Extranets (Computer networks)   2. Business enterprises—computer networks.
3. Internet (Computer network)   4. Computer networks—Security measures.   I. Title.
TK5105.875.E87F69 1999
650'.0285'46—DC21
                                        99-13845
                                          CIP

To Peggy, my ever patient wife,
without whom nothing would be possible,
with whom anything is.

Foreword

Susan Scheer Aoki
Cisco Systems, Inc.

It is a new world in networking. The advent of the twenty-first century invites new ways of thinking about global networks. We are on the brink of a huge transformation. Enterprises are seeking value and network services from providers to support their intranet and extranet applications—integrated voice and data—and access options ranging from dial to broadband. Service providers seek to meet this customer demand for intelligent services by building global networks increasingly built on packets to offer customers complete service solutions tailored to their particular business. Virtual private networks (VPNs) are an excellent example of new world services that benefit both enterprise customers and service providers.

Increasing demands from feature-rich applications and an ever growing, widely dispersed workforce are causing enterprises of all sizes to rethink their network strategies. Network managers must continually find ways to connect dispersed sites to ever growing corporate intranets efficiently and cost-effectively. As companies expand their reach to include partners and suppliers, and the number of remote users grow, building a distributed enterprise becomes ever more challenging.

VPNs have emerged to provide an alternative to private networks. VPNs are enterprise-scale connectivity deployed on a shared infrastructure with the same policies as a private network. Businesses that run their intranets over a VPN enjoy the same security, prioritization, management, and reliability capabilities as in their private network. A VPN can be built on the Internet or on a service provider's IP, frame relay, or ATM infrastructure. Virtual private networks include access VPNs for remote access, intranet VPNs for site-to-site connectivity, and extranet VPNs for business-to-business communication.

In deploying a VPN, business customers have two choices in the extreme: One, business customers can build their own VPN over the public Internet; or two, business customers can purchase a VPN service from a provider. When customers choose to build their own VPN, they integrate the products and technologies from multiple networking vendors, they design the network, they deploy the network over the Internet, and they support its operation. When business customers purchase a VPN from a provider, they enjoy an outsourced network service. As with few things in life, the choices are not binary. Business customers who purchase a VPN service, at the very least administer their own authentication, authorization, and accounting (AAA) server, and they may elect to encrypt traffic over their VPN service.

The advantages of VPNs are clear. VPNs can save on average 40–60% costs over a private network, and they can simplify connectivity to remote locations through the global span of the Internet. As an outsourced service from a provider, VPNs can simplify the operations of the wide area network, provide access to scare networking expertise, and enable the business to focus on core competencies.

Because of these business advantages, the industry is abuzz with excitement. Clearly understanding the advantages of a VPN and its technical implications are a prerequisite regardless if you choose to deploy a VPN or purchase one from your service provider. Dennis Fowler provides an insightful view to both the business benefits and technical requirements to VPNs. He mitigates the complexity and objectively reviews the pros and cons in choosing a VPN. His examples of other customers' experiences with VPNs breathe life into the discussion. In this regard, this book offers the reader a practical understanding to VPNs and provides the foundation for evaluating if VPNs make sense for you.

Contents

Preface

Almost lost in the glare and thunder of the Web is the fact that, at its heart, the Internet is a communications medium. Like the telephone network, it can serve many functions. Several years ago a few pioneering businesses and organizations discovered that, by using the public infrastructure of the Internet and its ilk, they could tie offices and facilities together in a new, exciting, cost-effective way, no matter where they were located, by building virtual private networks (VPNs). VPNs use robust, redundant public networks such as the Internet, instead of expensive and vulnerable leased lines, for their wide area networks and extranets. These businesses also discovered that, by letting their road warriors log on to the home network through the Internet, they could be freed from the expensive tyranny of long-distance dial-up telephone networks for remote access to the home network.

This interest caught the attention of Internet and networking service providers and of major networking hardware and software developers and vendors, all of whom are now feeding this burgeoning market. These include communications giants such as AT&T, MCI, and Sprint; networking hardware stalwarts such as Cisco and 3Com; software players such as Microsoft, Check Point, and Novell; and hundreds of others.

As VPN technologies have developed, so, too, has massive confusion—confusion as to just what a VPN is, what it can do for you, and how to implement one.

This book is intended to clear away the confusion. It explains what VPNs are, what they can do for you, and how they work, and it lays out the choices you have in planning and implementing your own virtual private network. The book also tells you what to expect once you have a VPN up and running. It covers both the positive side of VPNs and the pitfalls to avoid as you consider this technology.

Audience

The book is aimed at executives, managers, and upper-level technicians who are unfamiliar with VPNs and the technologies that make them possible. If you are a manager looking for a way to connect your office network in New York with the factory in Potstown, or you are trying to cut the phone bills of your reps around the country, this is the book for you. It shows you how you can give your mobile sales force direct access to the home office network so they have the latest product information. It explains how the Internet can be used to tie together the local area networks in your satellite facilities into one super network so that the entire workforce can be brought to bear on an opportunity or problem.

A Road Map

To simplify your reading, the book is divided into three sections. If you are a manager or an executive unfamiliar with VPNs, you should begin at the beginning. The first three chapters will show you just exactly what a VPN is and, drawing on real-life examples of VPNs in use today, what it can do for you. To keep you from getting too rosy a view of the situation, however, you will also see that VPNs have their risks, just as they have their rewards. We attempt to give you a balanced perspective so that you can make a reasonable decision as to whether a VPN is really what you want to get involved with.

Chapter 4 is a bridging chapter, of interest to executives and managers as well as to the more technically oriented. It discusses the choices of networks you have for implementing your VPN. While it does carry information for the technically inclined, this information is also important for managers as well, to help them understand that the Internet is not necessarily the best choice for a VPN substrate, that there are other options that it is important to explore, what those options are, how they work in comparison to the Internet, and the advantages and disadvantages of the available infrastructures.

The middle section of the book, beginning with Chapter 5, is more technically oriented and is aimed more at the technician; it discusses the various elements that go into a VPN. One of the crucial problems is keeping your private data private as it traverses the public networks, and this is where encryption comes into the VPN picture. In Chapter 5, you'll get a thorough grounding in what encryption is, what the various types of encryption are, and how they are combined and implemented to protect your data. Chapter 6 continues this theme by discussing the problems that encryption itself raises: authenticating users for access to data, verifying the integrity of the data after it has been transmitted, and ensuring that only the right people get the keys needed to decrypt the data. Chapter 7 ties all this together with a discussion of the various protocols there are to choose from to implement your VPN, protocols that incorporate encryption, authentication, and key management along with tunneling and other elements needed to provide secure connections through public networks. This chapter discusses the latest work of the Internet Engineering Task Force to bring order to the chaos of VPN protocols. Chapter 8 discusses the basic architecture decisions you will need to make, whether in hardware or software, which will strongly depend on your own situation.

The book's last two chapters get down to the nuts and bolts of implementing a VPN. Chapter 9 steps you through the process of planning your VPN. It discusses the many factors—technical, financial, and human—that you must consider as you embark on your project and the step-by-step planning you should follow so you can implement a VPN that meets your needs. Chapter 10 tells you what to expect once you get your VPN up and running: the issues that you must be prepared to deal with and what you can expect when you are managing it.

Content

This book, quite deliberately, is not brand or product specific, although it does describe most of the proprietary and nonproprietary VPN solutions that are currently available. The market is changing too rapidly to be more specific. During the course of the writing of this book, new companies entered the market and others left; new protocols appeared and old ones faded. For example, it was just as the first draft was nearing completion that Sun Microsystems introduced Sun.NET, a new Java-based VPN technology.

What this book seeks to do is show you the basic principles at work and the strengths and weaknesses of major products that will be available when you have this hard copy in your hands, to allow you to select those that will best meet your needs.

To help deal with the jargon, this book includes a glossary of Internet and VPN terms for easy reference. A bibliography gives recent literature, both corporate and public. There are also two appendices. Appendix A presents a list of VPN developers, vendors, and service providers. This is anything but a definitive list—again, the technology and market are changing too rapidly for that—but the list will offer a wide variety of contacts for you as you plan your project. Appendix B lists a number of resources you can tap into that relate to the Internet and VPNs.

Acknowledgments

As with any book of this nature, there is no way that I could have done this alone. Throughout its creation I have been aided by many people. The willingness of busy IT professionals to share that most valuable resource, time, never ceases to astonish me. Foremost among them are Glenn Botkin of Galaxy Scientific Corporation, Pat Patterson of Mazzio's Corporation, and Ariel Friedman, Earl Evans, and Mike Gentry.

Then there was the assistance of those who are directly involved with making this technology available and workable: Mark Elliot and Keith R. Wilber of Check Point Software; Rob Spence, Director of Product Marketing, Aventail Corporation; Christopher Ian Ogg and Steve May of The Wizard's Gate; Tim Gerchar, Product Marketing Manager for Compatible Systems Corporation; Kevin Kalajan of Sun Microsystems; and Carey Knapper of Lucent Technologies.

For helping with the development of the original proposal and outline, and for their patient reviewing of my manuscript as it grew, I must particularly thank Glenn Botkin, *PC Week* Contributing Editor Brian D. Jaffe, DuPont's Mike Minnich, Freelink Communication's David Dennis, Sportsline's Dan Leichtenschlag, and especially Marcus Ranum of Network Flight Recorder, Inc. for his vitally valuable assistance as I wrestled with the labyrinthine complexities of encryption, authentication, and key management. I'm also particularly grateful to Susan Scheer Aoki of Cisco Systems, not only for contributing the Foreword for this book but also for her valuable suggestions, especially with regard to her insight on the developing trends in VPN technology.

Finally, I must thank my editor at Morgan Kaufmann, Jennifer Mann, and her endlessly patient assistant, Karyn Johnson, and my production editor, Cheri Palmer, for bearing with me as, together, we beat this project into shape.

1

Defining the Virtual Private Networks

Virtual private networks (VPNs) have become a hot issue, the latest industry buzzword, one of the new "killer apps" of the Internet. Everything from extranets to workgroup systems to electronic commerce solutions has been hit with the tag "virtual private network." VPNs are being touted as incredible cost savers, infinitely flexible, and infinitely scalable. They can leap the broadest ocean and connect your most peripatetic account executive to the home network from anywhere in the world. Within reason, VPNs really are capable of all of those things. By leveraging the connective power of the Internet or other shared-backbone networking services, they do offer tremendous opportunities for expansive but cost-effective connectivity.

But beware of the hype. VPNs can offer awesome opportunities and benefits, but there are also some hidden costs and dangers, and some of the claims made for VPNs are exaggerations. Furthermore, the lack of standards has resulted in a welter of competing and not always compatible VPN products arriving on the market from firewall, router, and other network hardware vendors, as well as from software developers. Add to that the number of different ways there are to create a VPN, the variety of network services on which they can be created, the number of ways it is claimed they can be used, and the alleged (and sometimes inflated) benefits asserted to accrue from VPNs, and the confusion is monumental.

For example, marketers of network services other than the Internet will assure you the Internet is not the only medium on which a VPN can exist, which is true. However, this leads to VPNs also being sold by providers of networking services often described as frame relay or asynchronous transfer mode (ATM) networks, networks that are frequently promoted or at least implied to be totally distinct from the Internet, which they may be. But part of the confusion on this score arises because the line between some of these "private" public networks and the extremely "public" Internet as we think of it is anything but distinct; because these network service providers are frequently also Internet service providers, the confusion is further compounded.

If you've done a search on the World Wide Web for the keywords virtual private network or VPN, you've probably even discovered that for years companies like Pacific Bell have been marketing an extended telephone service using the same terms.

Thanks to all this confusion, it can be very hard to understand exactly what qualifies as a VPN, how a VPN can be implemented, and exactly what a VPN can and cannot do for you. That's what we'll explain for you here.

1.1 What Is a VPN?

Very simply put, a *virtual private network* uses a public network's infrastructure to make the connections among geographically dispersed nodes, instead of using cables owned or leased exclusively for one single network's use, as is typical for a wide area network (WAN). To the user, a VPN looks just like a private network, hence the *virtual* in its name, even though it is sharing a web of cables with the traffic of hundreds or thousands of other users at the same time. It has all the characteristics of a private network—limited access to only authorized users, for example—even though it is sharing the same public infrastructure with other users. Another way to describe it is that a VPN is a logical local area network (LAN) that connects an organization's geographically dispersed sites in a way that makes them all appear to be part of one single network.

There are a variety of public networks that can be employed to make a VPN's connections, but the most prominent and most public network available is, of course, the Internet. Because the Internet is everywhere and the Internet is where most of the VPN development is taking place, and because it is, as we'll see, the most ubiquitous and cost-effective medium for a VPN, we'll concentrate on VPNs running over it in this book. We will devote Chapter 4 to VPNs implemented through other networking services, and we will explain the differences in detail at that time, but since the Internet is the predominant medium and the technology is essentially the same regardless of the network being used, the Internet is where we will concentrate our discussion.

To illustrate how a VPN differs from a typical WAN, let's look at a leased-line network, as shown in Figure 1-1, and then show how a VPN differs from it. For the sake of simplicity, this is only a three-node network, a company headquarters and two branch offices linked together with three leased lines.

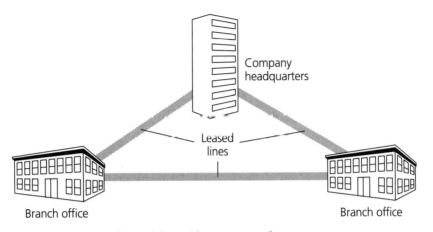

Figure 1-1   A typical leased-line wide area network.

Each office has to have a cable connecting it to each of the other facilities. Another arrangement would be to have the leased lines go through a hub, perhaps in the company headquarters.

Either way, with this type of network, the company actually owns the cable or pays a monthly fee for every mile of cable connecting its facilities, whether that cable is in use 10% or 100% of the time, whether it is being used to capacity or only a fraction of the capacity they're paying for. The costs escalate with every mile that separates the offices and with every node that is added to the network (requiring more strings of cable to connect it to the rest of the organization). Economies of scale are limited to what you can negotiate with the line provider, who is trying to recover from you all the costs for those cables.

Your message uses only those cables to get from point to point; there are no detours. Send a packet of data in one end of the cable and it travels right down that cable to the destination. It works much the same way the LAN connecting your office to the file server on your LAN does. This is a nice, secure connection, but it also means that if the cable is cut, perhaps by a backhoe operator putting in an irrigation line in an Iowa cornfield, that connection is down for the count. It will stay down until either the break is repaired or the traffic is rerouted manually around the break (if your agreement with the service provider offers that guarantee).

In a similarly simple three-node VPN, as Figure 1-2 shows, leased lines are dispensed with in favor of connecting each site to a public network. Instead of the hardwired pipeline between nodes of a standard wide area network using dedicated connections, the connections of a VPN are made through the web of cables, what is often described as the "cloud," of a public network such as the

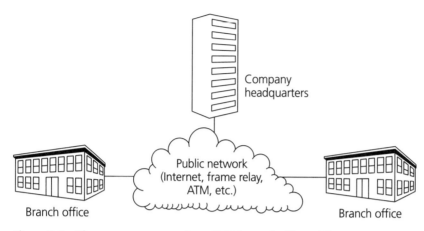

Figure 1-2   The same company using a VPN instead of leased lines.

Internet. Each office requires a single connection, most commonly a leased line and commonly referred to as a *local loop*, to the nearest public network *point of presence* (POP). That POP may be only a few feet away or it may be miles away. From that POP the data is carried by the web of connections—the cables, routers, and switches that make up the public network—to the POP serving the destination office, then through the local loop at that end on to their final destination.

As you can see, the connections—the local loops—between your company's offices and the public network are dramatically shortened. They can even be the "dry copper" connection provided by your local telephone service, perhaps an Integrated Services Digital Network (ISDN) connection. The costs for these short connections are correspondingly lower.

Within the cloud, however, as opposed to the leased-line design, there is no one single connection between point A and point B. Instead there is a web or matrix of cables connected by routers that the messages travel through. By using a public network—the Internet, for example—a network shared by hundreds or thousands or millions of other users, the cost of all those miles of cable is shared. We'll see further on in this chapter that this sharing can produce impressive savings.

It is also much more fail-safe than a single leased line, since a message can take any one of a number of different routes to its destination. It provides a redundancy, a safety net, that virtually guarantees that the traffic will continue to flow reasonably smoothly. If one cable is cut, the message will simply be routed automatically around the break to its destination, a service that is not generally available with a leased line.

1.2 What a VPN Is Good for and Why You Should Consider Building One

There are several uses for a VPN. It can be an extended intranet, connecting geographically distant facilities into a cohesive network. It can also be an extranet, linking, for example, customers and suppliers for increased efficiencies, such as electronic data interchange (EDI). Looked at this way, a VPN can do virtually anything that a more traditional leased-line WAN can do. In fact, so far it doesn't seem to offer services much different from any WAN.

But there is a third service that a VPN can offer that no leased-line WAN can offer, and that is in providing remote access services. A VPN lets road warriors with their laptops connect into the home office through an Internet service provider, riding through the public Internet to log on to the office network, rather than running up long-distance charges by dialing up to a remote access server thousands of miles away. As we'll see, that offers potentially impressive savings. While a VPN as an extranet or intranet offers some cost efficiencies over the typical WAN, the savings produced by using one for remote access are significant.

Hence the excitement that has developed over VPNs. Building a VPN would seem, at first glance, to be simple common sense. Why not take advantage of an existing infrastructure for the connections, instead of going to the expense of stringing your own cable or paying someone else to drag fiber through conduit to tie your facilities together? Or why go to the expense of leasing dedicated connections when they may only be used to a fraction of their capacity or for only a fraction of the time?

It does make sense, but as you'll see, there are downsides to VPNs. But before we take a look at the potential negative points to VPNs, let's see what the potential benefits are. As we said, there is a powerful logic to using an existing infrastructure to connect your facilities, rather than building your own.

The claims made for VPNs make them sound like the greatest invention since the electric light. The primary advantage cited is that a VPN is vastly less expensive than a network using leased lines. As we already mentioned, the VPN is also claimed to be more flexible and scalable, compared to a traditional WAN. Then, too, by using the international resources of the Internet, the vendors say that a VPN can offer connectivity virtually anywhere in the world. Finally, you'll hear that a VPN is an extremely cost-effective way to service a mobile workforce of telecommuters and road warriors.

To a degree, believe it or not, it's safe to say that most of these claims are true. Fortunately, some of them, such as actual dollar savings, are even measurable, while others are less tangible but no less real.

1.2.1 Economies of Sharing

It's a fact that a VPN escapes the cost of leasing the cables to connect your network. By using an existing public network for your VPN, you are sharing the cost of that public network with all the other customers. The cost of the public network is spread over a large customer base. You're not paying every month, by yourself, for every mile of each leased line, whether it is fully loaded 24 hours a day, 7 days a week or not. In most cases you're paying a flat, monthly fee that is a fraction of what you would pay for leased lines providing the same service.

Compare it to your personal telephone service, for example. While you pay a base charge for the local loop between your home and the telephone company's central office a block or two away, whether you are using it or not, you do not pay for every inch of cable between your home in Poughkeepsie, New York, and your daughter's dorm room at college in Palo Alto, California, whether you are using it or not, at least not directly. That cable is shared by thousands of callers, each paying perhaps a dime a minute for the time they are actually "online."

In the past, on long-distance telephone circuits, one call used one circuit, which was one pair of wires that could be traced from your home in Poughkeepsie to your daughter's dorm in Palo Alto. When you hung up on that call another took its place on the long-distance trunk, so at least you were only paying for time used. Today calls are multiplexed on that long-distance circuit, with the "silence" between words being filled with parts of other conversations. This spreads the cost of the wire over more than one customer, allowing each of them to enjoy the benefit of lower long-distance rates. From three dollars for 3 minutes the rates have dropped to three dimes for 3 minutes. But your conversation will still be carried over one circuit between Poughkeepsie and Palo Alto.

A packet-switched network such as the Internet allows even greater multiplexing, and thus greater efficiency, as each message is broken up into packets, and each packet is slotted in with others from other users and routed through a web of connections. No one circuit becomes overloaded, at least in theory, and every circuit, at any second, is efficiently utilized, carrying pieces of perhaps thousands of conversations. It also provides a safety net that a circuit-switched network or a leased line does not. If one link is overloaded or goes down, the traffic is automatically rerouted to its destination. (For a more complete description of how the Internet works, see Section 4.1.1.)

More importantly, the cost of all the fiber and copper and switches and routers is being spread over the millions of customers the Internet serves. You are leveraging to your advantage the investment in the hundreds of thousands of miles of cables and the uncounted routers and switches that go into making up the Internet. Your major expenses are only the cost of that short loop that connects your office to the network access server (NAS) or POP of your Internet service provider (ISP) and your monthly Internet fee. The average price for a leased T1 (1.544 Mbps) connection is about $1,800. A typical connection from a company's offices to the local ISP's POP costs $400 to $500 a month, because the chances are you'll actually use less than a full T1 line to your POP, perhaps even a 128 Kbps ISDN line or a digital subscriber line (DSL) of some sort at an even lower cost of $50 to $150 a month. If you're a small operation, your cost may be a monthly subscription for a dial-in connection to your ISP.

The savings can be considerable. According to a white paper by Infonetics Research, a study commissioned by Sun Microsystems estimated savings of from 20% to 47% by switching from leased lines to a VPN. In another analysis, Infonetics estimated savings of 20% to 40% for VPNs serving branch offices and 60% to 80% savings for a VPN serving remote access users. As we'll see later on in this chapter, when we look at the remote access aspect of VPNs, every analysis of VPNs produces similar savings estimates. The experiences of VPN users bolster those findings, as we'll see in Chapter 2.

Another source, *Data Communications* magazine, in their May 21, 1997, issue, ran their own numbers on a VPN, comparing leased lines, a frame relay service (see Chapter 4), and an Internet-based VPN solution (Table 1-1). The sample scenario was to connect three sites in the United States (Boston, Los Angeles, and Houston), plus one transatlantic link to London. All were connected at 64 Kbps. AT&T was the carrier and provided the charges, including local access circuits of 5 km to the nearest POP. Leased-line and frame relay figures were provided by Lynx Technologies, Inc. of Fairfield, New Jersey, a tariff tracking consultancy. Internet figures were based on average monthly ISP charges in the United States.

As the *Data Communications* analysis shows, the frame relay first-year cost is only about 17% lower than the cost for leased lines, but about twice the first-year cost for the Internet VPN. However, much of the frame relay

Table 1-1   *Data Communications* magazine VPN cost comparisons.

	Leased line	Frame relay VPN	Internet VPN
Annual charges	$133,272	$89,998	$38,400
Installation	$2,700	$5,760	
Four VPN encrypting devices		$16,000	$16,000
Total cost, first year	**$135,972**	**$111,758**	**$54,400**

first-year cost is the one-time charge for installation and the encryption devices. The annual charges (operating costs) are about two thirds of those for leased lines, though still more than double the annual charges for an Internet VPN.

By this analysis, the Internet is obviously the most economical choice for your VPN, but for the extra operating expense of the frame relay choice you do get added services that are not available on the Internet, as we'll discuss in Chapter 4. If you need those services, you'll see that, as economical as the Internet is, it is not the best choice for you.

Because of the way telephone charges are computed, the greater the distances and the larger your user base, the greater the savings you'll enjoy. Telephone charges are computed by the call, and the rates increase with the mileage covered. Distance means nothing to the Internet, and Internet service is usually billed at a flat rate, regardless of the number of times you use it or the amount of data transmitted. In Chapter 2 we'll look at some real-life VPNs and see how the savings can stack up in action.

1.2.2 Flexibility

It is true, also, that a VPN offers flexibility that is not available to a leased-line–based wide area network. To add a node to the latter requires leasing a new line, possibly more than one, perhaps even installing some cable. Leases have to be negotiated, perhaps rights-of-way arranged. Routers and switches have to be installed and configured.

Let's go back to our first three-node leased-line network. Your company, Giant Widgets, has long done business with Associated Grommets, a supplier of grommets for your widgets. Your company is flush with cash, the widgets market has been really strong lately, and you decide to buy the grommets factory. Once you've acquired it you want to put it on your existing network. Figure 1-3 shows what happens when you have to bring it into the loop of a leased-line network. Three new lines have to be leased and somehow integrated into your existing system.

Now let's take the same scenario if you're running an Internet-based VPN (Figure 1-4). You've purchased the grommets factory, and it just happens to already have a link to the Internet. They've been selling grommets through the Internet for years, after all. All that's needed is to slide into place the VPN system, generally a hardware box or some software, and they're on your network. Or suppose that instead of buying the Associated Grommets factory you just want to extend your VPN to it, turning your VPN from an intranet into an extranet. The scenario is essentially the same.

If you already have an Internet link on the facility you want to link to the VPN—for a Web site, for example, or email—getting your VPN up may be as

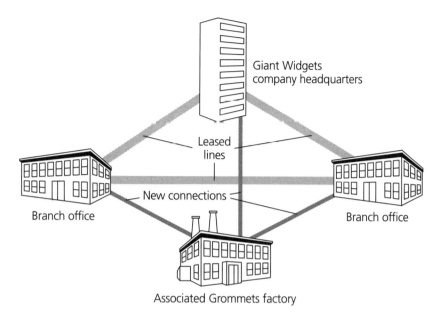

Figure 1-3   Adding one node to a leased-line WAN.

simple as installing a server and some software. For a small-scale VPN, if you're running Windows NT 4.0, adding a node to an existing VPN can be as simple as implementing the Point-to-Point Tunneling Protocol (PPTP) software that comes with the operating system and establishing a dial-up link to the Internet. A mobile user running Windows 98 can use PPTP to connect through the Internet for remote access to the home network from wherever he or she is. (But be forewarned: PPTP as implemented by Microsoft presents some serious security concerns, as we'll discuss in Chapter 7. Fortunately, it is scheduled to be replaced in Windows 2000.)

If speed is a requirement, you may need to call up your telephone provider and request a digital loop to their Internet service. If either ISDN or digital subscriber line (DSL) service is available, the existing copper that serves your telephone system may be put to use, saving the cost of stringing new cable, with only some terminators to be installed at your end. Another option worth exploring is the availability of Internet service through the cable TV network in your area, using a cable modem.

If your VPN is to serve as an intranet, connecting local area networks already up in distributed offices, it will require a router to connect you to the Internet and a firewall for protection from hackers. These may even be combined in one box that also integrates the VPN features along with its other functions. It still doesn't require leasing a thousand miles of dedicated cable.

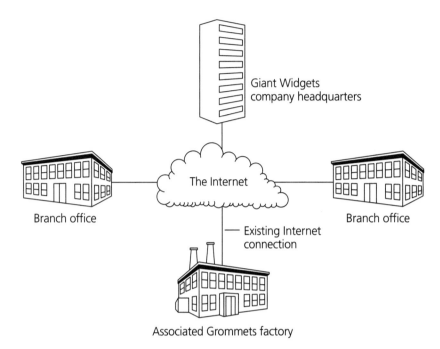

Giant Widgets
company headquarters

The Internet

Branch office

Branch office

Existing Internet
connection

Associated Grommets factory

Figure 1-4   Adding the Associated Grommets factory to your existing VPN. With an existing Internet link, it is almost plug and play.

So, turning your VPN into an extranet by adding a supplier or customer can be accomplished by negotiating a compatible VPN connection between you and them. As we'll see, this will not be as simple as plugging in a toaster, but it will still be less expensive than negotiating a dedicated connection. As the interoperability of VPN products improves, the problem will ease further.

1.2.3 Worldwide Connectivity on a Budget

With a VPN you can have a network node virtually wherever there is an Internet POP, and today the Internet is virtually everywhere, even on Tristan da Cunha, the remotest inhabited island in the world. For the cost of an Internet connection, a modest company that has overseas sales representatives can have them directly on their network, a luxury previously limited to major corporations with very deep pockets.

Even for a large corporation, the ubiquity of the Internet may prove to be a significant advantage. Frame relay and ATM networks are not as widespread as the Internet and are more expensive. International leased lines are costly and may not be available in areas where the Internet has a presence, or such lines may be available only from a very expensive government monopoly.

Also, the Internet is, to a great extent, oblivious to national boundaries. Certainly there are those countries where Internet service is limited or access is restricted, but the same or greater problems are likely to be encountered using any other form of networking as well.

As we'll see, the Internet may not be the solution to your VPN needs. However, in terms of accessibility it is hard to beat.

1.2.4 The VPN and the Mobile Workforce

It is in remote access services (RAS) that VPNs show the greatest savings. In the usual scenario, a road warrior must dial into the public telephone network to reach his home base remote access server (Figure 1-5). From his motel room in Los Angeles he immediately begins running up long-distance charges to the home office in New York City, where he goes on the network, perhaps to check his email. Furthermore, instead of logging off to read and respond to his messages and then logging on again to upload his answers, he is likely to stay online, while the telephone company counts up steadily increasing profits at your expense.

If there are any advantages to this they are only that your cost per minute for an 800 number call may decline, perhaps to as low as $0.07 per minute as

Figure 1-5   Accessing the network via dial-up service.

the time used goes up, and it may make it easier for the accounting department to keep track of the costs.

On the other hand, if your VPN supports remote access, that road warrior in Los Angeles can dial in to a local Internet POP there, perhaps through GlobalNet or WorldNet, perhaps using a local or regional ISP with whom he has an account. Once that connection is made, the Internet cloud connects him to the home office, avoiding all those miles at long-distance rates (Figure 1-6). Your cost is only the flat monthly fee he pays for his Internet service no matter how long he remains online, plus what the motel charges for a local call, not the per-minute charges for a long-distance connection. Even a series of 800 number calls at $0.07 per minute are not likely to be lower than the cost of a $20 per month Internet account with no time limits.

In terms of flexibility, a VPN can serve a mobile workforce or telecommuters in a way that no leased-line network can. A salesman in Dubuque can plug his laptop into the RJ 11 telephone jack in his motel room and dial the ISP that he has a subscription with, perhaps the local PSINet or WorldNet number. If he's staying in one of the upscale hotels that offer direct Internet connections, he can take advantage of that.

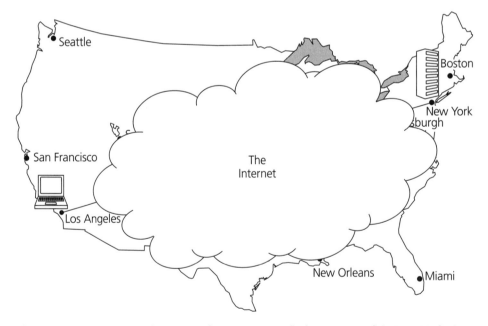

Figure 1-6   A remote user in Los Angeles connects to the home network in New York via the Internet through a secure VPN.

Once he's logged on to the Internet he can log on to his home network, turning his Toshiba laptop into a node on the network. He can check his email, upload new orders, review the status of last week's orders, download a new catalog and price lists, leave email to his assistant, check on his commissions, and log off. He can do virtually anything from that motel room that he could do from his workstation at the office.

The savings for such remote access can be even more impressive than for those in the more static intranet or extranet scenarios. VPN vendor TimeStep has created a cost analysis that is worth looking at because it puts some real numbers into the scenario (Table 1-2).

Notice that the capital costs for the Internet scenario are about six times that of the dial-in scenario. On the other hand, the monthly operating costs for the Internet scenario are only about one fourth those for the dial-up scenario. In less than 3 months, the difference in the capital costs has been recovered. The first-year return on investment is over 345%. Granted, these are numbers generated by a VPN vendor, but your own analysis is likely to return similar results.

More recently, Cisco Systems has analyzed the savings achieved by outsourcing a VPN-based remote access system using their Access VPN technology versus maintaining a dial-in remote access service in-house, using modem ports. As Table 1-3 shows, the estimated savings are 38% using this solution. Naturally, an in-house VPN solution is possible, too, with some trade-offs since you take on more management costs.

By their figures, a dial-in port for remote access costs about $1,500 a year, including local access line charges and the cost of a modem. Assuming a conservative ratio of users to ports of 5 to 1, the cost per user for such a port is about $300 per year. On the VPN side, a 1.024 Mbps dedicated line port and interface, including initial purchase, facility costs, and maintenance, runs about $2,500 per year. However, such a port can serve 20 users, resulting in a per-user cost of $125 per year, less than half the cost of the dial-up port.

If, instead of using the dial-in ports Cisco proposes in their chart, the remote users can connect to the VPN by making a local call to an ISP, the savings are even greater, since access charges are the minimal cost of the local call and a subscription with an ISP at $19.95 per month.

In the real world, the potential savings can be impressive. Mazzio's Corporation runs a VPN to serve their restaurants that we'll discuss in more detail in Section 2.3.1. They discovered they had more than 20 company users dialing in and running up a phone bill of $1,800 per month. By bringing them onto the VPN, that monthly cost will be eliminated.

Forrester Research set up a study comparing a leased-line network serving 2,000 remote users with a VPN serving the same number. As Table 1-4 shows, the 60% savings were about the same as predicted by other studies.

Table 1-2 TimeStep cost analysis of VPN savings with a mobile workforce.

Direct dial-up scenario

Item	Quantity	Unit cost	Extended cost
Capital costs			
Terminal server*	10	$550	$5,500
Total capital costs			$5,500

Internet scenario

Item	Quantity	Unit cost	Extended cost
T1 line startup**	1	$3,000	$3,000
Channel service unit/Data service unit**	1	$995	$995
Router**	1	$1,950	$1,950
PERMIT/Director***	1	$11,995	$11,995
PERMIT/Gate 2520****	1	$3,995	$3,995
PERMIT/Client****	75	$99	$7,425
			$29,360

Monthly operating costs

Long-distance charges****	1,500	$10	$15,000	ISP charges**	75	$20	$1,500
				T1 line**	1	$1,895	$1,895
				Local loop*****	1	$700	$700
Total monthly operating costs			**$15,000**				**$4,095**
				% operating cost savings			73%
				Payback period (months)			2.70
				Return on investment (for first year)			345.70%

*Average industry cost ("Intranets on the Road"; Forrester Report; June 1997).

**Price from UUNet (August 1997).

***TimeStep's PERMIT/Director is a Windows-based software suite that offers VPN user management, authentication, key management, and administrative tools. PERMIT/Gate 2520 is a tamper-resistant gateway that secures data for transmission over the Internet using a suite of hardware-based encryption and authentication protocols. PERMIT/Client is a software suite available for Windows and Macintosh operating systems that offers VPN services including encryption and authentication protocols.

****Price from MCI (August 1997).

*****Average local loop cost (varies region to region).

Table 1-3   Cost comparisons of an in-house remote access system vs. an outsourced VPN system. *Source*: Cisco analysis, July 1998.

	In-house	Outsourced	Savings
Ports and toll-free access	$957,000	$700,000	$257,000
Network backbone	$500,000	$450,000	$50,000
Staffing	$440,000	$0	$440,000
Security	$185,000	$100,000	$85,000
24 × 7 help desk	$750,000	$550,000	$200,000
Network management	$75,000	$0	$75,000
Totals	**$2,907,000**	**$1,800,000**	**$1,107,000**
Savings based on outsourced solution			**38%**

Table 1-4   Forrester Research found a 60% savings in a 2,000-user VPN.

	Private network	VPN
T1 lines	$48,000	$68,400
Routers and servers	$208,000	$44,800
Phone and ISP charges	$2,160,000	$1,080,000
User support	$600,000	(included)
Total	**$3,016,000**	**$1,193,200**

Notice, too, where the savings are made. The cost for T1 lines is higher, to allow the higher speeds needed for the consolidation to single-line access for the Internet, the extranet, and the intranet VPN. However, this is more than made up for by the consolidation of equipment (routers and servers), the phone and ISP charges, and the cost for user support. Again we see that the major savings come in operating expenses, not that the savings in capital costs from equipment consolidation are insignificant.

The consulting firm Gartner Group estimates VPN savings of at least 50% for remote access. For this reason they predict that by the year 2003, 70% of Fortune 500 companies will use VPNs for their road warriors. Telecommuters can benefit from a VPN as much as road warriors. If you have a VPN, telecommuters don't require a dedicated line between their home office and your headquarters. They can log on to your LAN through an account with their local Internet service provider. For speed, if the ISP offers it, they can use an ISDN or DSL local loop that offers digital speeds over copper telephone lines.

If that's not available, perhaps they will have a cable modem through their local cable TV service.

Similarly, with a VPN, managers who need to be on call at all hours can jump into a problem from home. When that late night call comes in from an irate customer in Tokyo, they can shuffle down the hall in their pajamas, turn on the computer in their study, and use their Internet account to log on to the company server to untangle the problem. A network administrator can log on and sort out a Paris-based user's account problem without making the 20-mile drive to the office at 3 in the morning.

1.3 Every Silver Lining Has a Cloud

All of this makes VPNs sound too good to be true. Putting in a VPN will boost your bottom line, satisfy your customers, turn your weary sales force into a jolly chorus line, and cure the common cold.

Well, not quite. There are challenges to creating a working VPN, especially one that uses the Internet. The Internet, as we all know, is an anarchic maze. It is rightly seen as a hostile environment, a tropical beach with appealing blue waters, which happen to be inhabited by sharks, jellyfish, moray eels, and stingrays. There are reefs and currents that must be negotiated and an occasional hurricane that may blow you on the rocks.

The primary concern on the Internet is, of course, security. For a VPN to work, the traffic it carries must get to its destination safely. It must be protected from sniffing and snooping, hijackers, denial of service, and from other hacker attacks (see Section 3.3 for a discussion of these terms).

As we'll see, VPNs, along with their Internet connections through firewalls and the like, are designed to cope with these hazards. But this also means that a VPN presents challenges that may not be encountered on a more secure internal local area network. There will probably be increased system management loads. These can be handled internally, or they can be outsourced, but either way they are going to result in some increased costs.

With regard to the Internet particularly, there are also issues of quality of service and reliability. The Internet can get bogged down. A fire in a manhole in Chicago fuses some fiber-optic cable into a useless lump and traffic all over the country slows to a crawl. Someone enters the wrong command and routers get confused and send everything off into a void until the problem is caught.

In Chapter 3, we'll explore some of the issues you need to consider before going the VPN route. We'll also go into more technical detail on how VPNs work in Chapters 5–7, but for now we'll take a brief look at how a VPN does what it does and some of the complexities it can deal with in the process.

1.4 How a VPN Works

How does a VPN make a private, secure connection through the very public Internet? What if you're running a LAN already that doesn't use the Internet's IP protocol, or that has IP addresses that are fine for your LAN but that would be banned from the Internet? Just as important, how do you keep unauthorized users from sneaking into the system? And how do you keep all those hackers out there from snooping into your data as it whizzes around the cloud?

To manage the first problem, that of making a secure connection and hiding your LAN's addresses from the Internet's routers, your existing network's headers are hidden using a process called *tunneling*. To keep unauthorized users out of the VPN, a system of user authentication is established, combined with security gateways such as firewalls that guard any Internet connection. To keep hackers from sneaking a peek at your company secrets, the data in transit is encrypted. To make sure someone hasn't tampered with the transmission en route, it is authenticated at the receiving end.

We'll go into the protocols that manage this and the details of how they do it in later chapters. For now, so you can understand some of the terminology, we'll take a quick look at the processes that are used to meet the challenges.

1.4.1 Tunneling

There's plenty of confusion in the terminology of VPNs, and a lot of it crops up right here. The term tunneling implies that, somehow, a pipe—a real, solid, direct route—is established through the Internet, a connection like you'd see in the telephone network, a circuit-switched network.

However, we know that the Internet is a packet-switched network. It simply doesn't work that way. In reality, a single message is broken up into packets, and each packet finds its own way to its destination, bounced from router to router in accordance with the address it carries, the route's routing tables, and the paths available. One packet may make its way from New York to San Francisco by way of Chicago, the next one by way of New Orleans. Once they arrive, the packets are reassembled in the right order to re-create the message.

So there is no such thing, really, as a "tunnel." However, there is a connection of sorts between sender and receiver in that the VPN equipment at each end has agreed on how to communicate (what protocols and security arrangements are to be used at each end). A control "circuit" may exist between them, a series of background messages that travel the Internet the same way as the message packets, taking care of administrative details of the communication, but it doesn't work like the solid link of a telephone connection.

Another term you'll hear in reference to the process is *encapsulation.* The terms tunneling and encapsulation seem to be used interchangeably. Probably the simplest way to differentiate between them is that *tunneling* is applied to the whole process of moving a message through the Internet for a VPN, while *encapsulation* refers to what is done to each individual packet that makes up the message.

In tunneling, each packet, including any existing header it has acquired from the LAN where it originated, is encapsulated—wrapped up, hidden—by a new envelope or capsule that carries the addresses of the source and destination VPN servers. In this encapsulation process, the VPN software, which we'll see may be running in a workstation, a network server, a firewall, or a router, appends a new header with new source and destination addresses to the packet before sending it out on the Internet. The original header becomes nothing more than part of the payload.

The Internet's routers and switches, which only know to look at that first header, are therefore oblivious to any invalid network addresses that may be buried in the packet, perhaps even one using a foreign network protocol, such as NetWare's IPX or Apple's AppleTalk. In this way, a company with NetWare or AppleTalk LANs in widely dispersed facilities may tie them together through the IP-based Internet with the Internet, and the local networks, being none the wiser.

1.4.2 Securing the Data

While tunneling allows non-IP data or data bearing illegal addresses to be moved through the network, it does not secure the data. While the network's routers may be unaware of the contents, anyone can intercept the packets and read and even tamper with their contents unless they are further secured. For security, a combination of encryption, verification, and authentication is required.

Encryption secures the data from anyone who does not have the key to decrypt it. A variety of encryption technologies are used, as we'll see in Chapter 5. Along with encryption there's the problem of making sure that only the right people can get access to the system and decrypt the data—there must be a way that users are *authenticated,* so that they are the only ones who get the key they need to unscramble the data. As we'll discover in Chapter 6, user authentication, and making sure users receive the keys they need to decrypt the data, is a vital part of a VPN, and a major challenge; the larger the VPN, the greater the challenge.

Finally there has to be some way of making sure that the data that is received has not been tampered with while in transit. For data *verification* yet another process is used.

1.4.3 Making the Combination Work

It is the combination of these elements—tunneling, authentication, encryption, and verification—that makes VPNs possible. To the user the process should be transparent. When Alice in her office at Giant Widgets logs on to the company network she should see the server in the former Associated Grommets factory in Malaysia the same way she sees the server down the hall from the cafeteria where she gets her morning coffee and bagel.

For this to be true, all the bits and pieces that make up a VPN's protocols have to work together. The Associated Grommets VPN server in Malaysia must communicate smoothly with the Giant Widgets server in New York. They have to agree on how every packet is to be encapsulated. Encryption must be agreed upon and somehow they must both have the right keys for the encryption/decryption process. They must be assured that some sneak hasn't gotten into the loop, that they are talking with authenticated users, and that the data has not been tampered with, and for all this to work they must be using the same methods.

It is in assembling all these pieces, and agreeing on them, that things can get a little sticky. Right now the VPN industry is like a teenage kid in the middle of a growth spurt. His arms and legs have suddenly grown out of his clothes. He bumps into chairs, drops the carton of milk off the table, his hormones are raging, his skin is bumpy, he suffers from selective deafness and blindness ("Take the garbage out? What garbage? Out where?"), and his mind is controlled from somewhere in outer space.

As you know, if you've done any reading about VPNs, there are a number of VPN protocols out there. Microsoft has offered up PPTP, Cisco Systems has developed L2F, and Digital Equipment has AltaVista; as of this writing, L2TP and IPSec are working their way through the Internet Engineering Task Force (IETF) development and approval process.

There are at least a half a dozen encryption algorithms to choose from, and different key lengths, some of which are legal in the United States but illegal to export anywhere outside the U.S. A number of different vendors are offering both hardware and software solutions to the VPN market. It seems that more than half the firewall vendors and router manufacturers are getting into the act, along with technology companies like Lucent. Every Internet security company that offers encryption has joined in the fray. Everyone has different ideas of how best it should be done, and few agree.

By means of protocols such as L2TP and IPSec, the IETF is trying to bring some order out of all this chaos. They have a number of different working groups studying these and other protocols in an effort to develop some standards. These working groups are made up mostly of volunteer software engineers, employed in academia and industry, who are often working for competing vendors. The process is one of negotiation, discussion, and clarification and works amazingly well. In the end, standards emerge from these working groups that we hope will offer a reasonably high degree of interoperability between those competing vendors' products that use the same standards.

The final step in the process rests with the vendors. Once the standards are published, it is up to the vendors to implement them. Just *how* they implement them is as important as all the rest of the process. They may not implement them exactly the same way, but for the industry to thrive, they must work together. A VPNet VPN should be able to talk to one from Shiva, Ascend, or Cisco. Fortunately, there are industry programs that are testing products for interoperability.

1.5 Where We Go from Here

The purpose of this book is to sort out some of this confusion. So far we've seen what a VPN is, some of the benefits it offers, and how it works. We've also warned that there are some downsides to running a VPN. We'll probe each of these topics more deeply as we proceed. Chapter 2 examines how VPNs are being put to use in the real world so that you can get some idea of how you might put a VPN to use for yourself and the benefits you should see from it.

2

How to Use a VPN

While it is only since late 1997 or early 1998 that the term VPN has gained widespread use and begun to attract significant attention, VPNs have been in use since the mid 1990s. This chapter gives us some examples to look at, so we can see how VPNs have been put to use and some of the issues being confronted in the industry. We'll see them being used by a variety of organizations, ranging from health care systems to restaurant franchises to entire industries. With regard to the latter, the adoption of VPN technology by industry coalitions is providing a badly needed standardization that will benefit the entire VPN industry.

In some of the examples cited here, the organizations requested anonymity, a reflection of security concerns. For that reason we do not identify them other than by their field of business.

2.1 The VPN for Remote Access

As we've already seen, it is as remote access servers that VPNs show the greatest potential monetary savings. By replacing the public telephone network with the more efficient and less expensive Internet for remote access, VPNs can produce impressive reductions in communications expenses, up to 60% or more by some estimates. Not unexpectedly, the potential is there, too, for faster data transfers than are possible using long-distance telephone connections (particularly international connections). So it stands to reason that there are already many examples of VPNs being used to give road warriors network access.

However, we're going to take a broad view of what we consider "remote access" and not confine it to the road warrior working from a motel room.

Certainly that is one important facet of remote access; however, in our view the concept extends beyond that. For example, we include providing access to the central office's network for a large number of widely distributed, small offices, as we'll see in the VPN being built by Prudential Insurance. Remote access also includes giving telecommuters who wish to work from home a way to get on the company network for more than just their email. Essentially, we're including any small unit that might hook into the company network using dial-in remote access but that is unlikely to qualify for a connection that is always "hot," such as a network link.

2.1.1 A Medical Software Company

As the current debates over managed medical care make clear, the medical industry is facing demands from government and the public to provide improved service while reducing costs. That may well be one reason medical service administrators have been so quick to adopt VPNs as a cost-effective way to meet some of these challenges. It's worth bearing in mind that medicine is a data-heavy industry—for doctors to make diagnoses they need information, often in high-density forms such as x-ray images. The protection of patient privacy is also a major consideration, so security is of paramount importance; this is one of the reasons our sources in this field requested anonymity.

VPNs serving medical organizations and services of many stripes have been established in areas as far apart as Boston, New Jersey, Georgia, and Texas. Some serve a locality, others stretch nationwide. A physicians' group headquartered in Georgia has been established with the intent of using a VPN to tie together geographically dispersed physicians' offices as they are acquired. The company plans to guide their administration through the network, providing greater efficiencies. A Boston-based VPN links together hospitals and physicians' offices to provide high-speed links for rapid consultations. A county health service in Texas employs a VPN to make their resources available to a large teaching medical facility, as well as connecting together their countywide clinics and services.

But where remote access is the goal, suppliers to the medical industry, with their traveling representatives, have not held back either. A medical software company that employs a total of 150 people uses a VPN to maintain contact with 50 roving users around the country. The home office of the company is served by a multisegment 100 Mbps LAN running TCP/IP, making the Internet connection relatively simple. The VPN runs on a Pentium Pro–based Windows NT 4.0 server. A T1 connection to the Internet provides more than enough bandwidth for the VPN connection at the home office end. While the company has 20 offices nationwide, interestingly enough there has been no effort to connect those offices to the network. Instead the VPN is designed solely to serve the sales and implementation personnel operating out of those offices when they are on the road, which is most of the time. Because these workers spend a great deal of time at customer sites, and are frequent travelers, a modem-based solution was selected, combined with ISPs with a nationwide presence, which allows the travelers to connect with the headquarters network from almost anywhere with a local call.

Instcad of being a replacement for an existing system, such as a dial-in remote access system, the VPN was actually a new service to the road warriors. The goal was to offer email, Web-based intranet connectivity, file transfer, and discussion groups. Before proceeding with designing and building their own VPN from the ground up, the company considered two other solutions: a dial-up server with a toll-free number and multiple dial-in ports, or a prepackaged VPN offering from a full-service vendor such as UUNet. Both alternatives were rejected because of the recurring costs involved. By doing the work themselves and tapping the Internet with $20 per month subscriptions, they estimate they save about $150,000 per year with the VPN.

The fact that they implemented the project in-house, rather than outsourcing it, is important. As we get further into our look at VPNs we'll see that designing, building, and managing a VPN can demand a high degree of technical expertise and resources. This particular medical software firm, being a technically oriented company, was confident they had the prerequisites to implement and manage a VPN in-house, but not all shops will be as well prepared. The company also went it alone because they wanted to maintain as much internal control as possible over security. They opted for a product from a single vendor, almost a necessity at this time considering the still-developing standards in the VPN industry. To get their remote users online, they provided them with a relatively simple turnkey installation of the client software.

The only disappointment they encountered arose primarily out of their choice of VPN product. Not all of the software they were using was compatible with it. As for the end users, while the system is widely accepted now, adoption of it by them was relatively slow, not because the field workers were reluctant to use it as much as because they were too busy to take the time to learn the new system. Now that it is widely accepted, there is a growing demand for expanding the service to offer access for telecommuters who want to work out of their homes.

2.1.2 The Prudential Insurance Company of America

Consumer insurance companies are an example of a business model that, of necessity, employs large numbers of widely distributed representatives. In the case of Prudential, there are about 12,000 field agents and support personnel who can benefit from close contact with the central office. Until recently that contact was primarily by telephone, mail, and limited online access to select information that was only available through agency-leased lines. To speed up and enhance this connectivity and to get their field force on the network, Prudential has signed a $100 million agreement with IBM to invest in a messaging and electronic commerce system, known as the LaunchPad project. Part of the investment will provide each of Prudential's field agents and support persons with an IBM ThinkPad notebook computer.

The intent is to provide full workgroup computing capabilities to their field force through a VPN. The agents will use Lotus Development Corporation's Notes and Domino platform to access messaging and workgroup applications and to file insurance policies over an IP-based VPN. From her ThinkPad an agent can access Prudential's system for contract management and customer needs analysis. Sales illustrations and marketing brochures are also available to her. Through Lotus Notes she can access email. Future enhancements may include electronic signatures for real-time policy approvals over the network.

One of the reasons Prudential went with the LaunchPad project was to standardize on a single platform. More than two thirds of the agents participating in the pilot project were already using PCs in their work. However, there were no clear standards for hardware or software. As a result, Prudential faced a serious compatibility problem, which they overcame by providing their agents with a uniform platform in the form of the ThinkPad preloaded with Windows 95, Lotus Notes, contact management and needs analysis software, and sales illustrations. An additional 2,000 administrative staff members will receive new desktop computers to provide the same standardization. To connect the field force, Prudential is using IBM's Global Network, which provides a secure, switched, dial-up network with more than 500 POPs available nationwide.

The Prudential example shows the scale on which a VPN can operate and how it can provide workgroup capabilities to a widely distributed workforce. By linking their field agents directly to the company network, Prudential gives the representatives on the firing line the latest data on rates and services. Contracts that need home office review can receive swift approval. The latest marketing tools are right at hand as well.

Before the full rollout, Prudential initiated a 6-month pilot program involving nearly 500 agents. Almost immediately some members of the pilot program showed returns in the form of dramatic increases in user efficiency and productivity. Some agents more than doubled the number of net paid-for life insurance policies sold, with net first-year commission credits increasing 153%. Turnaround times for new business applications were reduced from weeks to days. Agents who were part of the pilot program found that they were able to offer customers quicker access to information, which allowed them to come to informed decisions more quickly. This was all possible because the full resources of Prudential's central office were at the field agent's command instantaneously, thanks to the VPN.

2.2 The VPN as an Extranet

In today's fast-moving global economy, high-speed communications are vital. With major industries (such as automobile manufacturers) outsourcing more of their work, and imposing "just in time" inventory management, fast communications with vendors and customers has become even more important. For a manufacturer, being directly connected to both their suppliers and their markets can mean big bonuses in the form of increased efficiency. Inventories can be reduced, and by sharing design information, lead times can be cut. Electronic data interchange (EDI) transactions reduce paperwork and lower costs accordingly.

However, it is impractical to establish leased-line networks with the hundreds of small companies that make up the supply network for building a product such as a car. Just the cost of setting up all those dedicated connections would be prohibitive. The challenge of administering them would be monumental, and it is questionable whether the infrastructure even exists to establish all those connections. The Internet, on the other hand, neatly solves most of these problems, offering a web of connections and thousands of POPs worldwide, while adding a safety net of redundancy that leased lines can't provide.

On the other hand, Ford isn't going to want GM to be able to eavesdrop on their latest plans for the 2002 Taurus as they work with the dashboard instrument supplier, so privacy is essential, something the Internet does not inherently offer.

Enter the VPN.

2.2.1 Automotive Network eXchange

The Automotive Network eXchange (ANX) is a VPN extranet on a very large scale. A cooperative venture of the automotive industry, it will tie together the facilities of more than 1,300 automobile manufacturers and their suppliers into a single TCP/IP network. Bear in mind that in today's automobile industry, no company is an island. Certainly the big three (GM, Ford, and Chrysler) are still fierce competitors; however, they buy parts from a large number of suppliers and, while some of those suppliers may sell to only one manufacturer, others, such as a specialty steel mill, turn out components for several car builders. For the network to work, everyone must be connected to everyone, but confidentiality must be maintained.

The network must also be reliable. If an order for a transmission part doesn't get through, an entire plant could be idled, leading to a domino effect. As we saw in the latest strike against GM, if a single component factory goes down for any reason, the entire company can be crippled.

The ANX VPN offers the necessary combination of security, ubiquity, and reliability. By providing the security of tunneling and data encryption, it guarantees the user's confidentiality, so Chrysler can't be reading GM's mail. The Internet provides redundancy by offering multiple routes for messages to traverse. By requiring standards for its members who want to connect and providers who provide the service, ANX guarantees that users will be able to talk to each other over the network. These standards also guarantee performance, reliability, and management that the unadorned Internet usually cannot. By setting these standards, ANX is also proving to be a powerful driving force behind the movement toward greater interoperability and quality of service that will make VPNs more practical, efficient, and, hopefully, easier to implement.

ANX had its genesis back in 1994, when the Automotive Industry Action Group (AIAG) settled on TCP/IP as the common standard for an industrywide network to replace the patchwork of various networks in use in the industry. The AIAG is a not-for-profit industry trade association of more than 1,300 auto and truck manufacturers and their suppliers in the United States and Canada. Out of this first step evolved plans for a secure, business quality data communications network. The goal is to link automotive suppliers and original equipment manufacturers (OEMs) with a single connection, using a carefully monitored and managed TCP/IP network.

While ANX is, essentially, a part of the Internet, it demands of its providers guarantees of security and quality of service not normally available on the Internet. The architecture of ANX is worth looking at as a potential model for other similarly secure, large-scale Internet-based VPNs. As Figure 2-1 illustrates, while ANX looks like any other VPN using the network cloud, interoperability, security, and reliability are assured by having established standards for the trading partners (TPs) who use the network, the certified service providers (CSPs) who offer access to the network, and the Certified Exchange Point Operators (CEPOs) who provide ATM-based network services to interconnect the CSPs through the Internet. In more traditional terminology, CSPs are Internet service providers who have satisfied the ANX certification requirements, while CEPOs are backbone providers who have done likewise with their services. An overseer organization certifies them and makes sure the standards are maintained.

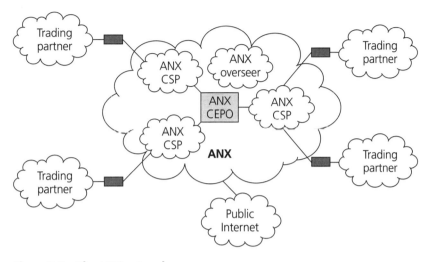

Figure 2-1   The ANX network.

Joining ANX is akin to joining a private club. In order to become a member, a potential user must first be sponsored by an ANX authorized trading partner. This is unlikely to be a problem if they are already selling to a manufacturer who would almost certainly be willing to sponsor them. The potential ANX TP must fulfill the ANX requirements by having an approved gateway to their CSP. To ensure interoperability, the VPN product used in that gateway has to be certified by the International Computer Security Association (ICSA), which tests VPN products for interoperability. A number of VPN vendors have already passed this certification, and the number will continue to rise. This is too big a potential market for them to ignore. There is also the incentive that having the ICSA stamp of approval gives a product a wider acceptance in the general VPN marketplace.

As for ANX itself, in the case of the service providers and exchange point operators, certification by the overseer company ensures the quality of service they will provide. They are required to meet high standards for network service features, interoperability, performance, reliability, business continuity and disaster recovery, security, customer care, and trouble handling. The overseer company chosen by AIAG is Bellcore. Among the first companies to be approved as CSPs by Bellcore to provide access for the trading partners are Ameritech, Bell Canada, and EDS. Ameritech has been certified as an ANX CEPO, and Ameritech, Bell Canada, and EDS Networks have been certified as CSPs for the network. The AIAG also offers two-day courses to help automotive trading partners and systems integrators understand and use ANX.

As an example of what ANX will mean to the auto industry, prior to ANX, Taylor Steel of Ontario, Canada, one of the first companies to sign on and qualify as a TP, was unable to justify the expense of dedicated lines to connect two of their Ohio plants with a WAN. Once the factories met the ANX requirements and hooked into the VPN, they had a connection between the two plants *and* their Ontario headquarters, as well as a link to the entire automobile industry in North America, at a fraction of what it would have cost for a WAN connecting just their two Ohio factories.

That ANX connection is also likely to offer Taylor Steel global access in the future, as AIAG is working on a cooperative agreement with the European auto association, Odette, to link up with them, and AIAG is also meeting with the Japanese Auto Manufacturers Association (JAMA) in hopes of establishing that connection as well. The automobile industry has not been confined by national boundaries for some time, with Japanese manufacturers operating factories in the United States, with Chrysler and Daimler Benz merging, and with Ford and GM owning plants in Asia and Latin America. Extending ANX overseas is almost unavoidable.

The exchange of data on ANX goes beyond simple purchase orders and email. Computer-aided design files, encrypted messages, and EDI transactions are supported by ANX. Taylor Steel uses the network to handle EDI traffic, to secure email, to access its suppliers' private Web sites, and even to transfer digital photos.

According to "The Business Case for ANX," a white paper by AIAG, ANX meshes well with the Manufacturing Assembly Pilot (MAP) launched by the AIAG in 1994, which implements electronic data interchange throughout the industry. MAP streamlines material and information flow by re-engineering business practices and implementing electronic commerce technologies. According to the white paper, the benefit to MAP of having ANX amounts to about $50 million per year overall. The big three auto manufacturers are heading toward 100% implementation of EDI throughout their supply chains. MAP, it is estimated, will offer savings of $1 billion per year ($71 per vehicle) to the industry.

Another project that meshes with ANX, the use of Collaborative Planning, Forecasting, and Replacement (CPFR) tools, may save as much as $1,200 per vehicle by speeding sales data to manufacturers and suppliers, thus producing faster delivery cycles and smaller inventories.

Compared to current connections, for medium and large trading partners communications costs may be cut in half, giving them a full payback on their ANX expenditures in less than 6 months. Small TPs will take longer to recover their costs—about 1 1/3 years—according to the AIAG figures.

As we'll see when we get to Chapter 3 and our discussion of the issues that must be considered before implementing a VPN, ANX faces and deals with most of these issues. Obviously, AIAG has resources available only to large industries. However, their trailblazing, by demanding interoperability for VPN protocols and setting standards for VPN clients (the trading partners), CSPs (ISPs), and CEPOs, will benefit the entire VPN industry and probably the Internet as a whole. With the certification process established for CSPs and CEPOs, and the work of the ICSA proceeding in certifying VPN products, the infrastructure is being laid for a more interoperable, reliable, secure VPN environment.

2.2.2 Open Access Same-Time Information Systems (OASIS)

Deregulation of the electric power industry quickly created a demand for a quick, efficient system of brokering electric power through the grid, to allow utilities to buy power where it was cheapest. Before 1997, electric power brokers operated under a system not much more efficient than the gathering back in the 1700s of stockbrokers under the buttonwood tree that was the nascent New York Stock Exchange. Before OASIS, electricity brokers, operating with phone and fax, were forced to make deals based more on who they knew, rather than who had the best price nationwide at that moment. There simply was no way to know, minute by minute or hour by hour, what utility had surplus power for sale at the best rate.

On January 3, 1997, the Federal Electric Regulatory Commission (FERC) ordered that wholesale buyers, sellers, and distributors of electric power must all have equal access to information about power transmissions, availability, and pricing. Suddenly everyone was on an equal footing, and OASIS was born.

OASIS involves more than 250 electric utilities in seven regions of the United States and Canada. It facilitates transactions of wholesale electricity to utilities and corporate customers throughout North America. In the first year, more than $25 billion worth of electricity deals were conducted, using a highly secure VPN on the Internet.

The FERC chose the Internet because it was the most economical medium for their network. OASIS itself was designed by the Joint Transmission Services Information Network (JTSIN), a consortium of electric utility cooperatives. The JTSIN service areas are shown in Figure 2-2. Development of the project was outsourced to TradeWave Corp., BSG Alliance/IT, Inc., and Cegelec ESCA Corp. TradeWave, now a subsidiary of CyberGuard, created one of the first VPNs in 1993 when its pilot version of TradeVPI enabled 1,000 Electrical Power Research Institute participants to swap information over the Internet. BSG Alliance, which has since become Impact Innovations Group, is a consultancy, while Cegelec ESCA is a leader in the development and integration of real-time power control systems for the electric utility industry in

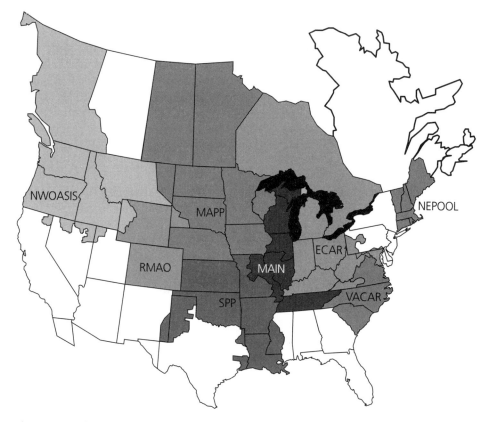

Figure 2-2   The JTSIN service area.

North America. This coalition illustrates the multidisciplinary nature of the project.

In a network such as OASIS, with billions of dollars of transactions taking place, as well as internal corporate data and operations potentially vulnerable, security is paramount. It was necessary to provide the VPN with a highly effective authorization mechanism to control user access to the network as well as what information they could view. Strong encryption was also provided, with accordingly secure authentication of the data so that both the source and recipient of the data would be verified.

However, speed and efficiency are also important to the network's operation. Without leaving his desk, a broker must be able to tap into the entire system quickly and easily. OASIS's centralized user authentication procedure provides it. When an electricity broker in Pennsylvania, for example, wants to access the Mid-American Interconnect Network (MAIN) located in

Wisconsin (one of the members of the consortium), he contacts a node local to him. He is first approved by a local registration agent (LRA) using the broker's encrypted sign-on. The broker is then provided with a security profile. The LRA of the MAIN site that he wants to access then confirms him with a certificate authority (CA) server located at a physically secure site, which happens to be in Texas. Once the broker is approved, he is admitted to the MAIN site. From this single log-on with his LRA, he also has access to any other OASIS node without having to log on again, because of his approval by the CA in Texas. This means he does not have to remember different IDs and passwords for each JTSIN account he has. Authentication and encryption key management are managed using a public key infrastructure (PKI), of which the CA is a part.

This PKI is one of the issues that must be addressed with any large VPN, particularly an extranet. As we'll see, encryption is a vital part of almost any VPN, and making sure that the right people have access to the right keys, in a secure fashion, is a major challenge. The certificate authority occupies a critical place in the public key infrastructure, as we'll learn in Chapter 6.

2.3 The VPN as an Intranet

While not as glamorous as an extranet or as cost-effective as a remote access server, a VPN can be an effective way to tie widely distributed facilities into a wide area network. It is particularly valuable for a business that has a large number of relatively small facilities that need contact with the central office.

2.3.1 Mazzio's Corporation

It's 7 o'clock at night and you've just gotten home from work, late again. You've been working overtime for the last month. While the bank account has been blessed, there's less food in your kitchen than in Mother Hubbard's cupboard, and in 20 minutes George will be home and hungry after watching the dials and turning valves at the refinery for the last 10 hours. The kids have eaten the last Twinkie.

Only a working mother can know this sense of panic—you must feed the starving horde or they'll start eating the curtains. Then you hear a commercial for Mazzio's Pizza on the TV and reach for the telephone. You dial a local number, and in less than half an hour, instead of football cleats on the table you have a steaming large pizza with cola and desserts for all.

What you don't know is that the call you're making to a local Springfield, Missouri, phone number—a call that, unknown to you, used to go to a call center six blocks away that served the eight Mazzio's restaurants in town—is now rerouted through an 800 number connection to the new Mazzio's call center in Oklahoma City. That nice young person you gave your order to isn't a pizza cook or a delivery driver a few blocks away, but a trained order taker hundreds of miles away who talks you into adding the cola and dessert and another topping (green peppers are good for your family after all, and somehow that nice young man knew you had them on your last three orders, and wasn't it nice of him to remind you, too?).

So how does your order get from Oklahoma City back to your local Mazzio's? From the call center it is sent out to the Mazzio's restaurant nearest your home via the Internet over the Mazzio's VPN. Getting the order off her terminal, the local chef bakes the pizza, bundles it with the cola and dessert, and tosses in a coupon for a free soft drink with your next order. As the driver heads out the door, he punches a code into the Springfield restaurant's computer to indicate that the order has been filled.

A VPN serving a pizza chain? Mazzio's has over 250 restaurants in 14 states (Figure 2-3). Mazzio's is gradually phasing out their local dial-in systems in favor of one centralized node. Callers will still call a local number, the same number for every Mazzio's in their town, which saves on advertising expenses. But that call will now be routed to the call center in Oklahoma City, even if the customer is located in Joplin, Missouri.

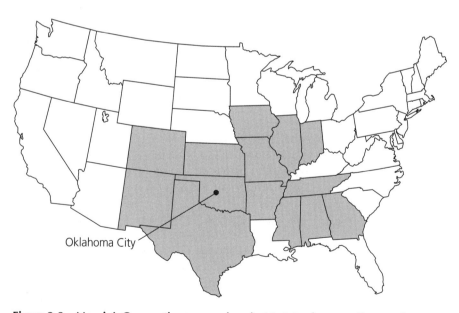

Oklahoma City

Figure 2-3   Mazzio's Corporation serves pizza in 14 states from a call center in Oklahoma City, thanks to a VPN.

Does it sound inefficient? Think again. Almost before you open your mouth, the order taker knows who you are and where you are calling from, thanks to phone ID information accompanying the call, combined with a customer database in the center's computers. If you've ordered from Mazzio's before, the order taker can even have your buying history up on her computer screen and could—but probably won't—say, "And will that be your usual large pizza with pepperoni, Mrs. Jones? And should we deliver as usual, or will you be picking it up?" before you can even tell her that's what you want.

Using another database, the computer routes the order over the VPN to the Mazzio's nearest your location. Once it is ready and the delivery driver heads out the door, a message goes back over the VPN. Oklahoma City is notified of exactly when the order left the restaurant. At the end of the driver's shift, the computer system lists every order the driver handled and computes the amount of money he should have collected for those deliveries.

In the highly competitive take-out restaurant business, the Mazzio's VPN offers a cost-effective, highly efficient customer service tool. Employees in the restaurants are no longer tied up taking calls, which allows faster service, while the staff at the call center aren't distracted by having to refill the water glasses at table 10. The order takers are trained to encourage buyers to add to their orders such extras as soft drinks or desserts, which have higher profit margins than pizza.

Although Pat Patterson, Mazzio's vice president of information systems, doesn't have the final numbers yet, the cost for the VPN is about $100 per month less per store than the current system, and the savings from shuttering the local call centers are expected to be considerable. A call center to serve 20 stores, for example, can cost $100,000 for the call distributing system, another $50,000 to $75,000 for the host computer, in addition to the personnel and rental costs. The VPN's 3Com routers, on the other hand, cost $1,000 to $1,500 for each remote site and $10,000 to $12,000 for the Oklahoma City call center.

There are other aspects of the VPN that are of interest. For example, in some areas there are clusters of Mazzio's restaurants that are already connected to each other by a frame relay network, but not to headquarters. In those situations, a single Internet connection can provide the VPN connection for all those stores. To provide redundancy, a dial-up Internet connection can be provided for each store in case the link goes down. Alternatively, two Internet connections can be used for a cluster of shops, with the routers balancing the traffic. Should one router or line go down, the other can pick up the load. Adding a restaurant to the Mazzio's network system is very simple: they open a franchise, set it up with an Internet connection, and it is on the VPN.

Another development with the Mazzio's system is typical of VPN deployment. While the initial intent was to use the VPN solely to connect the restaurants to the call center, the Mazzio's mobile workforce of area managers and the like are now being connected to it as well. Patterson did some research and discovered that they have over 20 people who dial in to the computer at a cost of $1,800 per month in long-distance charges. By the time you are reading this, they will all be connecting via the VPN, totally eliminating that monthly expense.

The VPN is also being used to download regular status reports from all the Mazzio's shops, which brings up the only hitch encountered with the system to date. As of this writing, for some reason FTP works in only one direction for the restaurants located in Arkansas. Go figure!

2.3.2 Galaxy Scientific Corporation

Galaxy Scientific Corporation's logo carries the subhead "Innovative Technology Solutions," which is about as good a summation of what they offer as anyone could come up with. Their business is broken down into four basic areas: information technology, aviation technology, navigation systems, and training systems. If you go to the pick list on the Products and Services page of their Web site, you'll encounter a long list of services ranging from 2D/3D graphics to Zyrcon, a computer game scheduled to be available in the first quarter of 1999. At the top of the product list page there are five categories: training development, training evaluation, instructional research, tool development, and multimedia production (where Zyrcon fits).

To give some examples, Galaxy Scientific offers expertise on Advanced Radio System Architecture and a training curriculum supporting the FAA's program for explosive detection systems. They operate and manage the Air Force's Training Research in Automated INstruction (TRAIN) program, which supports a large-scale basic research project in cognitive science.

In short, their interests and expertise are varied, and they operate through a number of satellite facilities which, as you'd expect, demand efficient connectivity. Today, thanks to their experience with their own VPN, one of their most prominent areas of expertise is systems integration, including virtual private networking and intranet and Internet solutions. As their literature puts it, "When Galaxy decided to extend our system integration expertise to include intranets and virtual private networks, we started with the toughest customer we know: Galaxy."

They learned a lot. In late 1996, before the term VPN became the buzzword it is today, Glenn Botkin, the company's intranet project manager, was asked to find a way to tie Galaxy's offices together in a network that would cut costs, improve productivity, and make it easier for the various divisions to collaborate on projects. The primary goal was to connect the seven core site offices. About a week before the company was going to sign off on the purchase of $160,000 worth of routers, the VPN possibility came to Botkin's attention.

Today those core offices are connected in a VPN using permanent virtual circuits (PVCs) provided by PSINet, with more of Galaxy Scientific's total of 28 sites being added using remote access services (RAS), ISDN, and the VPN. VPN access has also been extended to some 50 road warriors, and extranet capability allows direct contact with a few selected key customers and business partners. The international reach of PSINet has even allowed VPN access to a company team in China as well as other international travelers.

Their choice was to go with an Internet service provider that was offering an intranet service product—a type of service that has since become known as a virtual private network. Galaxy was a VPN pioneer. Galaxy's sites are linked through a VPN on PSINet's backbone, using frame relay switches that create PVCs that let PSINet guarantee a specific level of service, since the packets never leave PSINet's system even though it is part of the Internet.

By restricting the traffic to PSINet's switches, Galaxy's PVCs approximate the closed nature of dedicated point-to-point circuits, while still enjoying the efficiencies and redundancies of a packet-switched network. PSINet handles most of the management tasks, including the first level of security, that of knowing what goes on throughout their own network. Galaxy itself, of course, also monitors the VPN constantly to locate and plug any potential security holes. While PSINet can keep an eye on their own network, Galaxy is fully cognizant of the fact that only they can be directly responsible for meeting their own security needs.

To illustrate what a difference a VPN can make, before Galaxy's VPN was implemented their offices handled data traffic in a variety of ways. Email, for example, was managed by cc:Mail routers at each of five primary offices. These servers direct dialed each other several times a day. The corporate accounting system, on the other hand, was handled through direct dialing using modems connected to phone lines dedicated to that purpose. Botkin notes ruefully that the system was slow and prone to failure, and only two of the offices could connect at a time. Before the VPN was implemented, telephone charges alone were costing Galaxy Scientific close to $4,000 per month. If users wanted to exchange drawings, or timesheets had to be transferred to the central office, Galaxy resorted to Federal Express or fax to transmit them.

Now, with the VPN, the timesheets are handled over the network as part of the normal work flow to accounting. Sharing an engineering drawing is a simple drag-and-drop action through the VPN. While employees are encouraged to make such transfers at night when network traffic is low, it is infinitely easier than an email transfer and infinitely quicker than Federal Express. Furthermore, electronic transfer means that the drawings are instantly ready to be worked on by the recipient on her computer.

One other benefit of Galaxy's VPN architecture—and one that differentiates it from a WAN—is that it allows technicians anywhere on the network to monitor, manage, and provide administration to other remote offices. Remote users and extranet customers can even receive direct technical assistance in the same manner. While this level of service is possible with a WAN, it requires an investment in specialized software to provide it, something that is not required with Galaxy's VPN. We'll look more at Galaxy's experience in managing a VPN in Chapter 10.

We'll also take a closer look at the architecture of Galaxy Scientific's system in Chapter 4, where we'll see how a service such as that offered by PSINet can offer performance guarantees not generally available on the Internet.

2.4 Conclusion

In this chapter we've attached some reality to the theoretical benefits of the VPNs discussed in Chapter 1. In our illustrations it has become evident that VPNs are almost infinitely scalable, both physically and geographically. Whole industries have come to rely on them for efficient communication. Even governments have begun to employ them: the State of Kansas Department of Revenue has drawn favorable comment for its efficiency and attention to taxpayer service—such as issuing refunds—thanks, in part, to a VPN connecting their offices.

It is even possible to do things with a VPN that it would be virtually impossible to do any other way. How else could you provide 12,000 remote users scattered all over the country with fast, inexpensive access to a company network? How else could you trade electric power on a minute-by-minute basis using any medium other than a prohibitively expensive WAN? How else could you serve the entire automobile industry? The ANX system will be dynamic, flexible, and scalable, and the VPN will make it relatively simple to add or remove nodes in what is a massive, vital industry.

It is apparent, too, that while a VPN may be built with one function in mind, as it develops it rarely ends up as one discrete thing or another in terms of function, thanks to the flexibility inherent in the concept. What begins as an intranet project is likely to acquire both extranet and remote access functions and vice versa. Since the greatest savings are realized by using a VPN for remote access, that is frequently the reason one is installed in the first place, but as experience is gained, other functions are added. What starts out as a remote access server frequently gains value as the flexibility of the VPN is exploited. As you choose your VPN product, be aware that while all you see it being used for right now is an intranet, other applications may develop. Don't let yourself get boxed in.

On the other hand, there are reasons to proceed cautiously in implementing a VPN. In Chapter 3, we will look at the issues that you must address before committing yourself to one.

3

The Downside to VPNs

At this point, you are probably thinking that a VPN is just the thing for you. It sounds like the greatest invention since sliced bread. It will save you money. It will connect you with the world.

Not to dash cold water on the idea, but there are issues in implementing a VPN that you must take a close look at before diving in. Is a VPN what you need? Can you make the connections needed to a public network? How vital is security to you, particularly if your VPN would be on the public Internet? In addition, there are issues of performance and quality of service, particularly on the Internet. Will you have to train your personnel, and if so, how much time can you afford for that?

What about the problem of interoperability? How easy is it going to be to connect what you've got? What if you've got an AppleTalk network in Topeka and a NetWare network in Kalamazoo and you want to connect them? Are you thinking of an extranet, and if so, what does your proposed partner have? What costs are you likely to incur if you go the VPN route?

Let's take a close look at some of these issues and, as we go through them, realize that this is not an all-inclusive list. There are sure to be factors particular to your situation that we have no way of even guessing at.

3.1 Do You Really Need a VPN?

This may seem like a very elementary question, but it is one that too often is not asked. What do you want to do with a VPN? Or, to put it another way, what are you doing now that having a VPN will help you do better and less expensively? What do you think you need to do in the future that you cannot do now that having a VPN will make possible? If the only reason the CEO is asking for a VPN is so he can log on to the network from home, you might want to consider setting up a remote access server for him instead.

If you have a number of road warriors running up large telephone bills, chances are a VPN will save you money. If you have branch offices and factories that you need contact with, particularly overseas, a VPN is probably worth considering. If you have vendors and customers you could use EDI with, or could coordinate purchases and shipping with better, a VPN is a good option to consider.

But even if there are things you really want that require some sort of a WAN, don't fall for the hype that an Internet-based VPN is necessarily what you need, that it's a quick, easy, cheap way to get what you want. You may get into the project only to discover that it is anything but quick and easy, that cheap is a relative term, and that the VPN may not give you what you need, never mind what you think you want.

Look at all the other possibilities, even if only briefly. When we get into comparing VPNs on the Internet vs. other connection infrastructure options, you'll see that there are some issues of reliability, quality of service, and security that may, for you, tip the balance to a network of private virtual circuits through a frame relay service. On the other hand, while a leased-line WAN will cost you more, there may be good reasons to go for that level of service.

When we get into the actual VPN planning process, we'll go into this questioning in more detail. At this stage, probably the most important question you need to ask yourself is, "Is there something we are doing or want to do that can be done by a VPN, and is a VPN the best way for us to do it?"

3.2 Connection Availability

Is a VPN even possible for you? Believe it or not, there have been cases where a company has gone out and bought a VPN package, only to discover that they can't connect to the point they planned to because there's no Internet service to it. It's rare, but it can happen, and it has happened. Check out both ends of any connections. If your main goal is to connect your office in San Francisco to a facility in Siberia, while there's no problem on Market Street, the nearest POP to Ege-Khaya may be in Yakutsk, across 800 miles of tundra.

If your inclination is to go with a more "private" VPN by using PVCs through a frame relay service's cloud, the service provider you select must have POPs where you need them. The problem is the same if you are going to confine your users to a single Internet service provider for access. Remember, POPs restricted to a single provider are less ubiquitous than the sum total of Internet POPs for all providers, and while GTE may have a POP near you, maybe only MCI, or Al's General Store and Service Station, has a POP near your destination. You've got to make sure that there are POPs within a reasonable distance of all the major facilities you want plugged in to the VPN, otherwise the cost of connecting could obliterate any savings.

What level of service is available? If you're connecting to small offices, an ISDN connection may be sufficient. For road warriors, a dial-in connection is best, and the chances of locating one of those is no problem, except, maybe, in Siberia. But what if you want to connect a major facility that needs a lot of bandwidth for exchanging engineering drawings or holding videoconferences, can you get xDSL or a fractional T1 connection at a price you can afford?

3.3 Security

One of the most important issues to consider in implementing a VPN is security. By its very nature, having a VPN means that you are moving your company's data on a public network, making it vulnerable to possible exposure or attack. If you are not already connected to the Internet, implementing a VPN using the Internet will require that you be on the Internet. This opens you to all the hazards of the Internet.

Now don't get us wrong. We are all in favor of the Internet. However, any company connecting to the Internet without first learning as much as they can about the hazards it presents makes as much sense as a toddler taking a stroll down the middle of a busy interstate. Not everyone out there on the information highway is as careful or honest as they should be. There is even the occasional antisocial cracker who will attack your system through your Internet connection just for the pleasure of it.

If you are on the Internet already, you are presumably aware of the dangers. There are crackers who may try to penetrate your network just for the challenge. Others may do so for profit. Then there is the inconvenience of spam email, or the frustration of denial of service attacks in which someone, in a pique, floods your server with messages, clogs the channel, or even crashes the server. There is the contagion of viruses imported on email attachments or even downloaded by employees who found an FTP site with some interesting piece of software.

This is not a book about Internet security, so we won't go into the details here. But before you connect your business to the Internet, we strongly recommend that you consult the literature on the subject so you know what you're getting into and what steps to take to protect your resources.

When you implement a VPN, you are not only vulnerable to all of these hazards, but you are taking on some others, some of which are peculiar to virtual private networks. Guarding against these hazards adds a certain amount of overhead to the project, in terms of installation, data transmission delays, and management. Only you can judge whether it is worth the hassle, but let's take a look at the specific dangers to VPN traffic.

3.3.1 Snooping or Sniffing

There are programs available on the Internet that are designed to *sniff* transmitted packets. Packet sniffers are actually a part of some operating systems sold today. They have legitimate uses for analyzing network traffic and troubleshooting. Some people put them to less ethical uses. These people may simply be curious, or they may be indulging in a little corporate espionage. Either way, they could be studying your network. It is also possible to snoop, or actually read network traffic, exposing your secrets. "Sniffers" monitor network traffic (e.g., source and destination). "Snoopers" read the traffic.

The solution is to encrypt the packet, scrambling the data so it can only be read by someone who has the proper key. However, encryption imposes its own demands on the system and its management, as we'll see in Chapters 5, 6, and 7. It imposes computational overhead that has to be allowed for, along with user authentication and key management issues that add administrative overhead.

3.3.2 Capturing Addresses

A network packet carries a lot of interesting information with it, other than the payload itself. For example, it carries both source and destination addresses. Crackers like to sniff those out because it is then possible to mount assaults on those addresses. For example, a cracker might capture a server's address, then hit it with a flood of messages that overload it. When the server crashes, it often dumps all the data in its core so the cracker can capture it. That core dump might contain confidential information or passwords and log-in information that the cracker can then use to attack other parts of your LAN.

Captured addresses also allow *spoofing*, which is when an unauthorized user slips through your firewall by appearing to come from an IP address that is acceptable to your security system. Once in the door he may roam at will, perhaps trying to gain higher privileges, reading data on servers or vandalizing the system in some way. If the internal IP addresses of your network are revealed, it opens up individual servers or workstations to attack.

The solution, obviously, is to somehow conceal the true source and destination addresses of the packet. There are ways, of course, for this to be accomplished; for example, a proxy server or address translation can be used. As we'll see, most—but not all—VPN implementations add a new header in a process called encapsulation or tunneling, and many then encrypt (along with the data) the original header that contains the true source and destination addresses into a new payload. When the packet arrives, the receiving machine decrypts the original header along with the data and forwards the packet on to its destination. The hacker will have learned the addresses of the VPN servers involved, but, hopefully, nothing behind them. The VPN servers will filter out packets that don't originate from a known source.

Hiding the internal IP addresses is all well and good, unless your network administrator needs to track the true origins and destinations of your network traffic. Perhaps she's doing it to track loads on the network, or it gives her information about application utilization on your system. Suddenly she loses this capability. This problem can be one of the hidden costs of implementing a VPN.

3.3.3 Session Hijacking

VPN communication almost always takes place with an exchange of messages (a *session*). Unless proper precautions are taken, it is possible for a third party to take control of a session, or *hijack* it. Alice may think she's talking to Bob when she's really talking to Charlie. It's only when Charlie suddenly appears on the accounts payable list as being owed $10,000 that you realize you may have a serious problem.

In short, a VPN cannot be run like an America Online chat room; users must be identified and authenticated. This requires strong user authentication procedures and systems. As we'll see when we get into the technical details of VPNs, authentication is not a simple problem to solve even under the best of circumstances. How can you tell exactly who is sitting at that computer halfway around the world from you? We'll see that when we're looking at a large-scale VPN, particularly an extranet VPN, it is a major challenge.

There are solutions, of course. However, implementing and managing them becomes one of the costs of installing and running a VPN.

3.3.4 Data Tampering

If the data can be read, it can also be tampered with. If what Alice receives is not what Bob sent, the consequences can be catastrophic. This can be innocent tampering, or it can be malicious. Either way it calls into question the security of the entire system. For a VPN to work, a web of trust must be established so that every user is sure of whom he or she is talking to and that the data is arriving unchanged.

Again, almost every VPN system provides a means to verify the authenticity of the data. It's usually combined with the encryption process through the use of digital signatures. But once again it imposes some overhead on the process of exchanging data. Verification takes time. It can also require, again, some management burdens.

3.4 The Lack of Standards

As we said earlier, even though it has been around for 5 years or more, the VPN industry is still young. There are a number of different protocols, and standards are still under development. Once the Internet Engineering Task Force completes its work on IPSec, MPLS (Multi-Protocol Label Switching), L2TP (Layer 2 Tunneling Protocol), and whatever other protocols are brewing in the VPN industry or may impact VPNs, there will at least be some targets for vendors to shoot at.

However, if you think that once the IETF has signed off on a protocol you'll be able to buy products from several vendors and expect them to just plug into each other, you are sorely mistaken. All a protocol is is a verbal description of how something is supposed to be done, such as how to reach an agreement on encryption or how to exchange encryption keys. An IETF standard is made up of words, not computer code, and it is laced with words like *must* and *should* and *may*. These words are even defined in IETF drafts and requests for comment (RFCs).

- MUST   This word or the adjective "REQUIRED" means that the item is an absolute requirement of the specification.
- SHOULD   This word or the adjective "RECOMMENDED" means that there might exist valid reasons in particular circumstances to ignore this item, but the full implications should be understood and the case carefully weighed before taking a different course.
- MAY   This word or the adjective "OPTIONAL" means that this item is truly optional. One vendor might choose to include the item because a particular marketplace requires it or because it enhances the product, for example; another vendor may omit the same item.

So an IETF RFC may have wording in it like this: "Routing headers for which integrity has not been cryptographically protected *should* be ignored by the receiver. If this rule is not strictly adhered to, then the system will be vulnerable to various kinds of attacks, including source routing attacks." In other words, the vendor implementing this feature in his product may choose to ignore it, even though that may not be wise. When you get into the *may* area, things get even fuzzier.

Going from the words to the actual computer code is another long step. The IETF standards do not say *how* something that must be done shall be done. Implementation of the standards is up to the vendors. Every vendor—and every engineer—has a different twist on how he or she is going to implement a particular aspect of the protocol. On one VPN server, the protocol may be implemented in a way that is incompatible with the way it is implemented on another VPN server. Even within one vendor's product line, the way it is implemented on a server may not quite work reliably with the way it is implemented on the client side.

If you want a concrete example of the kind of confusion that can result, look at the state of the browser industry today. There are sites on the World Wide Web that are optimized for the latest version of Microsoft's Internet Explorer, while others are optimized for the latest browser from Netscape. Come into one of those sites with the wrong browser and, at the very least, you'll miss some of the features of the site. Some incompatibilities might even crash your browser. In the case of a VPN, incompatibilities like that usually mean that the darn thing just won't work, or that a vital security feature, such as encryption, will be seriously weakened.

This is not meant as a criticism of the IETF, their working groups, or the vendors. Developing these protocols is a painstaking process, involving endless discussions, with the language being steadily refined. But human language is imprecise, compared to the precise language required by computers, and the way human language is interpreted is very personal. Eventually, as vendors refine and debug their products, and as products are tested by organizations such as the ICSA, interoperability improves. But it takes time.

What makes it even more confusing is that there are at least a half dozen different protocols that can be used to build a VPN. There are different tunneling protocols that operate in different ways. Then there's encryption and key exchange, data verification, and user authentication, all of which can be done in different ways and combined with any of the tunneling standards. One vendor uses Layer 2 Tunneling Protocol (L2TP); another uses the Point-to-Point Tunneling Protocol (PPTP). Neither of those protocols, as they exist now, specify what kind of encryption *must* be used, and although they recommend the use of IPSec's encryption standard (using that vague term *should*), vendors are not bound by that recommendation.

At this stage, what this means for you is that unless you assemble your VPN solely out of one vendor's product line, you may be buying yourself a peck of trouble. Even within one vendor's product line there may be glitches. Naturally, if you are looking at a VPN that will serve as an extranet, the problem is compounded. Somehow you and your potential partners will have to reach some kind of an agreement to ensure interoperability. You have your favorite VPN vendor and they have theirs. Their network is NetWare; yours is TCP/IP. They use routers from Cisco with a proxy server, while you prefer 3Com with a firewall from someone else.

Fortunately, the situation is not as bleak as this may make it sound. With the demand by the auto industry for interoperability for the ANX network, and the ICSA testing products for interoperability, the problem of VPN inter-operability may be solved sooner rather than later. ICSA certification of VPN products will be extremely important to the VPN industry in general. The ANX project is so large that a significant number of vendors are currently sub-mitting their products for ICSA certification, which will soon give you a num-ber of competitors to choose from in building your system.

Fortunately, also, as the industry matures the problem of standards will di-minish. Compare the VPN industry, for example, with the modem industry. When a new standard emerged, such as the 56 Kbps standard, competing ven-dors offered up their version. The International Telecommunications Union eventually got into the act and offered up a compromise standard, v.90. Then the vendors implemented the standards, but it was still some time before 3Com modems were able to talk consistently with Hayes modems at high speeds. Eventually the incompatibilities were ironed out and things now work well, but it did take time. So will it be with VPN standards.

As it is now, however, the lack of interoperability is a serious issue, one that you ignore at your peril if you try to casually mix products from compet-ing vendors. Also, don't forget that an interoperability problem is like a soft-ware bug—it can lurk undetected in a system for months, perhaps bringing the system down when you implement some new service, perhaps suddenly appearing for no apparent reason at all or simply because the date changed.

3.5 Performance/Quality of Service

Quality of service (QoS) is a major issue on the Internet, as we all know, so much so that it has acquired an acronym all its own. We've all had experience with the World Wide Wait. We've seen days when the Internet has been dragged down by extremely heavy traffic. Even worse is when a cable fails somewhere and packets back up and are rerouted by way of Tibet to get from Chicago to St. Louis. If your VPN demands high reliability and QoS, then the Internet may not be the best place for it.

If you are thinking of using your VPN for videoconferencing, the issue is particularly acute. Dropped frames and sound can turn a conference into gib-berish. Voice transmission over the Internet imposes similar demands, al-though the bandwidth requirements are not as stringent. The technical term for packet delays is *latency,* and it is important even for uses other than the more obvious videoconference. No one wants to drag and drop a file and then sit there in frustration while the actual transfer slogs along waiting for pack-ets to arrive.

Getting a meaningful guarantee from an ISP won't be easy. While service level agreements (SLAs) are not unheard of with ISPs, they may come with so many qualifications as to be essentially useless. We'll go into SLAs in more detail later, but the reality is that no Internet service provider can guarantee the quality of service for packets that traverse any path other than their own backbone, and not all backbones are created equal.

As we'll see when we get into our discussion of the Internet vs. "private" public networks—such as frame relay services—the Internet should probably not be your first choice if the issue of reliability and quality of service are important to you.

Again, however, the situation is not as bleak as it may seem. The IETF is addressing the QoS issue by developing the Multi-Protocol Label Switching (MPLS) protocol, which we'll look at in a little more detail in Chapter 7.

3.6 Hidden Costs

When you prepare to make a deal with a VPN vendor, there will be a cost quote, of course. Then, too, you'll be negotiating with an ISP, perhaps, or the local telco, and they'll give you prices. Don't forget to look beyond those figures to costs that are less predictable but just as real. Training is one, and we'll discuss that issue in more detail further on.

Your first-year costs are almost unavoidably going to be hefty. As we've seen in some of our studies, they can actually run more than your current costs. You may need to add capacity to your existing Internet hookup. You'll have some hardware replacement costs. There will be installation charges. There are likely to be some pretty hefty staff costs as you bring the system on-line. Make sure you have the resources to carry you through this first period, with plenty to spare, because things will almost certainly go wrong somewhere, sometime in the process.

Don't think, either, that the moment the VPN goes online you can unplug your current system. Allow some overlap. That way, when problems crop up with the VPN, as they are almost certain to do, you have something to fall back on. Only after the VPN has proven itself can you safely dump the old rig. Only then will your savings really begin.

In short, be prepared to weather some storms. If there aren't any, then you are lucky and that much better off.

3.7 Management

How are you going to manage your VPN? Do you have the resources to manage it yourself? It goes beyond managing a simple LAN, after all. You have to be able to authenticate the users. You have to be able to track your traffic both internally and externally. You have to be braced to handle intruders or problem users who may be 10,000 miles away.

What about tech support for your users? If they are halfway around the world, they're going to be working while your office is sleeping. If they're having a problem, they may not be able to send you email to report it—they're going to want to talk to someone. If the work of the VPN isn't mission critical, perhaps it can wait, but it won't leave a very good impression if an important customer on an extranet doesn't get a prompt response. Can you afford to establish a 24 × 7 technical support crew, with toll-free lines, and to staff it around the clock?

When we get into discussion of the architecture, and further, when we start going into the planning and design process itself, you'll see that the management issue must be nailed down before you get very far into the process. You may find it preferable to outsource the entire project just based on the management issue, if your shop doesn't have the resources. User authentication may require establishing a relationship with a remote authorization server. If you want more than average security, you may want to talk to a company like Security Dynamics Technologies, Inc., with its SecureID product for tighter controls.

Encryption key management for a large extranet is going to require a relationship with a certificate authority (CA), unless you are prepared to run your own. If you do want to run your own key management, see if you still feel that way after reading Chapters 5 and 6, which dig into the complexities of encryption, data verification, and key management.

3.8 Fitting It In with Your Architecture

Will a VPN work with your current system? Are you running Banyan Vines or NetWare or token ring or AppleTalk on your local LAN? How hard is it going to be to find a VPN product that will work with your current network and do what you want?

Not all VPN protocols will handle non-IP packets, so if you're running NetWare or AppleTalk, your choice of vendors is reduced. Not all VPN protocols can provide for mobile users, or setting up the mobile clients may be cumbersome or expensive or may involve more user training and support than you can provide. If your goal is a VPN to serve your mobile workforce, can you find a VPN product that will do that and also connect to your LAN? The chances are that there is a way to do it, but you may have to search a little to find it. It may also involve compromises you're not willing to make.

What do you have in the way of firewalls, proxy servers, and routers? If you don't have them already, you're probably going to need them. Some firewall products come with VPN capabilities built in, as do some routers. Some VPN solutions require special servers. When we get to the chapter on VPN architecture, you'll see that there are myriad ways to design a VPN. Some of them will work for you; some of them will not be available to you, depending on what equipment you have and what you want to do.

3.9 End User Training

Even if they are already familiar with your LAN, your users are probably not going to be able to simply dive in and swim the VPN without some training. For road warriors with no experience beyond retrieving their email, the challenges are even greater. As Prudential rolls out the LaunchPad project, which will take a year or more, they are providing every one of the 12,000 field representatives and agents with 2 days of training in use of the new system. Twenty-four thousand person-days is a lot of time to have to pay for. Furthermore, the training of a field force that size is like painting the Golden Gate Bridge, a continuous process. Prudential is offering continuing training in the classroom, by way of interactive TV and CD-ROM.

Granted, this is a major paradigm shift for Prudential, a big company. They are migrating a huge workforce over to the use of Lotus Notes and Domino, but your VPN may entail a similar migration. They have the resources to devote to their end user training. Don't forget to allocate the resources you'll need for yours. These resources include accounting for the loss of productivity while the training goes on.

On a smaller scale, for example, when a medical software company established a VPN for their 50 road warriors, it was slow to gain acceptance. It wasn't that the users were unwilling. It was simply a matter of time available. The field staff was so busy, it was hard for them to find the time to learn to use the system, and the company wasn't able to set up a formal training schedule. Fortunately the savings—estimated at $150,000 per year—made the effort worthwhile, and the staff did eventually complete the migration to the VPN. It just took time.

The point is, don't underestimate the training that your people may require before they can use the new tools you're giving them. If they're going to have to install the client software themselves, they face another learning experience there as well, and you will have to be ready to help them through the process. Somehow the time will have to be found for them to train. Allow for it.

They'll also need some continuing support. Since the VPN will offer services they may not be accustomed to with their former system, they'll have to be given time to learn those too. In the end it will all probably pay off, but these hidden expenses should be anticipated, and plans should be made to support your users both in the beginning and in the long term.

3.10 Security, Again

We're returning to the security issue again simply to stress its importance. The security of your systems and your data is vital. A VPN unavoidably raises security issues that you would not otherwise face. As we discussed, in going on the Internet in the first place you are exposing your systems to security risks not present otherwise. If you then use the Internet for your VPN, the data traversing the VPN faces hazards it would not face on a leased-line network or even on an IP, frame relay, or ATM-based network that is not part of the Internet, simply because the service providers in these networks exercise at least some control over access to their own network.

How much risk are you willing to accept? How much are you willing or able to pay to reduce risk to an acceptable level? Are the savings you can expect from your VPN more than enough to cover the costs?

3.11 Conclusion

There are important issues that must be faced before deciding to implement a VPN. Leading the way is the simple question of whether you really need one or not. We all know it is very easy to get swept up in industry hype. Then there's the rather elementary question of whether a VPN is even possible for you. Before you waste a lot of time planning a VPN, find out if it will connect what and where you need to connect and do what you need done.

Look out for the various little "gotchas" that might turn around and bite you once you get a VPN up and running. Paramount among these is the security issue, followed by the current lack of standards in the VPN industry, which raise serious interoperability questions. Don't forget to analyze just what you need in the way of QoS and just how well you're equipped to take on the burdens of a VPN.

4

Internet Versus Other VPNs

As we've mentioned earlier, there's more than one foundation, more than one shared public network, on which to build a VPN. The medium for VPNs that has received the most industry attention is the Internet. However, it is not the only solution, and it may not even be the best choice for your situation. While this book does concentrate on Internet-based VPNs, we want to take at least a brief look at the reasons for and against using a VPN built on switched backbones, such as public frame relay and ATM networks run by companies such as Sprint, GTE, AT&T, and others.

As we look at their advantages and disadvantages, bear in mind how these may apply to your own needs. We'll find that, while Internet VPNs offer what appear to be undeniable cost advantages, there are other issues to be considered. As we saw in Chapter 3, these include security, reliability, and quality of service. On the other hand, there may be factors that make such a non–Internet-based VPN impractical for you.

4.1 Clearing Up Some Confusion

One of the big contributing factors to the confusion in the VPN industry is the way terminology is thrown around. For example, the term "the Internet" is used as if it were a single entity and as if it were the only place that the Internet protocols are used or where VPNs can be built. Then, too, "frame relay" and "ATM" are frequently used as if they were competitors of, or somehow excluded, the Internet protocols or competed with the Internet. Unless you already understand how the Internet works and is controlled—or rather *not* controlled—and how frame relay relates to the Internet and its protocols, these terms are misleading and confusing.

Most of this discussion may be very familiar to you. If it is, we recommend skipping on to Section 4.2 where we begin to compare the advantages and disadvantages of Internet and frame relay VPNs. But if you don't know what the Internet is and how it works and what frame relay and ATM can do, read on. This knowledge will later help you make intelligent decisions as you plan your VPN.

4.1.1 The Internet

Taking these in order, the Internet is not a single entity, nor is it the only place where the Internet Protocol (IP) and Transmission Control Protocol (TCP) are used; it is just the largest, most visible example of TCP/IP at work.

The Internet is actually an assembly of TCP/IP networks that are interconnected into a mass supernetwork. This assemblage is not under any one entity's control. Even the entity that assigns IP addresses on the Internet has no control over the actual operation of the network. It is just one of a number of groups that cope with various aspects of the Internet. For example, the Internet Engineering Task Force (IETF) works to develop standards by which various things are done on the Internet so that a router or server built by one vendor communicates reliably with a router or server from another vendor.

These standards, as discussed in Chapter 3, are called protocols, and are essentially detailed descriptions of how something is supposed to be done, such as how an Internet Protocol packet is designed, how it does what it does, and what information it contains (such as which set of bits in the header gives the destination address so the router knows what to read in order to know where to send it). The Transmission Control Protocol specifies how two hosts establish a connection, exchange streams of data, ensure delivery, and make sure the packets are placed in the correct order at the receiving end. The World Wide Web Consortium (W3C) attempts to do standardization for the World Wide Web by setting standards for the protocols that it depends on, such as HyperText Markup Language (HTML) and HyperText Transport Protocol (HTTP).

The important thing to realize is that there is no single body that oversees the day-to-day, hour-to-hour operation of the Internet. This lack of centralized control has important implications with regard to your choice about whether to put your VPN on the Internet or on some other network.

How the data moves through the Internet is another important thing to know, because it affects the speed and reliability of that movement, compared to other networks. To draw an analogy, within the Internet, to get from here to there data can take either an interstate highway (a *backbone*) or side streets (pass through local networks, moving from network to network). Like interstate highways, backbones are major pipelines that carry traffic at gigabit rates. The side streets are the paths from network to network through peer arrangements between cooperating networks. Data going from network A to network D can pass through networks B and C, instead of taking a backbone, thanks to these connections. A packet of data, or *datagram*, may travel across the country on one of the backbones, or it may be handed off from network to network through these peer arrangements. It's like the choice between taking I-95 from Boston to Miami or instead driving the side streets between the two cities, including wending your way through Manhattan. Just as with traffic through a city, where sometimes the side streets are less congested than the freeway, there may not be any real speed advantage between the two choices.

As Figure 4-1 illustrates, all of these elements are interlocked. The ovals represent networks within the Internet. Where they intersect with another network, there is usually a peer agreement allowing each to carry the other's

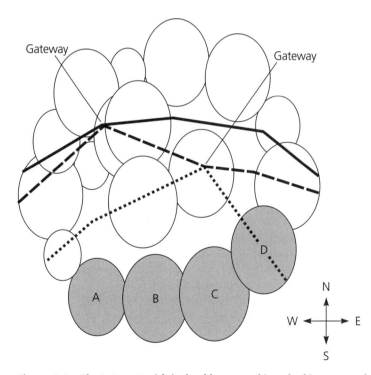

Figure 4-1   The Internet with its backbones and interlocking networks.

traffic on through the Internet. No peer agreement means no direct exchange of traffic between those two networks. The heavy lines represent three different backbones (there are actually about 40 backbones at latest count). Where they touch, the backbones interconnect at gateways. There are major gateways in the U.S. on the east and west coasts (where overseas traffic moving through undersea cables is handled) as well as within the country where backbones exchange traffic.

From this illustration, perhaps you can see why the Internet is usually depicted as a cloud.

The multitude of networks that make up the Internet, such as those run by local ISPs, are connected to one backbone or another, either directly or through a peer agreement or series of peer agreements to a network that is connected to a backbone. For example, network A doesn't have a peer agreement with the network to its west, but does with network B to its east, which links to network C, which links to network D, which does connect to the backbone.

For the average packet moving through the Internet, more often than not the path it takes is likely to use a backbone in one place and to travel through a network or series of networks in another. It may take a backbone partway, with network peer arrangements handing it off in other places. It may go partway on one backbone and then transfer to another. It all depends on where the packet originated, what its destination is, and how the Internet's routers decide to route the packet, and that is determined by what pathways are available at the time the packet arrives at the router. The router chooses the most efficient path available *at that particular moment.*

Unfortunately, what may be the most efficient path available at that moment may mean that the packet takes a long detour because other, normally more efficient paths are not available because of heavy traffic or some other problem. In this way, each packet picks its own way through the maze, even packets that make up parts of the same message, so the first packet that makes up part of a message may be routed on a backbone from New York by way of Chicago to Los Angeles, while the next will wend its way through networks in Georgia and Alabama and so forth, until it is reunited with the first packet at its destination. You won't see the message until all the packets have made their way to you and the message is reassembled.

As we've said, no one entity has responsibility over the day-to-day operation of the entire assembly of cables, bridges, switches, routers, networks, and gateways that make up the Internet. The backbones are run by 30 or 40 different companies such as AT&T, GTE, PSINet, and WorldCom. Every network involved in peer agreements is under the control of its own owner. Peering is negotiated between these networks on an individual basis. The usual deal is a quid pro quo: "I'll carry your traffic and you carry mine and we're even."

The backbone owners watch their own backbones and the connections with other backbones, and networks watch themselves and their connections, but no one oversees the whole. This lack of centralized control means that, as it operates now, there are no guarantees as to how well the Internet will function at any given time or how quickly a message will necessarily get through (which they sometimes don't). Also, it means that it is very hard to find anyone to call when things fail or anyone to sue when things go seriously—and inconveniently—wrong. As anyone who has run any kind of a network knows, things will fail from time to time and go seriously and inconveniently wrong every once in a while, usually at the worst possible moment.

However, this does *not* mean that the Internet is inherently weak, unreliable, or inferior. In fact, it is extremely robust and reliable, particularly considering the speed with which it has grown and the demands that have been placed on it. It works and works well, most of the time. In terms of cost-effectiveness, it cannot be beat.

The Internet is robust because it was embodied in the initial idea of a nationwide computer network, and it is actually a product of the architecture of connections and routers. If one node fails, the routers automatically find paths around it so the traffic continues to flow. While it's possible that any one cable, subnetwork, or router may fail, it is highly unlikely that all—or even a significant portion—of the bits and pieces that make up the Internet will fail all at the same time. When there is a major failure, which usually shows up at your end as a slowdown in traffic, the wizards who watch over the backbones and primary networks quickly collaborate to solve the problem.

But the lack of a centralized authority does mean that there is a lack of guarantees. Your ISP is unable to give you any meaningful promises that your messages will get through in a timely fashion simply because, unless the company is a backbone provider and can guarantee that only their backbone will be used to move your data, they have no control over the other systems the messages may have to traverse.

Not all backbones and networks are created equal; some work better than others. Routers get jammed up and packets get lost. Messages get delayed. In studies done by *Boardwatch* magazine and published in the September 1998 issue, depending on the backbone used, the median download time for a 50 Kb Web page ranged from 1.840 seconds all the way up to 7.610 seconds. Within the tests on each backbone, sometimes the download took 1 or 2 seconds, sometimes more than 30 seconds, or sometimes didn't make it at all. This study looked strictly at the backbones. While it may not be definitive, it does illustrate the capricious nature of the Internet. We all know that the Internet is faster during some hours of the day than others, and there are times when something major goes wrong and traffic slows to a crawl as packets are rerouted around the problem.

4.1.2 TCP/IP on Other Networks

The Transmission Control Protocol and Internet Protocol are the protocols most commonly used to transmit messages on the Internet and to make sure they get there intact. They are not the only ones, but they are almost certainly the ones a VPN on the Internet will use. However, they also can be and are used on a multitude of networks that have no connection with the Internet. These may be private networks, or they may be public networks run by a service provider. TCP/IP is also used on networks that connect to the Internet but that are not what we may think of as really part of the Internet, such as a TCP/IP LAN that connects to the Internet but doesn't itself carry Internet traffic to other Internet users.

4.1.3 Frame Relay, ATM, and TCP/IP

Frame relay and ATM are data transmission protocols that are spoken of as if they are used in place of IP, which is incorrect. They are switching protocols that direct the traffic through a particular kind of network. Both frame relay switches and ATM switches can be and are used to transmit IP packets. In fact, it is entirely possible that, if you are already connected to the Internet, it is through a frame relay connection. Hence, while you may choose to sign on with a frame relay or ATM service provider for your VPN, that does not mean you can't use an IP-based VPN product. On the other hand, you are not limited to IP for your VPN either, although most VPN products are built around TCP/IP.

Technical details aside, there are two major differences between frame relay and ATM. The first is speed. Frame relay offers speeds between 56 Kbps and 45 Mbps. ATM is faster, offering 25 to 622 Mbps. The second is that ATM offers bandwidth on demand, which allows the system to dynamically adjust to the needs of a customer. As such it is offered as a service for people who eed high data rates and quality of service for tasks like videoconferencing. It is also used for moving large amounts of data. For example, as we saw in our discussion of the automotive industry's ANX network, ATM switches are used within the Internet to move IP traffic for ANX. Unless you need great speed and flexibility, your chances of needing an ATM service are relatively slim. For the sake of simplicity, we'll concentrate here on frame relay networks.

4.2 The Internet Versus Private Services

One important element of what we are looking at here when we consider a frame relay service versus the Internet for our VPN is actually a matter of having a VPN built on a single, coherent network with a visible owner and administrator, such as WorldCom or Sprint, as compared to having your VPN on the more amorphous creation known as the Internet. The advantages in terms of security and maintaining quality of service should be obvious.

However, there are also specific technical advantages to be found in using a single frame relay service for your VPN, and it's worth looking at how they are implemented. Thanks to them, as we'll see in Section 4.2.2, it is possible—and not unusual—to set up a VPN using the frame relay services of one of the Internet's backbone providers. For the sake of sanity, we'll use the term *frame relay VPN* to mean a VPN that is somehow insulated from the Internet itself, even though the service provider may be an Internet service provider as well and the VPN may even use the same backbone that carries Internet traffic.

4.2.1 The Frame Relay Advantages

As we've said, frame relay switching offers some special advantages over the Internet's system of routers and switches. The overhead on a frame relay frame is only 5 bytes, compared to 20 bytes on an IP packet, making frame relay more efficient, although if you're moving IP packets using frame relay some of that efficiency may be lost. The other, more important advantages arise because of the way the traffic is handled and how frame relay deals with problems such as damaged packets and congestion on the network's switches. These differences allow frame relay networks to guarantee a level of service and to maintain it even when traffic starts to get heavy, unlike the Internet that slows down greatly when routers get overloaded.

Damaged Packets
One of the requirements of frame relay is high line quality. The error rate is extremely low on the fiber that is usually used for frame relay networks. Still, things happen, and packets do get damaged. On other networks, such as an X.25 packet network, if a switch detects an error (a damaged packet) it sends a message requesting that a new packet be sent. This results in a series of messages back and forth as the error is corrected, which both increases network traffic and results in waiting periods for missing packets.

Frame relay service, on the other hand, doesn't offer any error correction of its own. If a frame fails an integrity check at a switch, it is simply discarded. Instead, frame relay relies on higher-level protocols at the receiving end to request a resend of missing frames as they are detected. Thus, the second requirement for a frame relay network (aside from clean lines) is that end devices must run an intelligent higher-layer protocol, such as TCP. With this system, instead of every switch getting into the act of checking for missing packets and requesting resends, only the receiving node sends a message asking for a repeat of the missing data. This results in fewer delays and less traffic to clog the network.

TCP nodes communicate in the background, using an exchange of house-keeping messages, to keep things running smoothly. For example, the sender needs to know that the mail is getting through. To accomplish this, the receiving end will send an acknowledgment when a given number of packets or frames has been received in good shape. If there is a problem, such as a missing packet or frame, instead of an "everything's OK" acknowledgment being sent, a request for a resend of the missing packet or frame goes out and the sending node responds accordingly by resending the missing packet or frame.

Congestion

Because of the high line quality used for frame relay networks, damaged frames are rare. Consequently, the largest cause of frame loss is congestion. When congestion occurs, jammed up switches must discard frames because once their buffers are full, they have no place left to store new frames while frames already in the buffer are being processed. To minimize such loss, frame relay provides a system for anticipating congestion, instead of just reacting to it once it starts.

In a normal network, as the graph in Figure 4-2 illustrates, as the offered load (the traffic being sent) increases, the network throughput rises smoothly until congestion begins to show up (point A). From there the rate of increase of throughput slows until congestion reaches a critical stage (point B) and the switch begins to discard more and more frames because its buffers are full. At this point, frame loss becomes acute. As each frame is determined to be missing, perhaps at the next switch, perhaps at the receiving end, a request for a resend on each of those lost frames results, pushing traffic even higher, increasing congestion, and causing network throughput to begin to plummet.

This means that, on something other than a properly configured frame relay network, nothing is done to ease congestion until it begins to show up in degraded performance, and the very act of trying to replace the lost frames only makes things worse. Usually, on networks where the load limit is unknown, using what is called *implicit congestion notification*, higher-level protocols such as TCP operating in the end devices detect congestion when there's a loss of frames or when the round-trip time begins to increase (in other words, when congestion is actually beginning to affect throughput). Only then do the protocols react, reducing the number of frames or packets transmitted (the window size) before an acknowledgment is received.

In other words, the sending node, which has been sending 10 frames or packets before waiting for an acknowledgment that they were received, senses that things are getting clogged because it is detecting a lot of missing frames incoming or getting an increasing number of requests to resend

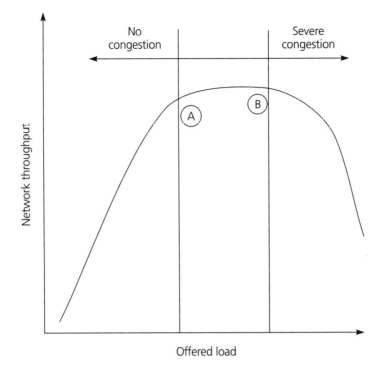

Figure 4-2 How congestion affects network performance.

missing frames. The node reacts by reducing its window so that now it is sending only seven frames before waiting for an acknowledgment. Obviously, this slows everything down, reducing the load on the switches and cutting down on the number of discarded frames or packets (and subsequent resend requests). But by then it is too late; congestion has already shown its face in the form of discarded frames and degraded performance.

On a frame relay network, however, each frame's header carries—among other things—two fields, one called Forward Explicit Congestion Notification (FECN), the other called Backward Explicit Congestion Notification (BECN). As Figure 4-3 illustrates, when a switch's buffers begin to get full or the queue of packets waiting to be processed gets to a preset level, but *before* congestion actually begins to result in discarded frames, the switch will reset the FECN of all passing frames to tell the next switch in line that things are getting jammed up, and the message will be passed along to all potential destinations. All the nodes downstream to the end will be informed of the impending problem and, if they are capable of responding to the FECN, they will react by reducing their contribution to the network's traffic.

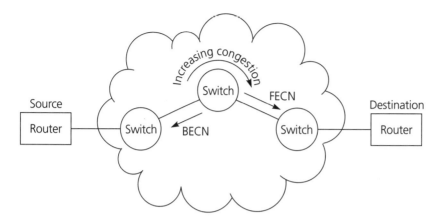

Figure 4-3   Frame relay's use of FECN and BECN to avoid congestion.

Even better, the switch also looks for frames headed in the opposite direction, back to the sources of the traffic, and resets their BECN field. This is done to all the traffic through the switch, so that all network access devices whose traffic is passing through that switch are notified and react accordingly to the extent of their ability. If the end user devices are able to respond to the FECN and BECN fields, they don't wait for actual congestion to slow down traffic before taking action to reduce the load; they slow down the rate they are sending data so that congestion is avoided before packets start to be discarded and have to be resent. Performance may slow some, but this method avoids the drastic plunge in performance that is triggered by frames being discarded, the subsequent extra traffic of requests for resends, and the resends themselves.

Most peaks in network traffic are temporary—the traffic is said to be *bursty*—so before congestion becomes severe the load is eased and traffic continues to flow smoothly. If traffic peaks too quickly even for frame relay's FECN and BECN to cope with, or if the switch buffer thresholds are set too low, or if some end user devices are incapable of responding to the FECN and BECN and fail to reduce traffic, then the switch will have to discard frames when its buffer becomes full.

However, to maintain promised rates of service—a *committed information rate*, or CIR—frame relay switches do not discard frames at random, which might penalize a circuit with a CIR as opposed to one that does not have a CIR. In order for service to be maintained for customers who have a CIR, there's another field in the frame header, set by the sending device, that indicates the discard eligibility (DE) of the frame. If the frame is eligible to be discarded, it will be dropped in favor of a frame that is not eligible for discard. Only if congestion continues will frames with the DE field set to "not eligible" be discarded.

Thanks to this DE field, a frame relay service provider can offer a more reliable service by guaranteeing a minimum level of service. The service can be made even better with permanent virtual circuits, which we've mentioned before. A PVC is a logical link whose endpoints and class of service are defined by the network management. A specific amount of bandwidth is guaranteed to a PVC, ensuring a given level of service. Each endpoint of a PVC is identified by a unique number called a data link connection identifier (DLCI). This information is one of the fields carried in the header of a frame relay datagram.

This capacity, along with frame relay's ability to set a CIR for a customer, allows frame relay networks to maintain traffic flow and to guarantee specified levels of service—if, that is, the service is properly managed. It does require the service provider to be aware of the traffic flow and to make adjustments to things such as the threshold settings on switch buffers and queue lengths in order to keep things running smoothly.

4.2.2 An Example of a Frame Relay VPN

As this capability to carry TCP/IP shows, the VPN choice between using the Internet Protocol and using a frame relay network is not an either/or proposition. A frame relay network can carry IP packets, belong to an Internet service provider, be an Internet backbone, and yet still offer private service through its PVCs.

A good case study of a frame relay network is Galaxy Scientific, the high-tech company we discussed in Chapter 2. When Galaxy, working with PSINet, developed their virtual private network, the term VPN had been limited to tunnels between firewalls; it did not yet extend to ISP-based VPNs and the like. Galaxy established a corporate intranet using PSINet's networking services. PSINet was one of the early frame relay services and one of the first to offer PVCs. PSINet is also an Internet service provider, with 225 POPs in the U.S. and 450 worldwide. PSINet's frame relay network is one of the Internet's backbones. As Figure 4-4 illustrates, Galaxy has PVCs on the PSINet network that tie their facilities together in a virtual private network.

Galaxy Scientific's PVCs actually share the PSINet backbone with Internet traffic, although the PVCs keep both Galaxy's traffic and sites insulated from the Internet and from other traffic on PSINet's backbone. Using PSINet's network offers the reliability and security of a frame relay service, with service guarantees, even though the network it uses is also a part of the Internet itself.

The benefits are tangible. Glenn Botkin of Galaxy Scientific notes that a cross-country PVC connection using PSINet's frame relay switches requires only four to six hops, while as many as 20 to 30 hops might be required using the Internet's IP routing. This offers not only high reliability, but better performance, since every hop adds time to the trip as the packet passes through each switch or router.

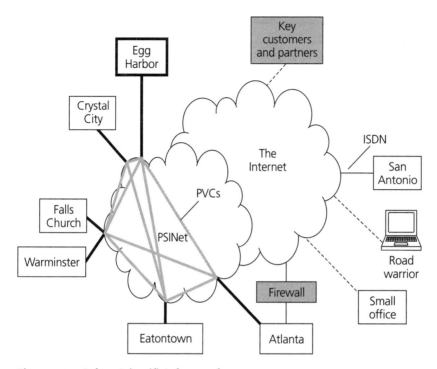

Figure 4-4   Galaxy Scientific's frame relay VPN.

PSINet ensures that Galaxy's traffic traverses only PSINet's network—it won't be routed over anyone else's network. This, plus frame relay's capabilities, lets PSINet guarantee a minimum level of service for the PVCs running through their switches and cables. Contrast this with the Internet's routers, which will route packets on the basis of whatever link is available. Even though the router chooses the most efficient link available at that moment, there are no guarantees. As we'll see when we discuss the VPN protocols in Chapter 7, even a VPN tunnel, which implies a logical, but not a physical, connection between endpoints, is not a PVC.

As we've noted, PSINet's consistency provides Galaxy with both speed and quality of service that are not available on the Internet. Right up front, Galaxy pays more to get this service than a VPN on the Internet would cost them. There are other costs, too, because for a Galaxy Scientific office to get a PVC it must connect to a PSINet POP, not just any ISP's POP. If PSINet does not have a POP near a given Galaxy office, something has to be done to cover the distance to the nearest one. In fact, the Galaxy Scientific home office in Egg Harbor, New Jersey, itself faces this problem. The solution, in this case, was to have the telephone company put in a circuit (a leased line) from the nearest central office where there was a PSINet POP to Galaxy's head office. Another solution would have been to establish ISDN dial-up service into PSINet. This would have required additional security measures to protect the site and the network.

Road warriors and small offices may dial in to a PSINet POP, or even into another ISP for a connection through the Internet itself, using typical VPN tunneling to provide the security but without the service guarantees of a PSINet PVC. Galaxy maintains its own firewall between the Atlanta office and the Internet. The final option for a private, non-Internet connection would be to dial directly in to the nearest Galaxy Scientific server using remote access.

In spite of these extra costs, Galaxy Scientific's VPN is less expensive than the system they had initially planned and more efficient than the dial-up system they'd been using, which cost them $4,000 per month in telephone charges. Botkin heard of PSINet's service just before he was about to lay out $160,000 for firewalls at Galaxy's six major sites, firewalls that turned out not to be needed since PSINet would insulate them from the Internet itself. The cost for the PVCs was about $1,600 per month (using the initial 56 Kbps connections), with the breakeven point coming at about 8 years. Since then, all but a few of their sites have gone up to 256 Kbps connections. Even so, breakeven is still only 3 to 4 years out, and this does not include the costs they would have incurred in managing multiple firewalls.

Managing firewalls can be costly. Another alternative Galaxy Scientific considered was a fully managed firewall/security solution from BBN Planet (now GTE Internetworking). It would have cost $2,500 per month *per site*, in addition to line service costs. Part of that monthly charge would have been to recover the $10,000 to $20,000 cost of putting a firewall on each of Galaxy's sites, but a big chunk would have arisen from having BBN Planet manage, monitor, and maintain the system.

However, even with the efficiencies offered by a system such as Galaxy's, the need for local PSINet POPs is obviously an important consideration. If your VPN will primarily be used to serve your road warriors, it will probably not be cost-effective to incur the added expense of PVCs. In the case of small offices, PVCs would restrict their access to a service that has POPs only where they are regularly needed. No matter what, the mobile user who every day connects by dialing in from a different town will not get the benefit of a PVC because PVCs can't be set up and taken down on a whim. Galaxy Scientific has made provisions for remote users and has selected special customers and business partners to be able to access their network through the Internet using the typical VPN tunneling for security. But these users don't get the guarantees that PSINet can otherwise offer, and additional security arrangements have to be made for them.

Looking at it from the other side, going with an Internet-based VPN allows your mobile employees to use any ISP with whom they have an account and to make the connection through the nearest POP to your network. It is more convenient—and less expensive—but you're left with coping with the vagaries of the Internet.

4.3 The Trade-Offs

As this discussion shows, there are trade-offs that have to be made when you choose one or the other of these two routes (the Internet VPN vs. the frame relay VPN). Primarily the trade-off is between lower cost and more flexibility versus better security, reliability, and accountability.

4.3.1 The Cost Factor

Reliability and safety are the upsides of using a frame relay or ATM provider for your VPN, as opposed to just dumping it on the Internet. The primary downside is the cost factor. By using the Internet, the cost of all that infrastructure is sliced millions of ways, and there is, essentially, no administrative cost of an Internet management structure to be defrayed. With a more private service, those costs are not divided as finely, there is a management structure to be accounted for, and there is a profit the owners want to make. In short, going the frame relay VPN route will cost you more.

How much more? In 1997, TimeStep, a virtual private network vendor, performed a financial analysis of the benefits of a VPN serving five separate facilities using the Internet compared to a VPN serving the same offices using permanent virtual circuits (PVCs) through a frame relay network (Table 4-1). In the TimeStep analysis, the PVCs are contracted connections through the frame relay network, with a guaranteed minimum service level of 768 Kbps on each connection (i.e., half that of the T1 lines connecting each facility to the network). While the computations are 2 years old, the situation still gives us a valid comparison between the two topologies because, if anything, costs have generally declined in the entire communications infrastructure.

For the financial analysis, TimeStep compared these scenarios using their VPN equipment to create the Internet-based VPN. The TimeStep cost model assumes that both networks are newly created and that they do not use existing network connections. No discounts have been considered, and the following formula is used to calculate the payback period:

IS = Internet scenario

FR = frame relay scenario

Table 4-1 TimeStep VPN comparison of frame relay vs. Internet.

Private line scenario

Item	Quantity	Unit cost	Extended cost
Capital costs			
Routers*	5	$1,950	$9,750
Channel service unit/Data service unit*	5	$995	$4,975
T1 installation	5	$300	$1,500
Total capital costs			**$16,225**
Monthly operating costs			
T1 ports	5	$1,768	$8,840
PVCs	10	$1,400	$14,000
Local loops***	5	$700	$3,500
Total monthly operating costs			**$26,340**

Internet scenario

Item	Quantity	Unit cost	Extended cost
Capital costs			
Routers*	5	$1,950	$9,750
Channel service unit/Data service unit*	5	$995	$4,975
T1 startup	5	$3,000	$15,000
PERMIT/Director**	1	$11,995	$11,995
PERMIT/Gate 2520**	5	$3,995	$19,975
Total capital costs			**$61,695**
Monthly operating costs			
T1 ports	5	$1,895	$9,475
Local loops***	5	$700	$3,500
Total monthly operating costs			**$12,975**
% OC savings			51%
Payback period (months)			4.62
ROI (for first year)			160%

* Prices from UUNet (August 1997).

** TimeStep's PERMIT/Director is a Windows-based software suite that offers VPN user management, authentication, key management, and administrative tools. PERMIT/Gate 2520 is a tamper-resistant gateway that secures data for transmission over the Internet using a suite of hardware-based encryption and authentication protocols.

*** Average local loop cost (varies by region).

CC = capital cost

OC = monthly operating cost

Payback period = CC of IS/(OC of FR − OC of IS)

Return on investment (ROI) is calculated based on one year's operational cost savings.

ROI = [12 × (OC savings) − CC of IS]/CC of IS.

Notice that the monthly operational costs using the Internet are roughly half the monthly costs using the frame relay scenario. While the capital investment cost is higher for the Internet scenario (witness Galaxy's planned $160,000 for firewalls), the payback period for that extra expense is only 4.6 months and the ROI for the first year is 160%. As we saw in Chapter 1, were TimeStep to include a leased-line scenario in their analysis, the leased-line operational costs would be considerably higher than under the frame relay scenario, while the expense of the VPN devices would be avoided, lowering the capital costs.

Even bearing in mind that this is a comparison generated by a VPN vendor—and it was created in 1997—it is reasonable to assume that savings in that range are still feasible.

4.3.2 Flexibility

As we noted in the discussion of Galaxy Scientific's VPN in Section 4.2.2 above, there are connectivity issues with regard to a VPN built on a service less distributed and more granular than the Internet. For a VPN on a private service to work for you, the service must have connections where you need connections. Otherwise any savings over a leased-line WAN will be eaten up in making those connections.

PSINet offers only 250 POPs nationwide, and they're distributed unevenly. Service tends to be concentrated in high population areas, since that's where the customers are. *Boardwatch* magazine lists an ISP as offering "national dial-up service" if it serves 25 or more telephone area codes, which is a rather liberal definition for "nationwide." There about 200 ISPs that meet that criterion, ranging alphabetically from 1 VEI NET to Zeke's General Store, Inc. In addition to these, there are thousands of small ISPs that fill in the gaps, serving small communities all over the world. Even a service as big as that run by WorldCom cannot possibly have POPs as widely accessible as the Internet.

If the goal of your VPN is to provide connectivity to a widely distributed workforce, particularly a mobile workforce, there may not be a frame relay service that will have POPs where you need them. Even if there is, your mobile workforce can't get the benefit of PVCs. An Internet-based VPN, on the other hand, is accessible from wherever there is an Internet POP. Granted, under the worst circumstances it may require your road warrior to cobble up a subscription or perhaps even dial from where he is in Fargo to his service provider in Minneapolis, but that may be better than accessing the nearest frame relay POP in St. Louis. If your road crew is on the move to a lot of out-of-the-way places, the Internet may just be the only viable option.

It's not necessarily an either/or situation. As we saw with Galaxy Scientific's VPN, there are ways to create a VPN that offer guarantees to your fixed facilities through PVCs while still providing road warriors with access to the network directly through the Internet via any Internet POP.

This is all a reflection of the fact that a private frame relay service is not as flexible a medium as the Internet. Establishing a new node on an Internet VPN is simply a matter of establishing a connection to the Internet, perhaps an ISDN link to a local ISP. A new node on a frame relay VPN requires a connection to the frame relay service's nearest POP. If you want a PVC, that's another setup to be accomplished. Where the service has a convenient POP, this may be relatively simple; otherwise it may require asking the local telephone service provider to establish a loop to the nearest POP.

4.3.3 Security

The Internet is not a secure environment. This is one of the issues you must be aware of before you start sending your corporate data hither and yon through the Internet's routers. The Internet is open to anyone with a computer on his desk and $20 in his pocket (and even to some who have connected without paying for admission). Paying or not, not all of them are nice people.

Going with a private service, therefore, would appear to offer greater security, which it does, although perhaps not the armor-plated security you might expect. Yes, private services such as frame relay networks are more secure than the Internet simply because there is more control over who has access to the system, but that access may not be as tightly locked as you would think. Remember that PSINet, for example, carries Internet traffic over the same cables and through the same switches that serve Galaxy Scientific.

But this doesn't mean, by any stretch, that PSINet's security is compromised. They still maintain control over their own lines and switches. They *can* keep tabs on what is going on on *their* network and protect their VPN customers, who are paying for that oversight and security. PSINet's switches are also harder to hack than the Internet's routers, increasing the security of the system. In addition to filtering all traffic, PSINet's routers know where internal VPN traffic is physically coming from and going to, making it hard for anyone from outside to use a stolen IP address to spoof their way into the system. Then, too, if you happen to notice an intruder that PSINet should miss, you can pick up the phone and set PSINet's hounds on his trail even as you close your own gate.

Even so, it would be naive to assume that even a system such as PSINet's is totally secure. No computer network accessible in any way to the public can ever be considered totally secure, any more than the Titanic was unsinkable back in 1912. Still, limiting your VPN to PVCs using a single provider's frame relay network is certainly more secure than the Internet.

4.3.4 Reliability and Accountability

The fact that frame relay providers keep an eye on their systems also means that they can offer you greater reliability and guaranteed levels of service. If PSINet says you have a PVC that gives you 768 Kbps service between two nodes, then either that is what it gives you or you can start asking for your money back.

You may even be able to track the quality of service you are getting. Frame relay offers the option to keep the end user posted as to the state of her connections. Special management frames may be passed between the network and the user's access device (a router, for example). These frames provide information on whether the interface is still active (a "keep alive" or "heartbeat" signal), the valid data link connection identifiers defined for that interface, and the status of each virtual circuit (for example, if it is congested or not).

While service level agreements are starting to be available from ISPs (see Chapter 10), it is not possible to guarantee Internet service. As we've pointed out, packets can get lost or delayed and there is no one you can turn to. If you need assurances such as that, then the Internet is not the way to go.

On the other hand, as far as reliability goes, there is a potential disadvantage to a frame relay VPN—it lacks the degree of redundancy that the Internet offers. If a cable should happen to get cut, it's possible that your frame relay service will be interrupted completely, the same way it would be on a leased-line connection. Since your frame relay traffic is restricted to a single service provider's fibers, and a PVC may further reduce the possible routing choices, there may be no way to route around the break. Granted, you may get a refund, but that's small consolation if a major project is delayed beyond its deadline. Traffic on the Internet, on the other hand, may slow down but it rarely stops.

4.3.5 Customer Service and Technical Support

Finally there is the issue of customer service and technical support. One of the reasons for going with a frame relay service is the value-added services they can provide that you'd otherwise have to provide yourself. In the case of Galaxy Scientific, for example, PSINet authenticates the users as they connect in using the same user ID and password you'd find on any dial-in ISP account. A more secure system (SecureDial) is available and is being evaluated by Galaxy. As we'll see when we get into authentication, encryption, and key management in Chapters 5, 6, and 7, these are major issues that you may want to hand off to your provider.

PSINet is in charge of a large part of the security for Galaxy's VPN. For example, Galaxy Scientific does not have to maintain firewalls at each site—only at a single one—since PSINet protects them. The VPN does serve as an extranet, with Galaxy's partners and select customers able to connect to the VPN by coming in through the Internet. To protect that connection, all traffic from the Internet is filtered through a single firewall maintained by Galaxy at their Atlanta office, where the central node for the intranet is located.

There's no encryption for Galaxy Scientific to worry about, with the accompanying burden of encryption key management. PSINet guarantees the security of Galaxy's communications through their network. PSINet has the staff and expertise to deal with the challenges of security on the Internet and on their own network, and Galaxy gets the benefit of that expertise, instead of having to provide it themselves at considerable expense.

If there is a problem, Glenn Botkin also knows exactly who to call. If the VPN were on the Internet he would not have that option. For a problem with his VPN installation, he should be able to get help from his vendor, but for a problem on the Internet he'd be out of luck.

4.4 Conclusion

So how do you decide which scenario to implement? Obviously, it depends on a number of factors. What are you going to use the VPN for? If it's for remote access for road warriors, then the Internet is your best option. Then there are the matters of your budget, how important speed and reliability are to your VPN, how well you can handle the security demands of being on the Internet, and the technical resources you bring to the project. How well can you handle security on the VPN yourself, for example? When we get into the actual VPN planning process in Chapter 9, we'll look at these elements in more detail. At least now you have some idea of how the two scenarios differ.

5

Encryption

Encryption is what puts the "private" in virtual private networks. Without encryption, information flowing over a public network such as the Internet is transmitted openly. Such traffic can be intercepted and read by common sniffing techniques, making it anything but private. Readily available programs such as protocol analyzers or the network diagnostic tools built into some of today's operating systems can easily see the information as it is sent. Encrypting the data ensures that it won't be read by unauthorized users, ensuring confidentiality; confidentiality, authentication, and integrity are the three properties of a cryptosystem.

In this chapter, we'll look at the two basic types of encryption, known as secret key, or *symmetric*, encryption and public key, or *asymmetric*, encryption. The importance of key length in security will be discussed, along with the danger of relying strictly on key length to judge the strength of a cryptosystem. We'll see how the different types of encryption are used to build systems that provide for secure key exchanges and effective and fast encryption of VPN sessions. Finally, we'll discuss authentication, or the use of what are known as *digital signatures* so that the recipient can be certain of whom the data came from and that it hasn't been tampered with.

One important point to be made here is that when we refer to "users" in this chapter, we're not necessarily talking about individual people. Every entity on a VPN that needs to exchange data with other entities needs the ability to encrypt and decrypt messages. This can be a person, or it can be a file server or print server, or even a router. In a VPN the encryption and data authentication are handled almost entirely automatically by the VPN's hardware or software. In fact, the data may not ever even be seen by a real live human being, because in a VPN a server, printer, router, or some other piece of hardware can have the same encryption/decryption privileges as a person.

Also, as we'll see in the discussion on architecture in Chapter 8, the encryption/decryption may be done where the VPN terminates—at the workstation, the server, the firewall, or the proxy server, or even at the Internet service provider level. In a LAN-to-LAN VPN, the decision may be to terminate encryption at the firewall (leaving internal LAN traffic unencrypted) or it may be to handle encryption at the user level, with all VPN traffic inside the LAN encrypted.

For the sake of convenience, we'll use the term "user" to designate the endpoints of a cryptosystem, regardless of whether the endpoint is a human being or hardware. In addition, to keep things on a more personal level, we'll invoke the seemingly universal "Alice" and "Bob" to be our users. (Alice and Bob are to encryption discussions what John Doe and Richard Roe are to legal discussions.)

5.1 An Overview of Encryption

Encryption is a way of scrambling data so that only those people who are supposed to read it *can* read it. Using a special key at the sending end, the data is scrambled into cipher text that can only be read by someone who has the proper key. At the receiving end, the key that decrypts the message is put to work and the encrypted data is converted back to what it was, which is known as *plain text*. As we said before, in VPNs the process is done automatically and is totally transparent to the users, just as it is in a secured transaction using a Web browser such as Netscape.

Generally speaking, encryption does not increase or decrease the length of the message, so there's no change in the transmission time as a result of that operation. As you'd expect, however, encryption and decryption processing requires both computing power and time, although with a properly designed system (note that qualification, it is important) it should not be intrusively obvious; remember that credit card transactions on the Web use encryption, for example. The encrypted pages generally appear just about as quickly—or slowly—as the unencrypted pages.

On the administrative side, there is the overhead of managing the encryption system: making sure the right user, and only the right user, has the authorized keys, for example. While a secure credit card transaction usually implements a one-time use key, reducing management overhead, a VPN requires managing keys for more persistent connections. Key management is a major challenge. We'll get into that issue in Chapter 6.

The entire package—encryption and decryption, the sender and the recipient—make up what we'll call a *cryptosystem* (Figure 5-1). Bear in mind that Alice and Bob are not necessarily people. Alice encrypts the message with a

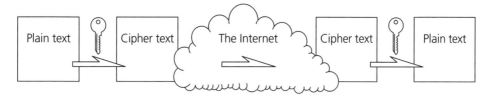

Figure 5-1   A cryptosystem.

key, sends it to Bob, who then decrypts it using a key. As we'll see when we get into asymmetric encryption, they may not necessarily be using the same key for both operations.

The strength of a given cryptosystem is determined primarily, but not solely, by its key length. The more bits there are in the key, the more difficult it is for someone without the key to decrypt data by applying many computers or one powerful, highly specialized computer to try to calculate and test all the possible key combinations until the right one is found (this is known as a *brute force attack*). Once a key has been cracked for one message, all other messages using that key can be read. If, as is sometimes the case, subsequent keys are generated using the one just cracked, they, in turn, can be easily cracked, making even more traffic vulnerable.

Look at key length the same way you might a combination lock for your locker . . . the more numbers there are available, the harder it is to try each possible combination until the right one is found. A combination lock with three dials, each with numbers 0 through 9, offers only 1,000 different combinations, 0-0-0, 0-0-1, 0-0-2, . . . , 0-1-0, 0-1-1, . . . , 9-9-9. If there are four dials with numbers that can be from 00 through 99 there are suddenly 100 million different combinations to try, a much greater challenge.

Since encryption algorithms use strings of bits as keys, a 40-bit-long encryption key offers 2^{40} possible keys, 56-bit encryption offers 2^{56}, and so forth. Every time a bit is added, the number of possible keys doubles. A 40-bit key provides 1,099,511,627,776 different keys. Using 56-bit encryption means that there are 72,057,594,037,927,936 keys to be generated and tried in a brute force attack. Move up to 90 bits and there are about 1,237,940,039,285,380,000,000,000,000 combinations; at 128 bits, there are roughly 340,282,366,920,938,000,000,000,000,000,000,000,000 combinations to be tested. Since there are only about 6 billion people in the world, there are plenty of spare keys to go around, even in a 56-bit system.

On the other hand, the same technology that makes VPNs possible endangers their security. The speed with which computers can crunch numbers has increased exponentially in the last 20 years. With only old PC XTs readily available to the public, it used to be that a few billion possible keys were enough to stymie the average snoop. But in June of 1998 a message encoded using a 56-bit key was cracked in 56 hours using a standard PC controlling an array of specialized computer circuit boards (which cost about $200,000) that were able to test 93 billion keys per second. At that rate that machine could chew through every combination in a 40-bit encryption system in less than 15 seconds. It's generally agreed that a 128-bit key length is essentially uncrackable using a brute force attack with today's technology, while 40-bit and 56-bit systems are no longer considered secure.

However, don't be lulled by the sales pitch of key length when it comes to encryption strength. Length alone is not the only factor that determines a cryptosystem's security. To be any good, an algorithm must also produce encryption that is highly resistant to attacks by methods such as frequency analysis of characters in the encrypted data. Even the way encryption keys are generated and exchanged can determine the security of the system. Fortunately, the algorithms in use in VPNs today have been exhaustively tested both for brute force and other, more subtle attacks. Unfortunately, as we'll see when we discuss some of the VPN protocols, the same attention has not always been given to key generation and exchange.

If you are planning a VPN that stretches overseas, it's important to realize that different countries have differing restrictions on encryption technology. As of this writing, the United States government requires a special license for the export of "strong" encryption, which, for secret key systems, they define as key lengths of over 40 bits. While it is relatively easy today to get permission to export 56-bit encryption, security experts do not consider 56-bit encryption strong, let alone 40-bit encryption. The data encryption standard endorsed by the U.S. government, which uses a 56-bit key, is due to be replaced, and new algorithms are being tested. However, the new standard is not scheduled for final approval until the year 2002.

The government also wants key recovery incorporated into encryption products that are exported. This is called *key escrow*. With key recovery in place, keys would be placed in escrow where, through the use of a court order, they could be obtained by law enforcement authorities so they would be able to decrypt messages in a form of cyber-wiretapping, in order to eavesdrop on messages from terrorists or criminals.

Encryption vendors and users are strongly resisting these government demands, on the grounds that they place the United States at a competitive disadvantage to vendors of encryption products and software developers from foreign countries that impose no restrictions on encryption technology. There is also the opinion that encryption weakened in accordance with government demands is not secure enough for ecommerce. The issue has been snarled in Washington politics for some time and shows no sign of being resolved in the near future.

Some countries prohibit the use of encryption entirely, or encryption systems over a certain key length, while other countries have no restrictions with respect either to use or export. So if you want a VPN with nodes in New York, Los Angeles, Paris, Moscow, and Tokyo, your encryption decisions are complicated. You can—and probably should—use 128-bit encryption between your New York and Los Angeles offices, but provision also has to be made to provide 40-bit encryption between Los Angeles and Tokyo. In Russia, encryption is the exclusive property of the military. France outlaws encryption unless you hand over the keys to the government. Violate any of these laws and you'll potentially find yourself in deep trouble.

On the other hand, no matter where your traffic is headed, your VPN's encryption/decryption process should be invisible as far as the end user is concerned. This means that, if your VPN encompasses foreign countries, it must be capable of dealing with these vagaries and with the fact that the laws are likely to change. It must be possible to configure your VPN to encrypt your domestic traffic using a 128-bit key, encrypt your Tokyo traffic with a 40-bit key, leave traffic to Moscow in plain text, and encrypt traffic to Paris using a key that is on file with the French government (bearing in mind, as you'll see, that to have a secure system you are constantly changing keys), and also to change these settings should the laws change.

Try to bear in mind, too, as we discuss encryption, and VPNs in general for that matter, that a potential eavesdropper or attacker can be anywhere in the world. Just because you are talking between Los Angeles and New York doesn't mean that an eavesdropper in Bulgaria isn't trying to listen in. Such is the nature of the Internet.

There are two different types of cryptosystems in use: symmetric, or secret key, and asymmetric, or public key, and within each type, several different algorithms are available. Each type of system has its advantages and disadvantages, and we'll find that VPNs use them in combination in a way that takes advantage of each type's strengths and avoids its weaknesses.

5.2 Secret Key (Symmetric) Cryptosystems

Secret key cryptosystems all work essentially the same way. In a *secret key* system, the same key is used for both encryption and decryption, meaning it must be a key that is somehow exchanged or shared secretly. For secret key encryption to be of any value, the key must be kept secret from anyone outside the system.

There are a number of different secret key algorithms in use today. These include Blowfish, CAST-64, CAST-80, CAST-128, RC2, RC4, RC5, DES, and Triple-DES. The two you may hear mentioned most often by VPN vendors are

DES and Triple-DES. If there's a "default" symmetrical algorithm it is DES. It will be found in most, if not all, VPN products.

DES stands for Data Encryption Standard. Developed initially by IBM, it has been the encryption algorithm certified by the federal government since 1977. DES can be used with several key lengths, including 40, 56, and 128 bits. Triple-DES is based on the same algorithm as DES, but, in an effort to overcome the weakness of 40- and 56-bit keys, the message is processed three times using two or three different keys. Since each key has to be found and then applied in the proper fashion (encrypt or decrypt) and in the right order, it is significantly stronger than straight DES. DES is scheduled to be supplanted by a new government-approved algorithm by 2002.

Another algorithm often found in VPNs is RC4. It is faster than DES, and it can accept keys of arbitrary length. Key lengths of 40 and 56 bits are common. Although it was originally proprietary to RSA Data Security, a source code claiming to be equivalent to RC4 has appeared in USENET newsgroups, and tests indicate that the claim appears to be accurate. RC4 has the advantage of being relatively easy to obtain an export license for at 40- and 56-bit key lengths. Although RC4 is hard to crack, it has been done to Netscape's exportable version of Secure Sockets Layer using 40-bit RC4; it took 8 days.

Another symmetric encryption system is the International Data Encryption Algorithm (IDEA). IDEA uses a 128-bit key and on that basis alone is considered to be stronger than DES. And although there is a large class of what are considered to be "weak" keys in IDEA, it is highly resistant to attacks by the analysis of encrypted data. However, IDEA has not gained widespread acceptance, probably because it is patented by a Swiss company. Noncommercial use is free, but commercial use requires a license. Also, its key length effectively prohibits it from being exported in products built in the United States.

Regardless of the algorithm used, all secret key cryptosystems work essentially the same way. As you might expect, the process is relatively straightforward, as shown in Figure 5-2. At the sending end, the plain text data is

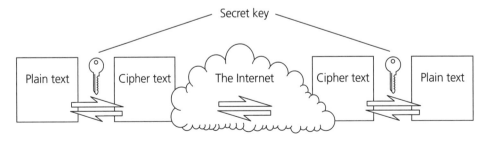

Figure 5-2   Secret key encryption.

scrambled into cipher text using the secret key. At the receiving end, the same secret key is used to convert the cipher text back into plain text for the recipient.

Don't make the mistake of carrying this simplicity of use over to the process of symmetric encryption itself. Encryption has become a complex branch of mathematics. Volumes have been written about it, and the actual mechanics of a commonly used algorithm such as DES are not simple. If they were simple, it would be too easy to decipher the encrypted data.

Secret key cryptosystems have the advantage of being fast. However, they also have drawbacks. For one thing, if someone outside the system acquires the supposedly secret key, then all traffic encrypted with that key is compromised. The longer a key is in use, the more data there is that is vulnerable. Then, too, when a lot of data has been encrypted using a given key, it gives a potential attacker that much more data to analyze using non–brute force methods to figure out the key. With the amount of data computers can generate and move over a network, the useful life span of a key is measured in minutes rather than days.

So, both to minimize the amount of data exposed to analysis and the amount of data exposed by a stolen key, it is wise to change the key frequently. Since both Alice and Bob must have the same key or, as is more likely, a shared pair of keys—one key used for traffic going from Alice to Bob, the other key used for traffic from Bob to Alice—key transfers must be made. These transfers must be done in a protected way so that the right key goes to the intended recipient and only the intended recipient. In "real space," as opposed to "cyberspace," this may require a direct face-to-face negotiation or a secure telephone call. In cyberspace it presents a similar challenge—somehow the key must be transferred in a secure fashion.

Furthermore, each discrete pair of users on a VPN should have a pair of keys different from any other pair of users. That is, Alice and Bob should use one key pair, while Alice and Charley should use a completely different key pair, and Bob and Charley share a third key pair, Alice and Diane share a fourth, and Diane and Bob a fifth, and so forth, and they are all different. That way users can't read each other's mail without authorization. More importantly, if the Bob to Alice key is compromised only his traffic to her is exposed, and analyzing that data won't give any clues to cracking either Bob and Alice's other key or any other pair's keys.

The need for all these key pairs of course quickly multiplies the number of keys and the number of key changes and transfers that have to be made. As long as there is only a relatively small number of users involved, even with frequent key changes, this rapid turnover may be manageable. But as the number of users on a VPN increases, the problem becomes more and more cumbersome. If there are 1,000 users in a symmetric cryptosystem, Alice and

Bob and everyone else would have to have a key ring the size of Texas (metaphorically speaking) to hold them all. Every round of key changes would devour that most precious of resources, time. In practice, many VPNs don't face this massive number of keys, because encryption is handled at the point of entry into the LAN—the router or firewall—rather than at every individual workstation, printer, or server.

Still, even those few keys must be exchanged and changed frequently. With every key exchange, in addition to the work involved, there's the danger that a key might be exposed to a potential attacker. This is the biggest single drawback to symmetric cryptosystems.

5.3 Public Key (Asymmetric) Cryptosystems

Asymmetric cryptosystems are relatively new, dating from about 1976, and they are really only practical thanks to the number-crunching powers of computers because they use difficult-to-compute mathematical problems, often involving the difficulty of factoring large near-prime numbers or calculating discrete logs.

In a *public key* or asymmetric system, Alice has a pair of keys she can call her own. The first key in the pair is a private key that is known only to her and is never exchanged with anyone. The second is a public key that can be publicly shared with others without endangering the system. Eliminating the need to secretly exchange keys would seem to solve the symmetric system's primary drawback, allowing asymmetric systems to supplant them. Unfortunately, there can be some danger involved even in a public key exchange, particularly in the Diffie-Hellman system, as we'll discuss in Section 5.3.1. Also, asymmetric systems are inherently slow compared to symmetric systems.

Public key encryption systems also use longer key lengths than secret key systems, although this does not mean that an asymmetric system using a 1,024-bit key is stronger than a 128-bit IDEA key. That would be comparing apples with oranges. The freeware email encryption program Pretty Good Privacy (PGP) is an asymmetric system that offers key lengths of 512, 768, and 1,024 bits. For public key encryption, the U.S. government's export limit is 512 bits. Again, today this is not considered to be strong encryption by security experts, who recommend a minimum key length of 768 bits for commercial use public key encryption.

There are two asymmetric cryptosystems in general use today, Diffie-Hellman and RSA. The algorithms operate differently, and the way asymmetric cryptosystems in general work, as you'd expect, is somewhat more complicated than a symmetric cryptosystem.

5.3.1 Diffie-Hellman Encryption

The first asymmetric cryptosystem was invented in 1976 by Whitfield Diffie and Martin Hellman and is known as the Diffie-Hellman (DH) system. The Diffie-Hellman public key cryptosystem can almost be seen as a hybrid of public key and secret key systems, because it is a way for two users to agree on a shared secret encryption key without having to exchange the secret key itself.

In DH, Alice has her own key pair—a secret key, and a public key that she generates as needed—and Bob has his own pair. When Alice and Bob want to communicate using DH, they agree to exchange public keys, which they each have generated independently using a special, complex mathematical procedure. Once the public keys are exchanged, Alice uses Bob's public key in combination with her private key to generate a secret key. When Bob does the same thing using Alice's public key and his private key, the result is an identical secret key (Figure 5-3). This works even though Alice and Bob have different public and private keys.

Note that Alice and Bob exchange only their public keys. The private keys remain private. Note also that it is not possible for an outsider to deduce either Alice's or Bob's private key by analyzing their public keys either singly or together, nor is it possible to generate their shared secret key from their public

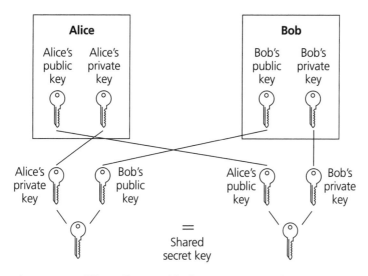

Figure 5-3   Diffie-Hellman public key cryptosystem builds a shared key.

keys. The shared secret key is the result generated independently by each of them using their private key and the public key they obtained from the other user. The shared secret key is never exchanged in any way; it is built in place and used there. The full process is illustrated in Figure 5-4.

Just as in a symmetric cryptosystem, messages passing in both directions are encrypted using the shared secret key. The advantage is that the shared secret key is never exposed on the public network. For security, DH shared secret keys are usually generated for each new session; this neatly solves the problem of distributing new secret keys that is faced in a secret key cryptosystem.

The danger in DH encryption is that it does involve exchanging the public keys that are used to generate the shared secret key. Since the public keys are being exchanged over a public network, an eavesdropper (call him Charley) could intercept the first message in the exchange—from Alice to Bob carrying Alice's public key—and could then substitute his own message (and key) for Alice's. Bob would have no way of knowing he's been deceived and would use

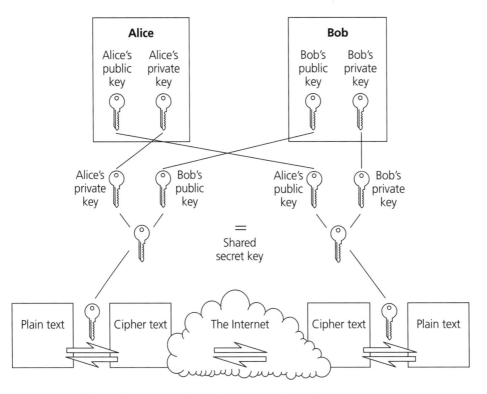

Figure 5-4   Diffie-Hellman shared secret key generation and use.

Charley's bogus public key to generate a DH secret key that he unknowingly shares with Charley, not Alice. Bob's next encrypted message to Alice would go, instead, to Charley, who could decipher it and read it. Not only that, but Charley could then re-encrypt the message using the public key he intercepted from Alice and forward it on to her and she would have no way of knowing the system had been invaded. This is called a *man-in-the-middle attack*. So, as deft as a DH cryptosystem is at avoiding the key management problems in a secret key system, it has its own weakness.

The way to avoid a man-in-the-middle attack is to somehow ensure that Alice is getting Bob's genuine public key and vice versa. The answer is called the authenticated Diffie-Hellman key agreement protocol, or the Station-to-Station (STS) protocol, and was developed by Diffie, van Oorschot, and Wiener in 1992. This protocol allows the parties in a DH public key exchange to authenticate themselves to each other by using digital signatures (see Section 5.4) encrypted in such a way that the man in the middle can't forge either of them.

5.3.2 RSA Encryption

RSA, the second primary asymmetric encryption algorithm, is named after its inventors Ron Rivest, Adi Shamir, and Leonard Adleman. RSA encryption technology is embedded in Netscape Navigator, Microsoft's Internet Explorer, Lotus Notes, Intuit's Quicken, Pretty Good Privacy (PGP), and hundreds of other products. It is used in firewalls, remote access products, electronic commerce, smartcards, and telecommunications, making it probably the most widely deployed publicly available cryptosystem in the world. Some of the products that use RSA come under names such as the Simple Public Key Mechanism (SPKM) developed by Entrust Technologies, Secure HyperText Transport Protocol (S-HTTP) from Enterprise Integration Technologies, and Secure Sockets Layer (SSL) from Netscape.

As with the DH cryptosystem, each RSA cryptosystem user has a public and a private key. However, these are not used to generate a shared secret key, but function by themselves. Information encrypted with a given RSA public key can only be decrypted with the matching RSA private key, and vice versa. This means that Alice can use Bob's public key to encrypt a message to him, who would then decrypt it using his private key, confident that no one else has read it (Figure 5-5).

Or Alice can use her private key to send a message to any user who has her public key, and that user can be confident that the message was written by Alice, since only she has that private key. However, used this way it's possible that anyone else who has Alice's public key can also read the message. Two-way secure communication can be established by making sure that Alice has

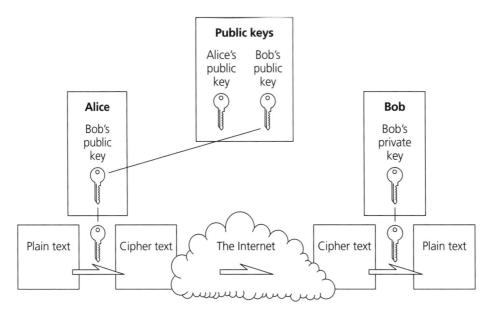

Figure 5-5   RSA encryption using public and private keys.

Bob's public key and that Bob has Alice's public key. Alice uses Bob's public key to encrypt; Bob uses his private key to decrypt. Bob uses Alice's public key to encrypt; Alice then uses her private key to decrypt (Figure 5-6).

However, when used in this way, RSA is not suitable for the high-speed work of a VPN because it is slower and more cumbersome than using a symmetric key cryptosystem or a Diffie-Hellman system with its shared secret keys.

One of the important things to remember about RSA is that what is encrypted by the public key can only be decrypted by the private key. It cannot be decrypted using the public key on it a second time. Similarly, a message encrypted using the private key cannot be decrypted by the private key, but only by the public key. Both the public and private keys are known as *trap door one-way functions*. One-way functions are mathematical functions that can be done but not easily undone. Trap door one-way functions, on the other hand, can be undone, but only if you have special knowledge (the trap door) to help.

A crude example of a trap door function is squaring a number and taking the square root of the result. It is simple to square a number—2 squared, for example, yields 4. But the square root of 4 can be either 2 or −2. Obviously, the trap door one-way functions used in public key encryption are much more complex. In the case of RSA encryption, the public key is the trap door to the

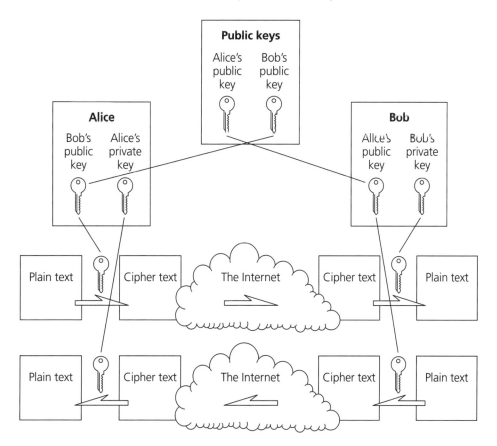

Figure 5-6   Secure two-way RSA encrypted communication.

private key, and vice versa. It is virtually impossible to determine the private key by analyzing the public key of the pair.

RSA is slow compared to other encryption schemes, particularly most symmetric ones. Depending on how it is implemented, RSA is 100 to 10,000 times slower than DES, for example. However, RSA is often used for security and authentication in the exchange of private keys. This is done using what is known as an RSA digital envelope (Figure 5-7). Alice first encrypts the message she wants to send Bob using a randomly generated symmetric (DES) key. Then she looks up Bob's public RSA key and uses it to encrypt the DES key. The DES-encrypted message and the RSA-encrypted DES key form the RSA digital envelope and are sent to Bob. Bob uses his private key, which only he has, to decrypt the symmetric key and then uses that key to decrypt the message itself. Once that is done, the symmetric key can be destroyed. This is a

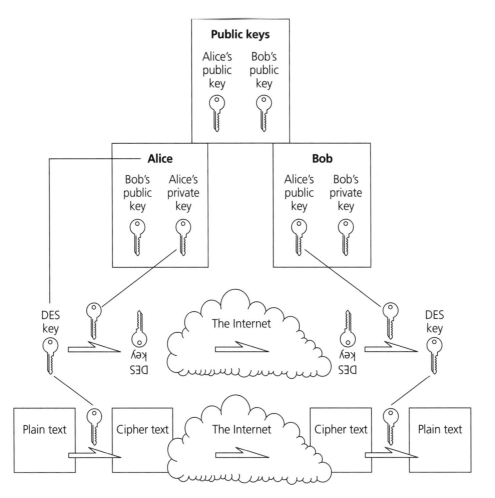

Figure 5-7   An RSA digital envelope at work.

one-time-use cryptosystem, where the symmetric key is used to encrypt and decrypt this single message. Since the amount of data being exchanged in such a case is relatively small, the slowness of RSA encryption here is not a serious problem.

RSA digital envelopes can also be used to overcome the man-in-the-middle threat to the Diffie-Hellman system. Instead of exchanging a message, Alice and Bob exchange their DH public keys, encrypting them with their RSA private keys. Even if Charley has Alice's and Bob's RSA public keys, he lacks their private keys, which he would need to fool them into taking his public key instead of those of each other, since Bob, using Alice's public key, could only decrypt a message from her and no one else, and vice versa.

After using each other's RSA public keys to decrypt each other's DH public keys, thereby assuring themselves that the DH public keys are genuine, Alice and Bob use those to generate the shared secret key they need for secure communication and proceed from there with confidence that Charley has not been able to slip into the middle position.

By incorporating digital signatures (see Section 5.4) in the initial RSA-encrypted exchange, they can be doubly certain that the DH public key received came from the right person and not a man in the middle capable of tampering with the data.

5.3.3 Other Public Key Systems

There are other public key encryption systems available. They all work essentially the same way as the RSA cryptosystem with its pairs of public and private keys, but they use different mathematical functions to do it. Some of these are based on mathematical operations on elliptical curves. One variant of this, using a mathematical problem called the discrete logarithm problem, is the basis for several digital signature methods, one of which is used in the Digital Signature Standard (DSS) that is approved for use by the federal government.

Both DH and RSA are well-developed and well-tested systems and have become the de facto standards, so it's unlikely you'll encounter these others. However, you may encounter some proprietary standards using different asymmetric algorithms. While they may offer some advantages within a proprietary system, the lack of interoperability outside that system is a drawback.

5.4 Digital Signatures, Hashing, and Message Authentication Codes

Digital signatures are generally not what we would normally consider a signature—that is, the literal application of a person's special mark at the end of a message—although that can be done using RSA encryption. Alice creates a literal signature, perhaps a tag line like "Alice likes special dark chocolate on her oysters," and encrypts it using her private key. After attaching it to the message, the entire package—message plus signature—is encrypted using Bob's public key. When the encrypted package reaches its destination, Bob decrypts the combined message and encrypted signature using his private key—he should be the only person in the world who can do that—and then decrypts the digital signature using Alice's public key, which by itself proves it came from Alice, since she is the only one who has the matching private key. Even if he's not the only one who knows that Alice likes special dark chocolate on her oysters, he still can be highly confident that the message came from her.

However, with respect to computer networks and encryption, the term *digital signature* is not a person's signature but rather the RSA private key encryption of a digest of the message, with the digest itself generated from the message using what is known as a *hash function.* Since the digest is scrambled using the sender's private key, the receiver knows the sender is who he claims to be since only the sender's public key will decipher the digest. Just as important, however, this type of digital signature proves that the message received is identical to the message that was sent. For that reason, this process is also known as "message authentication" as opposed to "user authentication."

So how does having a digest of a message authenticate it? The procedure begins with hashing the message itself. *Hashing* is a one-way mathematical procedure that takes a long string of bits—a message—and shrinks it down to a shorter string of bits of a specified length—say, 128 bits—called a *digest.* So far it sounds a little like compression, but unlike compression, hashing is a one-way conversion. Once it is performed, it is virtually impossible to convert the digest back into the message. A mathematician would call it a one-way function without a trap door.

A good hash function also has what is called *collision resistance,* which means that no two messages will produce the same digest. This, combined with the one-way nature of a hash function, provides the perfect way for a recipient to be sure that the message he receives is the message that was sent, while the sender, by encrypting the digest using her private key, proves that she is the person who sent it. The process works as shown in Figure 5-8.

Alice applies a hash function to the message, producing a digest unique to that specific message. She then encrypts the digest using her RSA private key. The result is the digital signature. The digital signature is attached to the message and the entire package (message plus signature) is sent. If it's important that the message itself remain a secret, the message + signature package can be encrypted before being sent, perhaps using a secret key cryptosystem such as DES or a public key system such as DH or RSA.

When he gets the message + signature package, Bob decrypts it, then he decrypts the signature back into the digest form using Alice's public key, thereby assuring himself it came from Alice and not somebody else. Then Bob applies the same hash function Alice used to the copy of the message he just received from her, producing another digest of it. Then he compares this

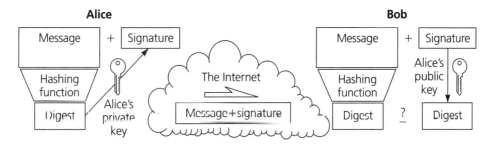

Figure 5-8   Creating a digital signature using hashing and RSA.

digest with the decrypted one that came with the message: they should be identical. As long as the two digests match, all is well.

For this to work reliably, the hash function used must meet two criteria. First, it must be hard to invert; that is, it must be mathematically infeasible— i.e., "require too much computing power and time to be practical"—to derive the message from the hashed result. (In theory, a computer could start churning out every possible message that would yield that digest until it stumbled on the right one. Practically, it would take so many years to do so that the inversion would be useless.)

Second, as we noted before, the hash function must be strongly collision free, which means that it must be extremely unlikely that two messages could be produced that would yield the same digest. If the hashing operation is not strongly collision free, it might be possible to create a message that yields an identical hash but that has a totally different meaning. For example, Alice's message might be a contract that says, "I, Alice, promise to send you, Bob, 10,000 kumquats." If our eavesdropper Charley can create a message with the same digest that says, "I, Alice, promise to send you, Charley, $10,000," he can substitute it for the original message. Digests of the two messages will agree, but Alice will find herself sitting on a pile of rotting kumquats and owing Charley $10,000, while Bob can't meet the order he has for kumquat pies.

There are a number of hash functions. The ones generally used for message authentication are MD5 (message digest), Secure Hash Algorithm (SHA), and SHA-1. You may also encounter MD2 or MD4. MD2, MD4, and MD5 all produce digests of 128 bits. While MD2 is optimized for use on 8-bit hardware, MD5 is optimized for 32-bit machines and fixes the problems with MD4. MD2 and MD4 are both considered "broken," and MD5 has been shown to have weaknesses that make its long-term viability questionable.

As a result, SHA-1 is becoming the preferred choice. SHA was developed as a federal information processing standard and is the algorithm published as the federal Secure Hash Standard (SHS), part of Project Capstone, a government effort to produce a digital standard for companies doing business with it.

SHA-1 is a revision that corrected an unpublished flaw in SHA. The SHA-1 algorithm takes a message of less than 2^{64} bits in length and produces a 160-bit message digest. It is slightly slower than MD5, but the larger message digest makes it more collision resistant and more resistant to brute force attacks.

Hashing has other uses, as well, since it can generate a random string of bits of a specific length from some other longer string of bits, such as random typing. For example, in PGP, the MD5 hash function is used to generate the 128-bit keys used in the IDEA secret key algorithm by hashing a string that can be created in any number of ways, perhaps something typed in by a user or a string derived from the system's time and date.

Message authentication codes (MACs) are similar to hashing in that they are used to authenticate a message. Some use hashing; others use stream or block ciphers. The MAC you're most likely to encounter is the DES-CBC MAC, which uses a DES-based cipher block chaining. Keyed-MD5, on the other hand, is a MAC that is based on MD5 hashing. MACs, like secret key cryptosystems, are computed and verified using the same key, so they can only be verified by a receiver who has that key. This differs from hashing-generated message authentication signatures that use the sender's public key for decryption, which could let someone who intercepted the signature decrypt it if he or she happened to have the sender's public key. MACs provide an added bit of security.

Remember, too, that intercepting even an unencrypted digest will do an attacker little good, since the digest results from a one-way function and cannot easily be inverted to convert the digest back into the message.

5.5 Putting It All Together

As we noted in Section 5.2, symmetric key systems, while fast, present a problem that results from the number of keys a system of any size requires and the need to exchange and change those keys frequently. On the other hand, while public keys can be exchanged more easily than secret keys, asymmetric systems have their own drawbacks. They are slow, and in the case of DH cryptosystems there is the man-in-the-middle attack threat when the public keys are exchanged.

The solution in VPNs is to use both systems together, because they do complement each other rather handily. For example, when combined with a digital signature, the RSA digital envelope is a highly secure way to exchange public keys. RSA envelopes can be used to exchange symmetric keys, perhaps just to send a symmetric key along with a message for one-time use or even to allow a long-term symmetric cryptosystem to move large amounts of data quickly over a connection that remains up indefinitely.

More likely, RSA digital envelopes and digital signatures are used to exchange Diffie-Hellman public keys. These DH keys are then used to create a shared secret key for a DH communication session. Alice and Bob will generate new public keys for every session, so every session has a new shared secret key.

In reality, all of this is done invisibly, often by a trusted third party known as a *certificate authority* (CA). Alice and Bob receive each other's RSA public keys from the CA, DH public keys are generated automatically and exchanged using RSA envelopes, and the DH public keys are used to generate shared secret keys; but Alice and Bob will never see any of this. The encryption will even change frequently as new public keys are generated and exchanged (which is called *rekeying*) and then used to generate new shared secret keys.

The challenge of key management is reduced to making sure that Alice gets Bob's public key and that Bob gets Alice's. Once that is done, that first secure connection is established and secret keys can be exchanged safely. Not that this first exchange of public keys is necessarily a simple problem in a large VPN. It still involves huge numbers of keys that must be managed and exchanged in a way that assures Alice and Bob that they are getting the right keys. As we'll see in Chapter 6 on user authentication and key management, an entire infrastructure is growing up around the process.

5.6 Conclusion

In this chapter we've discussed a number of different algorithms, both for encryption and for message authentication, which may be confusing. In reality, you're likely to encounter relatively few in use. The asymmetric algorithms DH and RSA are used primarily to exchange encryption keys securely, while work that requires encrypting and decrypting large amounts of data is turned over to the symmetric algorithms because of their speed advantage. Of these, the ones you are most likely to encounter are RC4, DES and Triple-DES, and possibly RC5 and IDEA. For data authentication, you'll most likely find MD5 or SHA-1 being used.

These have all been well tested, and DES, Triple-DES, and RC4 are becoming de facto industry standards. If something else is being offered to you, research it thoroughly before being sold on it solely on the basis that it uses a huge key length (for example), because key length isn't everything. You could be buying inferior security, to say nothing of opening yourself up to interoperability problems with products from other developers.

Without encryption, VPNs on the Internet would be useless. Anyone with a good packet sniffer could eavesdrop on the sessions and indulge in all sorts of mischief. For that reason, a VPN demands secure encryption. By using the strengths of asymmetric and symmetric encryption to overcome each other's weaknesses, and by combining them with data verification methods such as digital signatures, it is possible to provide the secure key exchanges needed for a reliable cryptosystem and a viable VPN.

None of this will work, however, without being able to be certain about whom you are communicating with. In Chapter 6 we'll discuss the various ways that user authentication is implemented in a VPN, along with the entire matter of key management, which involves making sure that the right keys get to the right people—and only the right people—in a timely and reliable fashion.

User Authentication, Authorization, and Key Management

Encryption is only as effective as the system that controls the access to keys. In a VPN, as with almost any network, there are essentially two stages to a security system. The first is authenticating the user, that is, making sure that whoever is logging on is who he says he is and has a right to enter. Once the user has been authenticated, there's the issue of exchanging and managing the keys that the users need to communicate as their permission (authorization) allows. Creating and managing the keys has to be done in a way that protects them from being stolen or tampered with and makes sure they get only to a user whose identity has been authenticated.

In this chapter we'll look first at who guards the front door and how users are authenticated. Once we've covered that layer, we'll move on to the pure key management systems. This is where we will get into encryption key management, which we'll find involves more than simply exchanging keys. The entire issue of key management, encryption and message authentication (hashing and signatures), and protocol negotiation must be addressed carefully.

6.1 User Authentication

It may seem strange to begin a chapter on key management with a discussion of user authentication, but one of the greatest challenges a VPN administrator faces is making sure the right person *and only the right person* is getting the right keys. To do that, the key management authority, whatever and wherever it may be, must have some way of being sure that the person getting the key is who he claims to be. It is one of the most difficult problems in VPNs or any other kind of networking.

As any network administrator can tell you, one of the most challenging aspects to any network security program is making sure that only the users who are authorized to have access get in the front door. If attackers somehow make it over that first hurdle, the amount of mischief they may get into is frightening. Once inside a system, even as low-level users, they may have access to important data. They may be able to steal higher-level passwords that will give them access to more critical functions, and they may perhaps even get super-user status through which they can commit wholesale mayhem or theft. The more securely the front door is locked, the better.

But securing that front door has become more and more challenging. You want it to be secure enough to keep attackers out, but you don't want to make it so hard for legitimate users to get in that they wind up frustrated. When networks were limited and essentially in house, the problem was relatively simple: strangers could be kept away from computer terminals with relatively unsophisticated techniques, such as locked doors or a security guard at the entrance. As networks expanded, it became more difficult. There were more doors, and not all of them were under the control of the network's owner. Then road warriors began to get remote access capabilities so they could dial in to the network from wherever they were. Attaching the network to the Internet or establishing an extranet only compounded the challenge, and the result has been firewalls and proxy servers.

That's still simple compared to a network that is supposed to be accessible to people from outside the host's control. How do you control the access of people from an entirely different organization, ones whose names don't appear in your own user database but have a legitimate right to be there?

Instead of simply locking the door to a terminal room, it has become necessary to develop a procedure where the system can somehow identify who is knocking and then decide whether to let them in or not. At first it was simply a matter of extending the original username/password system. That is still probably the most widely used system. But usernames are easily figured out, and passwords can be easily stolen. Also, for that system to work, the user has to already be registered with the system, with a password on file. What of an extranet VPN, where users from one organization are allowed access to another organization's system?

6.1.1 The Username/Password Challenge

As we've mentioned repeatedly, one of the weakest points to any VPN is the user password. During log-on is the one time when the end user, everyone from the secretary or clerk up to the CEO, has direct contact with the security system. If an attacker can, by giving a correct password, con the gatekeeper of the castle into lowering the drawbridge, the castle can be taken without having to storm the walls.

It may seem elementary to cover this here, but the reality is that this is where most security systems are vulnerable and most frequently attacked. Basic security consciousness can never be emphasized too much. Good security policies—policies that employees are regularly reminded of—are the first line of defense, and the first row of barbed wire is the username/password exchange.

Probably the most common form of user authentication uses the Password Authentication Protocol (PAP). The user enters her username and password, which are passed along to the authentication server. The authenticator looks up the username in its database, matches the password, which is usually stored in an encrypted fashion, and admits or rejects accordingly. The weakness here is that if the password is not encrypted during transmission, it can easily be intercepted.

In response to this weakness, there is the Challenge Handshake Authentication Protocol (CHAP), which counters the eavesdropping threat and provides a way to periodically reauthenticate the user at the client keyboard. In CHAP, the host responds to the username with its hostname and an encrypted, randomly generated challenge string. The client uses the hostname to look up the appropriate secret stored at its end, combines that with the challenge to generate an encryption key, and uses this key to encrypt the username and password, thus protecting them from eavesdropping. The result is returned to the server, which then decrypts and verifies the response and admits the user. CHAP can also reverify the user periodically by challenging for the password again, making sure that an impostor hasn't settled himself at the terminal.

The weakness of both PAP and CHAP involves the process of selecting a password. If Bob creates his own password to the VPN, there are two possible scenarios. Either he's going to make it something that's easy to remember or, if he follows good security policy, he'll create a random string of characters that is hard to remember, in which case he'll probably have to write it down somewhere. If it is a system-assigned password, Bob is likely to have the same problem of remembering it and will go for the same solution—he'll write it down.

If the password is easy to remember, like a name or a real word or a birth date, an attacker may be able to guess it by snooping Bob's records or by using a demon dialer to run through all the possibilities. If it's a random string, whether his own or a system-created string that is given to Bob—which should avoid the known word hazard—he'll be even more likely to write it down. If Bob writes it down, someone may just stroll casually past his cubicle and read it off the Post-it note on his monitor. Unless they are encrypted, passwords can easily be sniffed as they are moved over the network; more often, however, they are found by "dumpster diving" or when someone is conned into revealing a password by a telephone call from someone posing as, perhaps, a security specialist. In the security trade, this is known as "social engineering." A hacker, posing as someone from the security office or the network manager's office, simply calls and asks for a naive user's password, perhaps to track down some mythical problem in the network. Once the hacker has that password, he's in the door.

There are services, such as SecureID, that offer more secure authentication methods. Usually these are similar to the systems used in automatic teller machines, which employ a token in the form of a magcard or smartcard, combined with a personal identification number that is known—it is hoped—only to the user. On the cutting edge are systems that rely on fingerprint identification, or retinal prints, or even a user's facial bone structure.

For now and the foreseeable future, however, the username/password method is the most common. For a VPN to be safely secured, it is vital that users be taught the importance of protecting their password. On the administrator's side, minimizing the exposure of unencrypted passwords on the network is crucial. We come back to this issue in Chapter 10.

6.1.2 VPN User Authentication: The Simplest Scenario

If a VPN is confined to a single business entity that runs common software, the user authentication problem is relatively straightforward, since there's no need to involve a third party in the process. A good example is a small VPN running nothing but Windows and PPTP, perhaps involving a few dial-in users and a Windows NT LAN at the central office (Figure 6-1).

Between the dial-in client and the ISP's network access server (NAS), PPTP users are authenticated using whatever procedures the ISP uses. Once beyond the ISP's NAS, the user must be authenticated by the remote PPTP server, which uses a standard Windows NT–based log-on requiring a username and password. Authentication is the same used for any remote access server (RAS) client dialing directly into a RAS server.

Microsoft supports the Password Authentication Protocol (PAP), the Challenge Handshake Authentication Protocol (CHAP), and the Microsoft Challenge Handshake Authentication Protocol (MS-CHAP). Remote users' accounts are filed on the Windows NT server and are maintained through User Manager for Domains, a centralizing administration of both the VPN and the private network's user accounts.

6.1.3 Central Authorities

For larger, more complex VPNs, the problem is more complicated. How can the VPN administrator be confident of users who are entering the VPN from

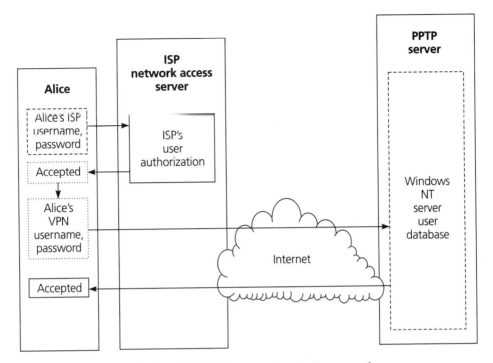

Figure 6-1   A simple Windows PPTP VPN user authentication procedure.

entities over which he has no control? Suppose that Giant Widgets has a VPN that serves as an extranet, and Associated Grommets, one of their vendors, is part of it. How can the VPN administrator at Giant Widgets authenticate a user coming in from Associated Grommets?

Then, to complicate matters, add in the Giant Widgets sales staff, who are on the road with their laptops. They're probably dialing in to an ISP, maybe an AT&T WorldNet POP in Bangor, Maine, or Madrid, Spain. How do they get authenticated?

For this purpose, there are central authorities that have developed to support extranets and larger, more complex remote access systems, such as Internet service providers, which essentially face the same problems. The Remote Authentication Dial-In User Service (RADIUS) and Terminal Access Controller Access Control System (TACACS) were both created to meet the challenge of managing remote access systems.

It is not necessary for your VPN to use one single authentication server in order to be able to authenticate all users. If Alice at Giant Widgets is registered on one authentication server, and Bob over at Associated Grommets is on another, the VPN can still work by accepting authentication granted by the other party's authentication server. The fact that Bob is coming to Alice from Associated Grommets can be assurance enough that he has permission on the VPN. As we saw in the discussion of digital signatures in Chapter 5, there is another layer of authentication available to Alice that allows her to be certain it's Bob she's talking to. This will come into play when they get down to exchanging encryption keys.

RADIUS

RADIUS is an authentication and accounting system used by many ISPs to authenticate their users. As the name implies, it was developed to serve dial-in users, but it can easily be extended beyond that market.

When the user logs on to a network access server that is a RADIUS client and enters his username and password, the information is passed to a RADIUS server, which checks that the information is correct and then authorizes access to the system. A RADIUS server can, of course, serve a number of different clients. RADIUS server software is readily available from many sources, so you can set up your own RADIUS server, or you can sign on with a company that provides RADIUS server authentication for you. While it is not an Internet standard, per se, there is an IETF working group that keeps an eye on RADIUS.

A RADIUS authentication is relatively straightforward, as Figure 6-2 shows. The authentication request from the RADIUS client contains the username and password (encrypted), the identification number of the RADIUS client, and the port number the user is binding to. The RADIUS server and client are authenticated to each other through the use of a shared secret key. If the primary RADIUS server should be down, the client passes the request along to a secondary RADIUS server.

The RADIUS server validates the client request, then decrypts the packet to get the username and password. This information is then passed along to the appropriate authentication method (PPP, PAP, CHAP, etc.). If a challenge/response authentication is required, the server initiates that exchange. If the authentication succeeds, a message goes back to the client accepting the user; otherwise the server passes back a rejection.

RADIUS servers can also provide accounting services. They track a variety of information, such as username, network services, times of log-ons through the RADIUS server, and so on. The client can send an accounting request packet and the server returns an accounting response packet. Both are protected by a shared secret key.

Note that RADIUS only authenticates users. It doesn't have any key management capabilities.

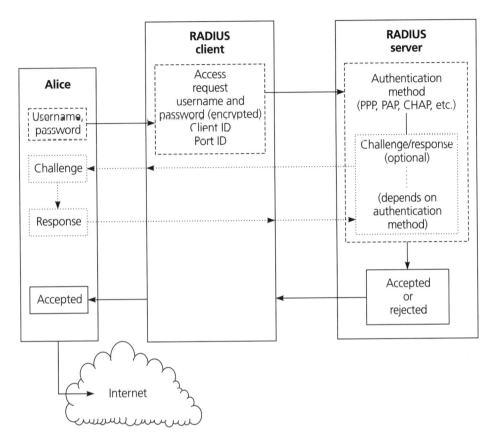

Figure 6-2   How RADIUS user authentication proceeds.

TACACS
Although it has been around since 1989, making it older than RADIUS, TACACS has been overtaken in popularity by RADIUS, primarily because the latest version of the protocol, TACACS+, is proprietary to Cisco Systems. It works in much the same way as RADIUS, the main difference being that RADIUS uses the User Datagram Protocol (UDP) between client and server, while TACACS uses TCP. If you are already using TACACS, you should be able to continue to use it with your VPN. Otherwise you should probably go with RADIUS or Kerberos.

Kerberos
Kerberos is named after the three-headed dog who guards the gates of Hades in Greek mythology. It emerged from MIT, and a free implementation is

available from there as is the source code. It is also found in a number of commercial products; version 5 is the current implementation of Kerberos. The current version of Kerberos uses DES encryption.

Kerberos is interesting because it both authenticates users and generates and manages encryption keys at the same time (Figure 6-3). In this way, it serves as both user authenticator and key manager.

Instead of authenticating a user to a client for the client to admit, a Kerberos server authenticates the user using a username/password authentication scheme and then issues the user a "ticket" that gives the user access to Kerberos-enabled servers and applications.

If Alice and Bob are using Kerberos, the process begins with Alice getting herself authenticated by a Kerberos server and getting a ticket and an authenticator (Figure 6-3, paths 1 and 2). The ticket, encrypted using the server's private key, contains the random session key, her name, and a time when the session key expires. This time window is usually short—5 minutes—for increased security. The authenticator includes, among other fields, a current time stamp, a checksum, and an optional encryption key. This authenticator is encrypted with the session key from the ticket.

When Alice wants to talk to Bob, she knocks on Bob's door, metaphorically speaking, and hands him her ticket and authenticator. Bob decrypts the ticket using the server's public key and then uses the session key to decrypt the authenticator, which Bob uses to assure himself that it did, indeed, come from

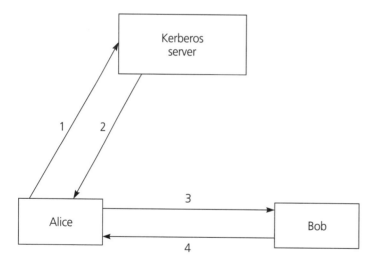

**Figure 6-3   A typical Kerberos exchange. All exchanges are encrypted and authenticated.
1. Alice requests ticket and key from server. 2. Alice receives ticket and key from server.
3. Alice presents ticket and key to Bob. 4. Bob verifies ticket and gives Alice access.**

Alice. As an additional check, he looks at the time stamp to make sure the ticket hasn't expired. The ticket also establishes the encryption protocol and the key, so the key exchange takes place at that point as well and he admits her (Figure 6-3, paths 3 and 4).

Alice will need a ticket for each user she wants to communicate with. So for every new connection she will first contact the Kerberos server for a new ticket.

6.2 Key Management and Certificate Authorities

Once we get user authentication established there's still the issue of encryption key management to be addressed. The authenticated user must receive the proper keys and must be assured that they are the proper keys. The security of the entire VPN relies on a secure method of generating, registering, distributing, and managing these keys. If one key is compromised, the entire network may be compromised. As we pointed out earlier, the longer a key is in use the more data there is available to analyze to crack the key, and the longer it is in use the more data there is that is vulnerable if a key is compromised.

Since one vital aspect to key management is to make sure that keys are registered to a certain user, the entity performing that task has to know exactly who the user is. If a public key is to be distributed, the entity needs to know that the recipient is who he says he is. For that reason, key management and user authentication are intimately interlocked. While a RADIUS server does authenticate a user, it doesn't do key management (unlike Kerberos, for example). The key management facility depends on the RADIUS server's authentication in that, once a user has been authenticated, the key management authority issues her the proper keys.

Key management consists of certain basic steps. Keys must be generated, registered, and then distributed. They must be activated and/or deactivated, replaced, or updated. When they are no longer to be used, keys must be revoked or terminated, and it may be desirable to archive keys that have been removed from service so that old messages encrypted with them can still be accessed.

As we discussed in Chapter 5, users are usually assigned a key pair using one of the asymmetric algorithms, either Diffie-Hellman or RSA. In practice, users usually have pairs of both types assigned, since an RSA envelope may be used to exchange DH public keys to establish a DH session. Anyone who wishes to sign messages or to retrieve encrypted messages must have key pairs. They may need several different pairs, perhaps one for work and one for personal communications, or one for interdepartmental messages and one for intradepartmental messages. As we've pointed out before, every device on the network must have a key pair, including modems, workstations, servers, terminals, and printers. Larger organizational entities such as departments may also need a key pair.

This adds up to a considerable number of keys that must be generated. They must be distributed in some secure fashion, activated, deactivated, retired, replaced, updated, revoked, terminated, and archived. In a VPN of any size, an entire structure must be created to handle the process.

While key pairs can be generated by the user, they rarely are in a VPN. Since large prime numbers are used, the only feasible way to generate keys is using a computer and special software. Since users on a VPN may be routers or servers, automatic generation is a necessity. It can possibly be done locally, but more likely will be done at some central service.

With VPNs, keys required for a single session are usually generated for each new session. These shared secret keys are usually generated using Diffie-Hellman encryption, but that still requires exchanging public keys in a secure fashion. In the case of Microsoft's implementation of PPTP, instead of using DH the secret key is generated using the user's password, which is available at both the client end and at the PPTP server where the user database is maintained. But, as we'll see when we look into the workings of PPTP, this system has its weaknesses.

Some secret key authentication systems, such as Kerberos, do not allow local key generation. Instead, Kerberos uses a central server to generate keys.

No matter where a key is generated, somehow the user must be assured that this is a valid, unique key or key pair; that somehow the private key will be transferred securely to him; and that the public key will be made available only to those who should have it. The recipient must be confident that any public key she receives is the right key and not one from some third party.

That means that whoever does the transferring has to be trustworthy, and the transfer itself has to be secure. The process usually involves a digital envelope, authentication, and something to certify that the key is genuine. Bear in mind, too, that virtually all of this takes place untouched by human hands and invisibly to the user.

If we go back to our example VPN linking Giant Widgets to Associated Grommets, you can see the need for some central entity to handle all this. If each company has its own key management, the confusion will be monumental, and as the VPN adds outside members the problem becomes worse. In addition, the road warriors must also be brought in safely. It should be obvious for this to work at all that some central office must be responsible for the process, and something has to accompany the key to authenticate it. Here is where certificate authorities come into play, which are discussed in the next section.

6.2.1 Certificate Authorities

As commercial use of the Internet has grown, the need for a security infra-structure has become apparent. For commerce to take place, there has to be some way of assuring users of who they are talking to, and there must be a way to handle the encryption key exchanges that are necessary for secure transactions to take place. Hence, key management specialists called certi-ficate authorities (CA) are being established to meet the need for encryption key management. While a company VPN might have its own CA, most CAs are third parties, providing key management services to a diverse group of cli-ents. Although the main thrust behind them is ecommerce, VPNs are going to benefit from their development as well.

CAs generally do not regulate admission to the system itself. For a user to acquire an encryption key, she must have already gained access to the system. User authentication has already been handled by something like a RADIUS server.

As you can see in Figure 6-4, the key management process starts when a key pair is registered with a CA by whoever generates it. Often, as in this case, the CA generates the key pairs itself. These RSA key pairs will be used later to exchange DH or symmetric keys for secure communications between Al-ice and Bob. The CA sends Alice her private key, along with a certificate at-testing to the validity of it, and does the same for Bob (in a secure fashion, of course).

Information on the certificate may include the key's expiration date, the name of the certifying authority that issued it, a serial number, and perhaps other information. Most important, it includes a digital signature of the CA (the issuer) so that Alice and Bob know that the certificate is legitimate. Every key transfer must be accompanied by a certificate.

When Alice needs Bob's public key, she sends a request to the CA, which first checks her authenticity, then returns to her Bob's public key. Likewise, Bob requests and receives Alice's public key in the same way. Both key trans-fers are accompanied by certificates guaranteeing the authenticity of the keys (Figure 6-5).

Once they have these, they can use them to safely exchange DH public keys they generate themselves. These DH keys are then used to generate the DH shared secret key for their communication session. Or they may use the DH session to exchange yet another key (a DES symmetric encryption key, for example) for their session.

The CA is the cornerstone of your VPN encryption key security system. Users depend on it to validate and register their keys. It is to the CA that users go to obtain other users' public keys. The CA must ascertain that each request

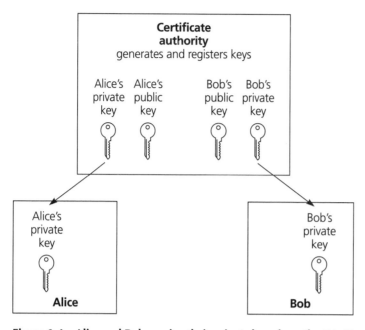

Figure 6-4   Alice and Bob receive their private keys from the CA. Key exchanges are accompanied by signed certificates that guarantee authenticity.

is valid and must return the appropriate public key to the user in a secure fashion. The CA manages and tracks all public key exchanges, guaranteeing that the right keys come from the right people and get registered and that the right keys get to the right people. It is the repository of all information on keys, including the users' names (and it must have authenticated those users) and the keys registered to them.

For this reason, the CA must have the highest level of trust, and it must be the most tightly secured entity. If the CA is compromised, then every key in the system is compromised. If an attacker obtains Alice's key, he might then pretend to be her and send a message to her bank transferring all the money to his own account. The certificate authority may be within your organization, but, as VPNs develop and become extranets, it is more likely the CA will be a part of the Internet's slowly developing public key infrastructure (see next sections).

Also, if VPNs are to be assured of any degree of interoperability, how the CAs communicate with them and how key exchanges are certified has to be standardized. A print server that receives a key from the CA has to be able to read the certificate it gets, whether that print server is running VPN software from Aventail or Cisco or VPNet.

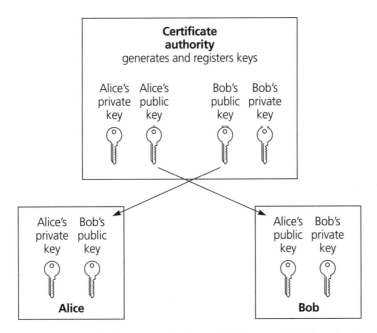

Figure 6-5   At their request, the CA sends Alice and Bob the other's public key. Key exchanges are accompanied by signed certificates that guarantee authenticity.

6.2.2 The ITU-T X.509 Certificate Standard and the Public Key Infrastructure

The most widely accepted format for certificates is defined by the International Telecommunications Union (ITU) in the ITU-T X.509 standard, which is often referred to as just X.509. Certificates complying with the standard can be read or written by any application complying with X.509. Since automated systems such as firewalls, modems, or printers require key exchanges just as human users do, this compatibility is important.

This brings us to the public key infrastructure (PKI), a system that is starting to be established on the Internet. It will consist of a system of digital certificates (probably meeting the X.509 standard), certificate authorities, and other registration authorities that verify and authenticate the validity of each party involved in Internet transactions.

There is no single PKI in place at the moment. There is not even a single agreed-upon standard for setting up a PKI. OASIS, the electric power industry's VPN, has set up its own PKI, so the technology does exist, although it is not yet standardized. With the push toward expanding ecommerce, however, this situation should change, making large-scale VPNs more practical as well.

6.2.3 Public Key Cryptography Standards

To help bring order out of potential chaos (or perhaps to increase the confusion, it can be hard to tell sometimes), there are the Public Key Cryptography Standards (PKCS), developed by RSA Data Security, Inc., in cooperation with an informal consortium that originally included Apple, Microsoft, DEC, Lotus, Sun, and MIT. PKCS #6 describes a format for extended certificates, which consists of an X.509 certificate along with a set of attributes signed by the certificate issuer. Mercifully—in view of the potential benefits of uniformity—PKCS #6 is being phased out in favor of v.3 of X.509.

The PKCS also define things such as mechanisms for encrypting and signing data using RSA, a Diffie-Hellman key agreement protocol, and a method for encrypting a string with a secret key derived from a password. The point of mentioning all this here is so you know to look for X.509 and/or PKCS compliance in your VPN solution.

6.2.4 Lightweight Directory Access Protocol and VPNs

The Lightweight Directory Access Protocol (LDAP) is a set of protocols for accessing directory information. Since public keys are stored in directories, LDAP may find applicability in VPNs for that purpose, too, among other uses. However, it appears more likely that authentication servers such as RADIUS and CAs will be the route taken as the PKI develops.

6.3 Making the Connection: More than Just Managing Keys

Key management, particularly distributing and generating keys for a session between two users in a large, complex VPN, is only one part of establishing communications within the VPN. Protocols and encryption and authentication algorithms must be negotiated between them, and keys must be exchanged. When Alice's node, part of Giant Widgets, needs to talk to Bob's office over at Associated Grommets, things can get complicated, since Alice's VPN server is running one brand of VPN and Bob's is running another. Alice's VPN client may be capable of handling DES, Triple-DES, RC4, and maybe even IDEA encryption. Bob's server, on the other hand, may not offer DES or IDEA, but does have Triple-DES, although a different variant, as well as RC4. Similar choices of hashing or MAC algorithms may be involved at either end.

If, in the beginning, Alice doesn't have Bob's public key and Bob doesn't have Alice's, those keys have to be exchanged. That's where the CA and the X.509 certificates come in. Then Alice and Bob need to negotiate a connection. They have to agree on what encryption and authentication algorithms to use, then they have to exchange the keys needed to make them all work. And all of this has to be done in a secure fashion so that no one can intrude on the session.

For the sake of Alice and Bob, let's at least agree that Giant Widgets and Associated Grommets are both running the same VPN tunneling protocol; in this case let's make it IPSec (see Section 7.3.5). This means, we hope, that they will both use the same key management and exchange method, which in IPSec is usually ISAKMP/Oakley.

6.3.1 ISAKMP/Oakley (IKE)

The Internet Security Association and Key Management Protocol (ISAKMP), combined with the Oakley key exchange protocol, is one of the more popular sets of protocols for negotiating and implementing VPN sessions. This integrated set of protocols automatically negotiates a connection and handles the exchange of keys between sender and receiver. The IETF has recently renamed the ISAKMP/Oakley combination to Internet Key Exchange (IKE), but you may hear either term being used; they are identical. As we discuss IKE, we'll separate out the two factors, ISAKMP and Oakley, to show how each functions.

IKE performs a number of complex functions to bring everything together. It provides a way to agree on which protocols, algorithms, and keys to use. It provides primary authentication so Alice knows she's talking to Bob, and vice versa. It manages the keys after they've been agreed upon and exchanges them. And it does all this in the shelter of what is called a *security association* (SA), an agreement about which encryption and authentication algorithms and keys to use, which prevents eavesdropping. The IKE process is worth looking at in detail, because it illustrates the problems that any similar system must deal with, and it shows at least one way it can be done.

IKE runs in two phases. In the first, two ISAKMP peers establish a secure channel in which ISAKMP works, called an ISAKMP Security Association (SA). In phase two, they negotiate general-purpose SAs. It is within these that the actual VPN session takes place.

We're facing a chicken-and-egg situation here. For an SA to exist, encryption and authentication must be enabled between Alice and Bob. But that involves exchanging encryption keys, and keys have to be exchanged in a secure transaction; i.e., they must be encrypted and authenticated, which requires an agreement on the algorithms and keys to be used for that encryption and authentication.

ISAKMP has two ways to set up the first ISAKMP SA, main mode and aggressive mode. As Figure 6-6 illustrates, *main mode* involves exchanging

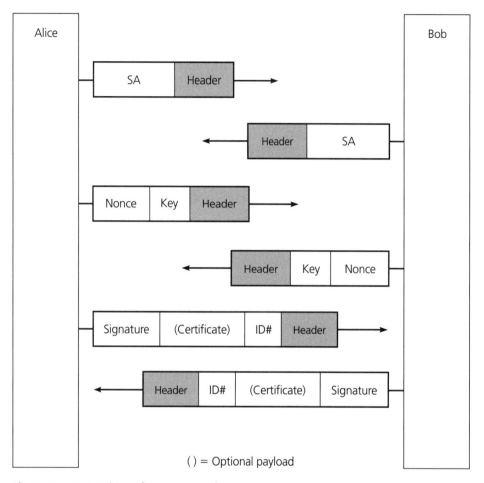

Figure 6-6 IKE main mode message exchange.

three pairs of messages. First Alice initiates things by sending a message proposing an SA, which consists of the following: an encryption algorithm, a
hash algorithm for preparing things for signing, an authentication mode for
signing data, a group (the material used to generate a DH public key; that is, a
seed and a large prime number) over which to do a Diffie-Hellman exchange,
and, optionally, a hash function called a *pseudorandom function* (PRF) used
to hash some values during the key exchange for verification purposes. Instead of sending a PRF, they can just use the hash algorithm already proposed;
it's optional.

Bob's response to this first exchange establishes the agreement on the basic
algorithms and hashes. In the second step, Alice sends Bob her DH public key
and, to make sure they're not being snooped by a man in the middle, Alice

sends along a *nonce*, a random number for Bob to digitally sign (using the hash and authentication mode just agreed to) and return with his public key, which he does. In this way they've exchanged their public keys in a reasonably secure fashion. At this point Alice may not be sure that Bob is really Bob, and Bob may not be sure that Alice is really Alice, but at least they know there is no third party in the middle. Finally they verify each other's true identities by exchanging identification and certification payloads in encrypted packets. Authentication between them may involve contact with a RADIUS server or may rely on a certificate from a trusted authentication server.

All that an eavesdropper can know is that an SA has been reached. He has no way of knowing who is at either end of the agreement, since their true identities weren't exchanged until they could be encrypted and authenticated.

You'll notice that each ISAKMP packet leads off with a header. This header identifies the step being taken. Each of the pieces is carried in its own payload, and any number of payloads can be packed into a single ISAKMP packet. The shared key that is generated by this first DH algorithm is hashed three times, first to generate a first derivative key that is used later to generate additional keys in quick mode (see below). The second hash is an authentication key; the third hash is the encryption key for the ISAKMP SA.

Aggressive mode lightens the workload of this initial negotiation, at the cost of some security, accomplishing the same thing as main mode by exchanging only three messages, as shown in Figure 6-7. Alice proposes an SA and sends her public key along with a nonce and her ID, all in one packet. Bob checks her ID with a third party (perhaps a RADIUS server), then responds by sending back everything needed to complete the exchange—the SA, his key, the signed nonce, his ID, the certificate, and his signature. All Alice has to do is confirm the exchange with a signature and certificate and they have their ISAKMP SA. Aggressive mode is faster, but since the identities are exchanged before a secure channel is established, an eavesdropper can identify who has just formed a new SA.

Once the ISAKMP SA is established, completing phase one using either main or aggressive mode, *quick mode* is used to negotiate general SAs in phase two. Quick mode is used for negotiating general security services and for generating fresh keys. Since it is already running inside a secure ISAKMP SA (using the protocols and hashes established by the first exchanges between Alice and Bob), it can be simpler, faster, and more flexible (Figure 6-8).

Quick mode packets are always encrypted. They also always begin with a hash payload, which is composed using the pseudorandom function agreed upon during the first exchange that established the ISAKMP SA. The quick mode exchange establishes the general SAs between Alice and Bob so they can exchange data safely.

Once all that is done, the actual working key exchanges can take place. ISAKMP can work with a number of different key exchange protocols, but it is

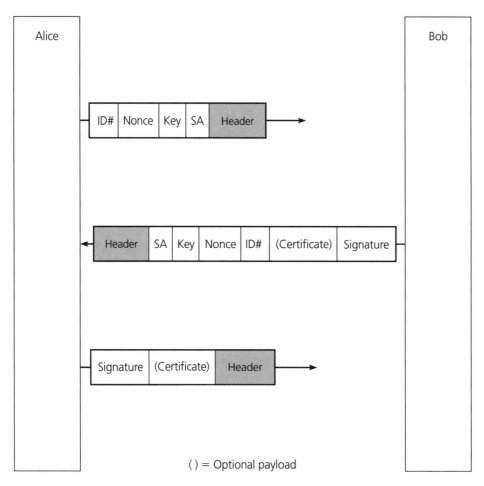

Figure 6-7   ISAKMP aggressive mode message exchange.

most often coupled with Oakley. Photuris is another protocol you might find with ISAKMP, but Oakley is the one that has been chosen to be incorporated into IKE. Oakley handles the key exchanges through general SAs negotiated in quick mode in a couple of different ways. The simplest method is an exchange of symmetric keys, such as DES keys, passed through the SA.

For even greater security, a property called *perfect forward secrecy* (PFS) can be used. A Diffie-Hellman exchange (see Section 5.3.1) can be used to build a system with perfect forward secrecy, where each key pair is generated pseudorandomly and is never permanently stored or used to generate future keys. With perfect forward secrecy, if an early key is cracked it does not mean that later keys can be cracked. PFS systems also lack "master" keys and "key

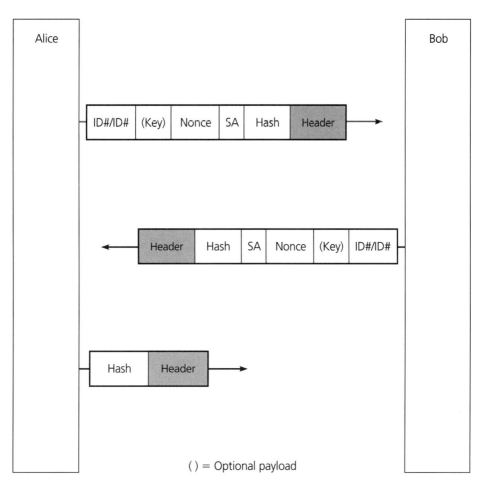

Figure 6-8   Quick mode exchange.

escrow" as well as key-generating keys. The ISAKMP SA contains a Diffie-Hellman parameter, which is where the agreement to use DH is set up. The parameter contains information on a group, which is the material needed to generate Diffie-Hellman keys. It consists of two numbers: a large prime number and a seed, which is a starting value for generating a random number. Using these numbers, they generate public keys, exchange them securely within the SA, use those to generate the shared secret key, and use that to encrypt and decrypt their communications.

By default, IKE always specifies two groups that are available to both parties for DH exchanges. If Alice and Bob wish to add new groups, they have the IKE *new group mode* available to them so they can generate new groups to make additional DH public keys for building new shared secret keys, which makes IKE's perfect forward secrecy scalable.

The point of all this analysis of IKE is to emphasize the amount of work that must be done by a VPN protocol to create a secure connection. Because of the many encryption and authentication options available and the security threats on the Internet, achieving security requires more than a simple generation or exchange of encryption keys. Both the encryption and hashing algorithms must be agreed upon, keys must be exchanged, and somehow all this has to be done in a way that keeps a potential snoop from getting in on the action. ISAKMP's phase one, either main mode or aggressive mode, neatly bootstraps a secure connection, in the form of that first SA, negotiating all the algorithms and exchanging keys in a secure fashion, and then proceeds to use that secure channel to generate keys for the real work of the VPN.

6.4 Conclusion

In this chapter we've addressed the issue of security, beginning with the problem of user authentication. Because authentication is such an important issue and because it is the first layer, we'll return to it when we discuss the problem of managing your VPN in Chapter 10. As you can see, everything else rests upon reliable authentication. After that has been accomplished, the problem of encryption key management is encountered. IKE (also known as ISAKMP/ Oakley) is becoming the preferred solution, in combination with CAs that adhere to the X.509 certificate format.

In Chapter 7 we'll be looking at the specific protocols and suites of protocols that fasten a VPN together. We'll see how these incorporate tunneling along with encryption, message authentication, user authentication, and key management to provide the security needed for a VPN to communicate safely over the Internet.

Tunneling and the VPN Protocol Suites

V PNs involve a multitude of protocols—for encryption, for authentication, for tunneling. In this chapter, building on what we've covered in the two previous chapters, we'll be concerned with the protocols that bolt the VPN together. These include the tunneling protocols, the protocols that make the connection, and the specifications within the protocols that make the connection private: encryption, authentication, and access controls.

All of these various types of protocols, algorithms, and specifications are mixed and matched in different ways to produce suites of protocols that provide the full range of services needed for a secure VPN. Although we may talk about IPSec or PPTP as if each of them is a single protocol, we're actually dealing with suites of protocols rather than a single entity. As we've already seen, even the IKE key management and distribution protocol is actually a combination of two protocols.

This suite or group structure can create problems because the internal protocols may not quite match from product to product, or the way they are implemented may differ. As we've already mentioned, most Internet protocols are designed by committees, by working groups of the Internet Engineering Task Force. Most Internet protocols work amazingly well, especially considering the hostile environment of the Internet. Nevertheless, if VPN products from different vendors—using what are supposedly the same protocols—are to work together, they have to be selected carefully and it may take a bit of coaxing, and you have to know the protocols within the protocols and how they are implemented.

7.1 Tunneling

Tunneling is the technology that puts the "virtual" in VPN by letting one system (or network) send its data to another system using the Internet's or some other network's connections. At its simplest, tunneling means that your network's packet is essentially hidden from the transporting network by hiding its original header behind one tacked on by the tunneling protocol. Seeing only that header, routers pass it through the Internet to the destination contained in the added IP header, where the VPN server strips away the tunneler's header and the remainder is forwarded on to its ultimate destination.

7.1.1 The IP Packet and Encapsulation

To understand what's going on, we need to take a look at the basic IP v.4 packet. As shown in Figure 7-1, it consists of several sections. The payload, of course, is the data. In front of that is the IP header.

We've labeled the sections of the IP header that are particularly applicable to the tunneling process. For example, one of the fields within this IP header,

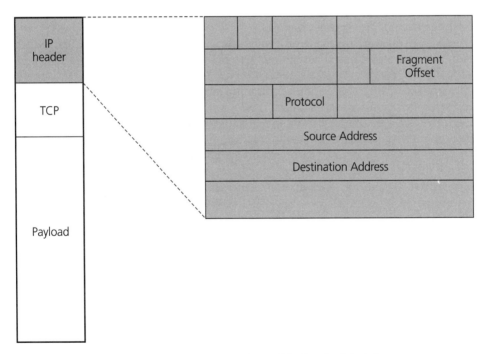

Figure 7-1   The IP packet with important sections of the header labeled.

the Protocol field, indicates what higher-level protocol is contained in the payload. Normally this is TCP or UDP, but a tunneling protocol like IPSec uses what is called an *encapsulated security packet* and for that reason sets a different value in the Protocol field, as we'll see, to tell the receiver what it's dealing with. The Fragment Offset field tells where the payload (higher-level protocols and data) begins in relation to the start of the packet.

The last two fields shown give the source and destination IP addresses so the routers know where the packet is going. The tunneling protocol appends a new IP header that contains as origin and destination addresses the VPN's client and host IP addresses, rather than the internal network addresses of the actual point of origin and remote destination. Other fields within the IP header are different as well, such as the Fragment Offset field. In Figure 7-2 we're tunneling an IP packet similar to the one illustrated in Figure 7-1. The Fragment Offset field in the new header indicates that the data begins at the beginning of the old IP header, rather than where the actual data begins, effectively hiding the original destination and origin from the Internet's routers. In real life, depending on the VPN protocol used and how it is implemented, the new payload, containing the concealed IP header, will probably be compressed and encrypted before the tunneling, further securing it from prying eyes.

As we've said before, this tunneling process allows a network that uses unregistered or illegal addresses to link to another network through the Internet by hiding those addresses from the Internet's routers. Tunneling can even transport a non–IP-based packet such as IPX over the IP-based Internet, complete with its data and headers intact.

If encapsulation of the packet were all there was to tunneling then it would probably be called "encapsulation." While it is a crucial part of the foundation of a VPN, encapsulation alone doesn't provide a tunnel. A tunnel is actually a set of connections through the Internet between client and server. A tunnel can carry more than one connection between client and server, so if two LANs

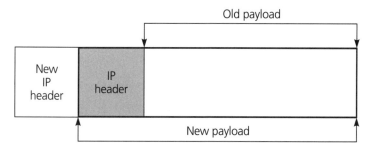

Figure 7-2   A tunneled IP packet with a new header. The Fragment Offset field in the new header indicates the new starting point for the payload.

are tied together using a tunnel, multiple users on each end may be using the tunnel at the same time.

Each packet in the tunnel is, of course, encapsulated, because the Internet routers themselves don't see the tunnel at all. It is nothing more than an agreement between client and host, no more substantial than a telnet connection.

As Figure 7-3 illustrates, using the Point-to-Point Tunneling Protocol (PPTP), when a client begins a dial-up VPN connection, the first thing established is a Point-to-Point Protocol (PPP) connection to a PPTP-enabled network access server (NAS) on the Internet. Once that is set, a second connection is made through the PPP connection, through the NAS and the Internet, to the VPN server at the far end. The server must authenticate the client and vice versa, providing confidence that the parties are talking with whom they are supposed to be talking. Once that is done you've made the connection and established the tunnel. Then it is through that connection that the encapsulated packets are moved. How the authentication is performed is directed by the tunneling protocol.

While this tunneling method provides the "virtual" of VPN, it does nothing about the "private." Even inside that tunnel, any packet sniffer can capture the encapsulated packets. An attacker can read internal IP addresses, read the data itself, perhaps spoof the server with a fake IP address, or hijack the entire session. As we discussed in Chapter 5, encryption is what makes the VPN private. As a result, the tunneling protocols that are implemented on VPNs

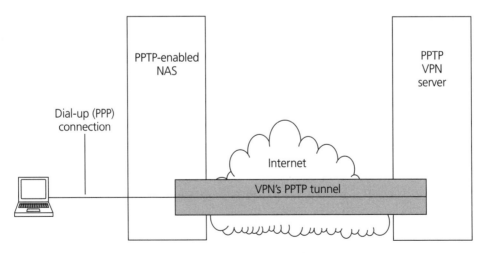

Figure 7-3   PPTP tunneling using a PPTP-enabled network access server.

make a place for encryption, authentication, and key exchange—all the details that make sure your data stays private on your VPN.

When we get down to discussing the nitty gritty of the different protocols, we'll find that what is left unsaid in the tunneling protocol can sink the entire project by keeping nodes from understanding each other, even though they are supposedly using the same protocol. Picking products that offer PPTP or Layer 2 Tunneling Protocol (L2TP) as your tunneling protocol is only the first step. After doing that you'll have to make sure that the various products on your VPN are speaking the same dialect within the language of that protocol; you will have to make sure that authentication takes place so the tunnel can be built, so that the system can decrypt the data and route it to its proper destination on the internal network.

Fortunately, as we'll see, there are strong forces pushing for standardization. The automobile industry is working on a massive VPN that will tie together all the major auto manufacturers with their independent suppliers. With these companies already running a variety of networks, and with hundreds of enterprises selecting VPN products that somehow all have to communicate, the need for interoperability is crucial.

The VPN industry (the vendors) do understand this need. The IETF IPSec Working Group schedules regular "bake-offs" to test the work of its members. Even more encouraging, at least two organizations, the Internet Computer Security Association (ICSA) and the RSA Data Security, Inc., project S/WAN, are testing VPN products for interoperability. If the products you choose have the stamp of approval from one of these testers, there is a reasonably high degree of probability that they will work together. (At least if they don't, you've got someone to scream at.)

Of course, if one product has been approved by one tester, and another has been approved by a different tester, things may not be as certain. If A equals B and B equals C, does A equal C? Not necessarily, when it's Widget Testing that says A equals B and it's Grommet Standards that says B equals C. They may not be testing exactly the same things or using the same methods, and neither is capable of testing all the possible situations encountered in the real world. As they say in the automobile ads, your mileage may vary.

7.2 VPNs and the Open System Interconnection Model

As you'd expect with any networking project, we can't possibly get through this book without referring to the Open System Interconnection (OSI) model.

As you can see in Figure 7-4, the OSI model consists of seven layers and essentially describes the structure of a networked system from the hardware up.

Each layer provides services to the layer above. Data destined for the network that originates at the top layer, the application layer, is fed down through the stack, with each layer doing what needs to be done to hand it on to the next. In a TCP/IP network, for example, layer 4, the transport layer, adds the TCP protocol. Then layer 3, the network layer, slaps an IP header on the packet and hands it off to the data link layer, which passes it to the hardware layer, which passes it out onto the network. Conversely, data from the network comes in through the hardware layer, is passed up to the data link layer, which passes it up to the network layer where IP does its thing, then up to the transport layer where TCP does its thing (which includes checking that the data got there without being scrambled or broken somehow) before passing it on up.

Figure 7-4 also shows where the protocols we will be discussing fit into the OSI model. You'll notice that some of the protocols are placed on the line

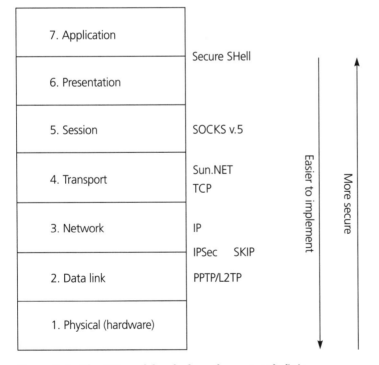

Figure 7-4   The OSI model and where the protocols fit in.

separating two different layers. This is because they may not neatly fit into one layer or the other, as we'll explain.

Also, notice that as you move down through the stack, implementation of these protocols becomes easier, while securing them becomes more of a challenge. Although this is generally true, it should not necessarily be an overriding factor in your decision about which products to implement. More important is whether the protocol will do what you need done. There are ways to secure the lower-layer protocols well and, if you choose vendors wisely, implementation of the higher-layer protocols may not be a serious problem. Bear in mind that the OSI model is only a model; it is not engraved on stone tablets. It is a handy way of describing the sequence in which things are generally done in networks, nothing more.

VPNs can also be said to be of two basic types, with a third type that builds its own layer into the OSI model. The most-talked-about VPNs are what can be called *packet-oriented* VPNs. They operate at the lower OSI layers (2 and 3). This type of VPN has gotten the most attention from the big vendors such as Cisco and Microsoft, as well as from the IETF with the development of the L2TP and IPSec protocol suites.

The second type of VPN works at a higher level by letting the application talk to a proxy service of some kind. While the packet-oriented VPNs work at layer 3 or below in the OSI model, the *application-oriented* VPNs such as SOCKS v.5 work at higher layers, closer to the user. Naturally, IP packets are still used to move the data through the network, but these protocols work above the network and data link layers, at a level where the packet is really built, rather than messing with the packets themselves.

7.3 Packet-Oriented VPN Protocols

The packet-oriented VPNs are the ones upon which most interest is focused these days. They generally operate at layer 2 and layer 3 of the OSI model. However, as we'll see, this is not a hard and fast situation. Life just isn't that simple. Some elements of these VPN protocols operate at one layer, some at another.

7.3.1 Point-to-Point Tunneling Protocol

The PPTP is an extension of the PPP used for dial-in Internet connections. It was developed by Microsoft, Ascend Communications, and 3Com, and it has been incorporated in the Windows NT 4.0 Server and Workstation, in Windows 98, and as an add-on to Windows 95. Earlier versions of Windows do not offer PPTP. PPTP drivers are also available for some versions of Unix, but otherwise it is not widespread. In the IETF draft of the PPTP, authentication and encryption methods are not spelled out. Hence, just having PPTP in common does not necessarily guarantee interoperability between different vendors' products.

Sometime in the future, PPTP is going to be supplanted by L2TP. That future is not here yet, however. Since it is available with virtually every copy of Windows that currently ships, PPTP is out there and easily available, which is why we feel it is important to discuss it here in detail. It has advantages beyond ready availability, but it also has grave disadvantages, as we'll see.

One of the advantages to PPTP is that, even though it requires IP, it can also carry data using protocols such as IPX or AppleTalk. This makes it useful for establishing a VPN between LANs running non-IP networking software, such as Novell's NetWare.

Because of Microsoft's involvement, it's simplest to discuss the Windows implementation of PPTP. As you might suspect, since it was an extension of the PPP protocol, PPTP was intended primarily to provide dial-up remote access through the Internet. Under Windows, it works in conjunction with Microsoft's Remote Access Server software. The PPTP client can be running under Windows 95/98, Windows NT Workstation, or Windows NT Server. As implemented by Microsoft, the PPTP server must be running Windows NT Workstation or Windows 95/98 as well, although more usually it will be running Windows NT Server.

Typically, the client makes a dial-up PPP connection to an Internet service provider, then a second logical connection is established that builds the VPN tunnel to the PPTP server at the LAN end. The PPTP packets are then received and processed by the PPTP server and sent on through the LAN to their destination. If the client is already connected to a LAN that is connected to the Internet, the initial PPP connection is not required, of course.

Another way to connect that doesn't require a PPTP-enabled client is to dial in to an ISP's network access server that is equipped with PPTP. In such a case, PPP runs between client and ISP, and the PPTP tunnel is established by the ISP's NAS to the LAN's PPTP server.

PPTP encrypts and compresses the PPP packets for moving them through the Internet. A modified version of the Internet's Generic Routing Encapsulation (GRE) protocol is used to create the IP datagram. At the receiving end, the PPTP server disassembles the IP datagram into a PPP packet and decrypts that PPP packet using the network protocol of the receiving network.

PPTP traffic uses TCP port 1723 and the IP protocol uses ID 47, as assigned by the Internet Assigned Numbers Authority (IANA), so PPTP can be used with most firewalls and routers by enabling them to admit traffic destined for that port and protocol ID. In terms of architecture, this means that the PPTP server can be deployed behind or in front of the firewall.

Authentication of a dial-in user begins with the ISP. After the user has been authenticated by her service provider, the connection to the PPTP server is made and the user is authenticated there, as we discussed in Chapter 6.

Once authentication has taken place, access to the private LAN follows the Windows NT–based security model. In Microsoft's implementation of PPTP, data in the packets is encrypted using the Remote Access Server shared secret encryption process, which is a private key system using the DES algorithm. Included with Microsoft remote access client software on Windows NT 4.0 or Windows 95 with Dial-Up Networking 1.2, it is called Microsoft Point-to-Point Encryption (MPPE). The shared secret key is derived from the hashed password stored on both the PPTP client and server. In the version shipping with the operating systems, RC4 is used to create a 40-bit session key. Users in the United States and Canada can obtain a 128-bit session key for use inside the United States and Canada. To further enhance security, packet filtering can be enabled on the PPTP server, making it harder for an attacker to slip through that opening.

It is because of the encryption scheme used that the security of Microsoft's implementation of PPTP has been brought into question by (among other security experts) Bruce Schneier, author of *Applied Cryptography* and a consultant from Counterpane Systems. He claims that an attacker can sniff passwords across the network, break the encryption scheme, and then read confidential data and mount denial of service attacks against PPTP servers. According to Schneier, the flaw is not within the PPTP itself, but in Microsoft's implementation of it, and fixing it would require Microsoft to completely rewrite it.

The weak point is the use of the password to develop the encryption key, instead of the use of a random number generated by a difficult-to-predict source, such as mouse cursor position, CPU instruction counters, and/or current interrupt timings. Believe it or not, date/time as a seed is relatively weak, since there are only 86,400 seconds in a day, a range that can be tested in milliseconds. Crypto keys must be highly unpredictable. As we've seen, the weak point of private key encryption systems is the need to exchange the key or, in this case, to develop it at each end of the system using some value that both ends can agree upon. If the private key is exposed, all the data is exposed as well.

Using the password to "seed" the encryption algorithm is very risky. As we've noted, passwords are always a vulnerable point for any network, virtual or real. If transmitted unencrypted, they can be sniffed. If they are real words, they can easily be guessed by readily available software. The safest password is a long, meaningless string that mixes letters, numbers, and symbols—the longer the better. However, if a password is not real words or easily guessed names or number strings it is hard to remember, which means that it may be written down by the user on a piece of paper that can fall into the wrong hands. With a PPTP password in the wrong hands, not only is the network accessible, but also, potentially, the session's encryption key itself.

In response to Schneier's critique, Microsoft has issued assurances that their product is sound and they claim to have received no customer complaints. They recommend that users remain current on Windows NT service packs and that North American customers use the 128-bit version of PPTP that Microsoft offers. This, of course, does not address the inherent weakness of the scheme of using the password to generate the encryption key. Windows NT 5.0 may remedy that weakness.

PPTP also has another drawback, which is that it implements the entire VPN process in software, software that is probably already running on a heavily loaded system. Encryption imposes a heavy load on the processor. In short, unless the machine is designed to handle the load, PPTP is slow.

One other drawback shows up when a PPTP user attempts to use a service such as America Online as her ISP. AOL and Compuserve both filter out PPTP, making the protocol unusable on their networks.

On the other hand, PPTP is being used successfully on many VPNs. Galaxy Scientific, for example, uses PPTP for their VPN. However, they also implement some hefty security measures, and they are looking at more secure and stable alternatives such as L2TP and/or IPSec.

7.3.2 Layer 2 Forwarding Protocol

The Layer 2 Forwarding (L2F) protocol was developed by Cisco Systems and, as its name states, it is a layer 2 protocol. In addition to being included in Cisco products, it is also supported by Northern Telecom, Inc., and Shiva Corporation. As with PPTP, no authentication or encryption standards were included in the protocol. The L2F protocol is not just an Internet tunneling protocol, either: it can be used on frame relay and ATM networks as well.

The L2F protocol was submitted by Cisco to the IETF as a proposed standard. The IETF PPP Extensions Working Group agreed to accept the proposal and to combine it with PPTP from Microsoft. The result is the Layer 2 Tunneling Protocol (L2TP). The L2F protocol is not a protocol you're likely to encounter in VPN products from vendors other than Cisco and its allies.

7.3.3 Layer 2 Tunneling Protocol

When the Internet Engineering Task Force was handed PPTP by Microsoft and the L2F protocol by Cisco, the Layer 2 Tunneling Protocol is what resulted. Cisco, Microsoft, Ascend, 3Com, U.S. Robotics, and others are members of the working group that is drafting it. Although the working group hasn't finalized it, L2TP is already being used. It is to be included in Windows NT 5.0 along with PPTP.

Like PPTP, L2TP offers the advantage of being able to tunnel non-IP packets such as IPX and AppleTalk. Also like PPTP and the L2F protocol, however, it does not specify encryption or authentication methods, although the IETF draft recommends using IPSec's encryption (see Section 7.3.5). Another important feature of L2TP is that, like the L2F protocol, it is designed to tunnel traffic over a variety of networks other than IP networks. These include frame relay, SONET, and ATM.

Backed as it is by major vendors, L2TP is an emerging standard. By combining it with the encryption standards incorporated in IPSec, it is likely to emerge as the industry leader for VPN usage.

7.3.4 AltaVista Tunneling Protocol

Another tunneling protocol you may encounter is AltaVista Tunnel, developed by Digital Equipment Corporation (DEC). Although AltaVista is a proprietary system, it is worth looking at the specifications because they illustrate the advantage to using a product from a single vendor. All of the details are spelled out carefully, and special features (such as SecureID for user authentication) are available, which may not be possible if products from different vendors are mixed in a VPN.

AltaVista Tunnel was conceived with the intention of linking DEC products. It consists of a Telecommuter Server and an Extranet Server. The former allows connections between an AltaVista server and mobile workers who connect to their home network via the Internet. The latter is used to tie together two or more networks, from a remote office to a central office, for example.

For establishing the connection in the first place, user authentication options include SecureID authentication tokens (SecureID Card, KeyFob, and PinPad). When contacted by an AltaVista client, if SecureID is implemented the AltaVista server instructs the tunnel client to prompt the user for SecureID credentials. Once the information is sent for processing, the server either authorizes the client to connect or unauthorizes it.

Encryption is just as clearly spelled out. AltaVista Tunnel uses a 1,024-bit RSA public key cryptosystem for user authentication and private session key exchange. RC4 is used for bulk data encryption. The keys are tied to the user's cryptographic identity, not to a specific workstation, which means that the IP address is free to be dynamically assigned. Once the tunnel is established, the server and client automatically switch from RSA public key encryption to RC4 private key encryption. At 30-minute intervals, the client and server exchange new keys. MD5 hashing is used to ensure data integrity.

For domestic use, AltaVista's RC4 secret key encryption for bulk data transfers uses a 128-bit key. In the international edition a 56-bit key is supported, and 40-bit key encryption is also available. When creating a multinational tunnel, an automatic arbitration, transparent to the user, reconciles any encryption discrepancies.

AltaVista Tunnel also specifies data compression in its protocol. If both client and server have compression enabled, Lempel-Ziv-Oberhumer (LZO) compression is implemented. Otherwise the data is sent uncompressed.

The fact that all of these details are spelled out and built into AltaVista Tunnel provides a high degree of assurance that interoperability problems just won't be a factor in the pure AltaVista tunneled VPN. On the other hand, when trying to build a VPN using clients and servers from different vendors, these details have to be negotiated, somehow, so that the nodes can connect up reliably.

7.3.5 IPSec

IPSec is rapidly becoming the VPN protocol of choice, even over PPTP. Windows NT 5.0 will reportedly offer it along with PPTP and L2TP. Cisco Systems has announced that they will have IPSec support built into their routers. IPSec encompasses most, if not all, of the elements required for a VPN. It can be used in its entirety as a VPN protocol all by itself, or elements of it can be used to establish standards for other VPN protocols. For this reason we need to look at it in detail.

IPSec is an extension of the standard IP protocol, securing the network at the IP level with authentication and encryption. The intent of the IPSec working group is to provide a security standard that will apply to the broadest possible range of Internet services, including VPNs.

To do this, IPSec is actually a suite of protocols, a set of extensions to IP. They do not all need to be used together, and the parts of IPSec that handle problems like negotiating security attributes and managing encryption keys can be used to enhance and standardize layer 2 VPN protocols such as L2TP or PPTP.

However, while tunneling is actually a relatively small part of the IPSec suite, it is an important one from our standpoint, because it does make IPSec a VPN protocol, one that promises to offer real interoperability in the market. Although it is still in draft form, IPSec is already available, which means that there are still interoperability problems as vendors play with the not-quite-standard standard. IPSec2 is already on the drawing board. It will offer enhancements such as multicasting.

IPSec attempts to ensure interoperability by spelling out certain defaults that any implementation must contain with regard to authentication of the payload and packet, and encryption. As we'll see, these defaults are set low and may not provide the degree of security or functionality you want in your VPN. But since IPSec also spells out ways to negotiate these agreements, it should be possible for IPSec-compliant products to reach a higher understanding if it is available (such as the use of strong encryption). There is also the use of the protocol negotiation and key exchange protocol ISAKMP/Oakley, which lets communicating users agree on how they are going to secure the stream and on how to exchange keys safely.

Mapping the IPSec Packet

Since IPSec can be used in place of standard IP, it makes sense to take a look at the IPSec packet and to see how it differs from the standard IP packet.

To begin with, an IPSec packet begins with an IP header that looks like any normal IP header. Because it uses this standard IP header, the network can route it using standard IP equipment. There's no need to develop new routers to handle the traffic. (Looking to the future of the Internet, the IPSec working group is even working with the IPv6 working group to make sure that IPSec will remain compatible with the new version of IP when it shows up.) The Protocol field of that header contains a number that says there's an encapsulation security payload (ESP) following, rather than an IP packet's more usual TCP or UDP protocol.

As Figure 7-5 shows, in addition to the header, the IPSec packet consists of two basic elements, both of which are optional. The authentication header (AH) lets IPSec users verify that the data has arrived unmolested and unchanged and that it came from its apparent source. The ESP encrypts the data, making it safe from eavesdropping in transit.

The IPSec Authentication Header

Use of the IPSec's authentication header is optional. The AH can be applied alone, in concert with the ESP, or in a nested fashion when used in tunneling mode, which we'll get to under "IPSec Tunneling" below. In the usual packet, the AH goes after the IP header, but before the ESP, if one is present.

The AH provides authentication, but it does not address confidentiality (it does not encrypt). The AH ensures the integrity of the entire packet, including those fields in the external IP header that do not change in transit. Since some of the fields in the external IP header must change as the packet moves through the network, and the sender can't predict those changes, those fields are left unprotected by the AH. As we'll see below, the ESP also offers authentication, but the ESP's authentication protects only the material in the ESP, including whatever headers it contains, not the entire IPSec packet.

As you can see in Figure 7-6, the AH itself consists of several fields. The Next Header field indicates what higher-level protocol follows the

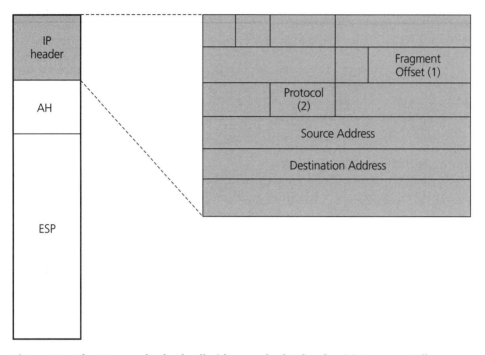

Figure 7-5   The IPSec packet leads off with a standard IP header. (1) Fragment Offset pointer indicates start of ESP. (2) Protocol field indicates that ESP follows instead of usual TCP or UDP.

authentication header (TCP or IPSec's ESP, for example). The Payload Length field is an 8-bit field specifying the length of the AH. The Reserved field is reserved for future use and is currently set to 0. The Security Parameters Index identifies a set of security parameters (algorithms and keys) to use for this connection; this information will come into play when we discuss the use of ISAKMP/Oakley for handling key management and distribution.

The Sequence Number field is a number that increases with each packet, used to keep track of the order that packets are sent in and to make sure the same set of parameters is not used for too many packets. Finally, the Authentication Data field is the actual digital signature, called an integrity check value (ICV), for the packet. All IPSec implementations must support at least HMAC (a symmetric signature scheme) with hashes SHA-1 and MD5 being used for the AH.

The IPSec Encapsulation Security Payload

The ESP is next in line. If there is no AH, then the ESP immediately follows the IP header. The ESP contains the data, as well as all higher-level protocol

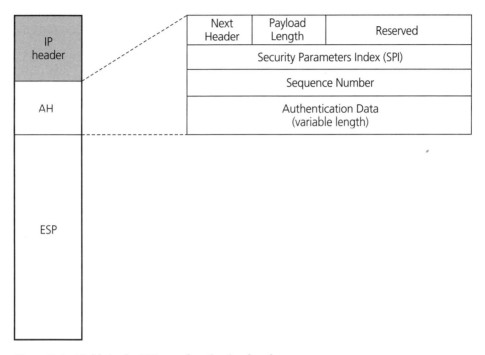

Figure 7-6   Fields in the IPSec authentication header.

headers such as TCP, and it offers some authentication of its own. The structure of the ESP is shown in Figure 7-7.

The first two parts, the Security Parameters Index (SPI) field and the Sequence Number field, perform the same functions as those used in the AH, as we'll see in a moment. They are not encrypted, but they are authenticated. The remaining parts—including the data payload, possibly a TCP protocol section, and the authentication data—are all encrypted during transmission and can really be considered to be one unit as far as we're concerned here.

Just like the SPI in the AH, the SPI that leads off the ESP tells the IPSec-enabled receiving device what security protocols are being used. This includes the encryption algorithms, which keys to use, and how long those keys are valid. This is where the receiving machine learns what algorithm it is going to use to decrypt the packet. IPSec can support any number of encryption protocols. By default, 56-bit DES-CBC (Data Encryption Standard, cipher block chaining mode) is required as a minimum in an IPSec-compliant product, but IPSec supports almost any kind of symmetric encryption. You can even use different encryption protocols for each party with whom you are communicating. As we'll see, the SPI ties in with the ISAKMP/Oakley key management protocol used by IPSec.

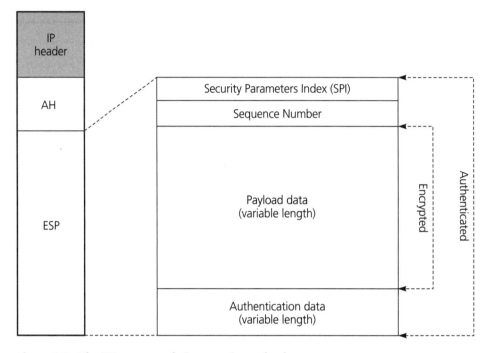

Figure 7-7   The IPSec encapsulation security payload.

Following the SPI is the sequence number. Again, as with the AH, this is a counter that increases each time a packet is sent to the same destination using the same SPI. It tells which packet is which and how many have been sent with the same parameters. The sequence number protects against replay attacks, in which an attacker sends a copy of a packet out of sequence to confuse communicating nodes or as a means of hijacking a session, or repeatedly replays a transaction, such as "buy 100 widgets," resulting in a massive oversupply of widgets in your inventory.

The final field in the ESP is the authentication field. As with many IPSec features, the authentication within IPSec's ESP is optional. If it is used, it consists of an integrity check value (ICV) computed only over the rest of the ESP (not the entire IPSec packet) once encryption has been completed, and exclusive of the authentication field itself. The authentication field's length varies, depending on the authentication algorithm used. The ICV uses hashing, and the current standard specifies the same mandatory minimum algorithms for IPSec-compliant equipment and software as are spelled out in the authentication header's specification (HMAC signatures and SHA-1 and MD5 hashing). The vendor is free to implement other authentication methods here, because as IPSec is set up, all of these parameters can be negotiated between IPSec hosts, using ISAKMP/Oakley. However, to be IPSec compliant, the minimums must be included.

User Authentication and Key Management with ISAKMP/Oakley

All of this security is wonderful. However, as we have discussed repeatedly, unless there is a structure for distributing keys and negotiating protocols between communicating parties, it isn't worth much. This is where IPSec's use of ISAKMP/Oakley comes into play.

As we saw in Chapter 6, ISAKMP provides a framework for key management on the Internet. It also offers specific protocol support for negotiating security attributes. The Oakley Key Determination Protocol provides the means to establish session keys on Internet hosts and routers. Combined into a hybrid protocol, ISAKMP/Oakley (now known as IKE) offers a complete package for negotiating security attributes, authentication methods, and key management.

It is here that IPSec's security parameters index, found in both the AH and ESP packets, comes into play. The SPI is a 32-bit number, picked by your system to represent the SA (security association) negotiated by ISAKMP. It identifies the SA, which contains the information on encryption and hashing algorithms used and the keys.

When Alice's system negotiates an SA, Bob's system assigns an SPI that it currently isn't using to reference it, preferably one that hasn't been used recently. It then communicates this SPI back to Alice's node. Until that SA expires, whenever Bob wishes to communicate with Alice, Bob's node uses that SPI. Alice's node reads that SPI to determine which SA it will use to decrypt and authenticate that packet.

IPSec Tunneling

IPSec's ESP provides the tunneling capability needed for a VPN. It does this by taking the original IP header and encapsulating it within the ESP, where it is encrypted with the rest of the data. Then it adds to the front of the packet a new IP header containing the address of the VPN's gateway. Doing it this way, IPSec not only hides the data, it hides the original source and destination addresses from Internet users, encrypting them in the payload, and thus making the packet immune from a traffic analysis attack. However, this same security feature is an impediment to network managers who would like to be able to track things using source and destination IP addresses by analyzing IPSec packets.

Summing Up IPSec

IPSec's wide range of security services, while intended for use on the many different services the Internet offers, makes it ideal for VPN use. By establishing at least minimum requirements for IPSec-compliant VPN products, it ensures a higher degree of interoperability than has ever been available before. With the ICSA and RSA Data Security, Inc., team both testing IPSec VPN products for interoperability, a real VPN standard is developing, making the creation of large VPNs possible.

IPSec need not even be the tunneling protocol. PPTP or L2TP can be used with parts of IPSec—the authentication header and ISAKMP/Oakley, for example—to handle authentication and key management. By using IPSec in this way, vendors can ensure interoperability in their PPTP or L2TP product.

The fly in the ointment, as of this writing, is that IPSec is still an IETF draft concept. There are parts of it that have not been nailed down. As a result, the interoperability issue remains. Once IPSec is set in stone, problems with that issue should be reduced.

7.3.6 Simple Key Management for Internet Protocols

The Simple Key Management for Internet Protocols (SKIP), developed by Sun Microsystems, could almost have been included in Chapter 6 on security. But since it goes beyond key management to provide tunneling, it can also be seen as a VPN protocol. Also, because it inserts itself into the OSI model between layer 2 and layer 3, it seems more logical to explore it in this chapter, where we first encounter the OSI model.

SKIP is also a proposed Internet standard, and a number of companies (Novell, VPNet, Toshiba, Internet Dynamics, Check Point) are supporting it. Although patented by Sun, SKIP is an open system because Sun put the patents into public domain. Reportedly, SKIP advocates would like to see it incorporated into the IPSec protocol suite instead of, or perhaps along with, ISAKMP/Oakley.

SKIP has actually been around since 1994, longer than ISAKMP/Oakley. It was developed by Ashar Aziz and Whitfield Diffie, so you might expect it to use a Diffie-Hellman key exchange and you'd be right. Initially, unlike ISAKMP/Oakley, SKIP did not support perfect forward secrecy. In response to criticism, PFS was added, but it is not available as a default mode; the default mode uses a master key for rekeying. To use SKIP, all that is needed is for both parties to have a DH key pair and to have SKIP implemented on their systems. If user authentication is used (an optional feature of SKIP), the recipient must also be on SKIP's access control list (ACL) or on a certificate authority. The ACL also lists IP addresses of hosts that use SKIP, as we'll see.

As we've said, looked at from the OSI model viewpoint, SKIP sits between the network layer and the data link layer (see Figure 7-4). SKIP is transparent to the user and to all layers above it, including the layer immediately above it, the network layer, where the IP header is appended to the data packet.

A packet of data comes down through the stack, picking up its IP header at layer 3 in the OSI model. When it reaches the SKIP layer, SKIP checks the IP address on the packet with the ACL to see if SKIP should be used at all, to see if encryption and/or authentication are needed for packets going to that address, and to see which protocols to use if they are. If the IP address is not on the ACL, the packet is sent on unchanged. If it is on the ACL, SKIP encapsulates the packet by building its own SKIP header on the packet. If the ACL calls for it, it also encrypts the packet and adds authentication as required.

Finally—and in this way SKIP functions the same as the encapsulation we see in all the other packet VPN protocols such as IPSec—at the sending end SKIP appends a new IP header to the packet ahead of the SKIP header and sends it out on the Internet (Figure 7-8). With the SKIP-added IP header, routers pass a SKIP payload along just as they would route any IP packet. The important thing about this new IP header is that it has the value 57 in the Protocol field, telling the receiver that it is a SKIP packet, instead of the usual code for TCP, UDP, or the code for ESP that IPSec uses.

The SKIP header has to perform essentially the same tasks as IKE (Figure 7-9). Among other things, it carries the information on where to look up the public keys that are needed to build a DH shared secret key at each end. It also spells out what algorithms are to be used for symmetric key encryption, hashing, and data compression. Finally, it actually carries the symmetric key, encrypted with the DH shared secret key, and everything is authenticated with digital signatures.

Because the public keys, which are not in the packet itself but must be obtained from a CA or some similar repository, are of no use without the DH private keys, and because everything is carefully authenticated, the exchange is secure. And because the packet carries, in a secure fashion, everything that's needed to unscramble the data, there is no lengthy negotiation process as we see in phase 1 of ISAKMP.

Once it is received by a remote SKIP host, the packet is delivered from the data link layer to the SKIP layer. SKIP examines the Protocol field of the IP header appended by SKIP. If the Protocol field is other than 57, the packet is simply handed off to the network layer. If the protocol number is 57, SKIP reads the rest of the header, gets the required DH public key, and generates the

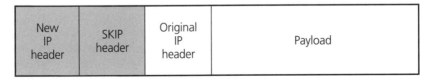

Figure 7-8   SKIP tunnels the packet by appending an IP header on the packet.

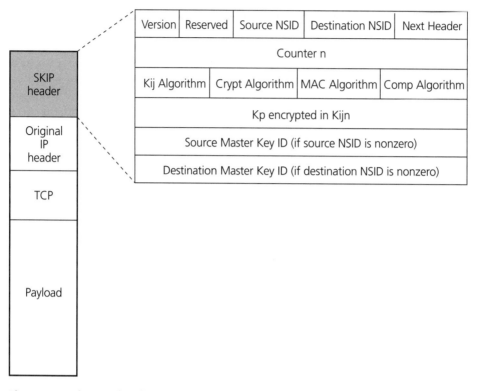

Version	Reserved	Source NSID	Destination NSID	Next Header
Counter n				
Kij Algorithm	Crypt Algorithm	MAC Algorithm	Comp Algorithm	
Kp encrypted in Kijn				
Source Master Key ID (if source NSID is nonzero)				
Destination Master Key ID (if destination NSID is nonzero)				

SKIP header

Original IP header

TCP

Payload

Figure 7-9   The SKIP header carries a lot of information.

DH shared secret key. It uses this key to decrypt the symmetric key, which is then used to decrypt the data. Along the way everything is authenticated according to the instructions carried in the packet, and the data is decompressed in accordance with the algorithm specified in the packet as well.

SKIP offers some interesting advantages over ISAKMP/Oakley. The main advantage is that a SKIP-equipped Internet host can send an encrypted packet to another SKIP host without requiring any prior message exchanges such as are required for ISAKMP/Oakley. It avoids a long exchange of messages just to establish a secure connection: compare that with ISAKMP/Oakley's main mode negotiations to establish an SA.

Since no exchange of messages is required, this also means that SKIP allows unidirectional IP encryption, so it can be used for IP broadcasting via a satellite link or cable, even making encrypted multicasting feasible. SKIP also offers a form of crash recovery: if an encryption gateway fails, SKIP can reboot and resume decrypting packets without having to renegotiate any connections. However, this property also means that when SKIP is used this way, it cannot offer perfect forward secrecy.

SKIP also permits nodes to share the same DH identity. In other words, from an encryption standpoint, multiple devices can be identical. This permits setting up redundant secured networks, where if one node fails another can take up the load instantaneously. SKIP gateways can be configured in parallel to perform instant failure takeover, letting one take over if the other goes down for some reason, a redundancy not readily available with ISAKMP/Oakley.

SKIP is included with every server sold by Sun Microsystems. It is available for Windows NT and Windows 95, SunOS, FreeBSD, and Linux. While it is not seen much in VPNs, it would certainly appear to be a viable alternative to ISAKMP/Oakley in IPSec, and it can even function as a VPN protocol on its own.

7.4 Application-Oriented VPN Protocols

As mentioned previously, there are VPN solutions other than the packet-oriented VPNs we've just discussed. These operate farther up the OSI model and present their own advantages and disadvantages, compared to the packet-oriented VPNs.

7.4.1 Secure SHell

Secure SHell (SSH) is probably the most straightforward of the application VPN protocols to deal with. SSH is a program to log on to another computer over a network, to execute commands in a remote machine, and to move files from one machine to another. In that way it sounds like rlogin. However, SSH adds security that rlogin lacks in the form of authentication and encryption, essentially turning it into a VPN protocol.

Looking at the OSI model, SSH works at the application level, at the top of the food chain. This limits the architectural choices for an SSH-based VPN. It can't be located at the firewall or router; it can only be implemented at the user to server level.

SSH exchanges random session keys (for Triple-DES encryption or the like) using RSA public key encryption. RSA digital signatures are also used for authentication. The key used to encrypt the session key is never stored on disk, but instead it is regenerated and the old key is deleted. The client RSA-authenticates the server machine in the beginning of every connection to prevent Trojan horses from being executed by routing or Domain Name Service (DNS) spoofing. The server RSA-authenticates the client machine before accepting anything. SSH is intended as a complete replacement for rlogin, rsh, rcp, and rdist. It can replace telnet in many cases.

You'll note, however, that SSH does not use tunneling or encapsulation as we'd see it in a packet VPN protocol such as PPTP. This means that, while the payloads are encrypted and authenticated, the source and destination IP addresses are not concealed from the Internet's routers or from someone using a packet sniffer. This also means that only traffic to and from legal IP addresses is allowed unless it is hidden behind a proxy server or some sort of network redirection is implemented.

The only security is the encryption, to prevent eavesdropping, and the authentication. Since the server will reject any packets that don't pass authentication, the session can't be hijacked unless the authentication is broken.

A free version of SSH that runs under a number of versions of Unix is available for noncommercial use. Commercial versions, which include patent licenses, are also available. Also, commercial versions are available for Windows (3.11, 95, and NT), for Macintosh, and a freeware OS/2 version is available as well. Two versions are available for Amiga.

Some commercial VPN products use SSH; one company, SSH Communications Security Ltd., specializes in it. The IETF SecSH Working Group is working on SSH2, which will add, among other things, support for the public key infrastructure, such as certificate authorities.

7.4.2 SOCKS v.5 Network Security Protocol

SOCKS, short for sockets, began life as what is known as a "circuit-level proxy." The release of SOCKS v.5 raised SOCKS itself to the VPN level when support for multiple levels of authentication was added, along with the ability to negotiate authentication, using the Generic Security Services (GSS) application programming interface (API).

With SOCKS, all communication flows through a central facility on the network, a SOCKS server. SOCKS-enabled client applications use the SOCKS protocol to communicate with SOCKS-based servers and to establish relay connections between internal and external networks. SOCKS is also used to establish proxy connections between segments on an internal network.

In the OSI model, SOCKS works at the session layer, below the presentation layer and above the transport layer. Requiring as it does a SOCKS server, a VPN can only be implemented through a server, rather than at the user level. The VPN also requires SOCKS-enabled client software, which may further restrict its use somewhat.

Once authentication is agreed to between a SOCKS v.5 client and server, SOCKS handles connection requests to the local workstation, creates a proxy circuit setup, and relays data between applications. By acting as a proxy server, a SOCKS v.5 server can handle communications from illegal IP addresses behind it. SOCKS v.5 also added support for UDP and TCP to SOCKS v.4.

In addition to authentication, SOCKS v.5 provides encryption through the GSS-API. The GSS-API does not specify security algorithms, but it does let a SOCKS v.5 server query a SOCKS v.5 host as to its encryption capabilities and then lets them negotiate a protocol to be used. Since no minimum encryption algorithm is specified, as it is in IPSec, SOCKS v.5 servers must be configured to be able to negotiate a secure connection.

7.4.3 Sun.NET

Sun.NET is a late entry into the VPN marketplace from Sun Microsystems. It developed out of Sun's acquisition of i-Planet and their Netlet and Remote Passage technologies. This interesting protocol operates at layer 4, the transport layer, on the OSI model. It is Java based, which liberates it from virtually any operating system platform problem on the client side. When a Sun.NET-enabled site is contacted by a Java-capable browser, after authentication a Java applette is transferred to the client side. Once it has been activated, it establishes a VPN connection with the server. Encryption is accomplished using a DH exchange and RC5 (from RSA) symmetric encryption. The key length available for it ranges from 0 to 2,048 bits.

The obvious advantages of Sun.NET are the ease with which it is implemented on the client side and its platform independence. It is also, obviously, a client/LAN (or, more accurately in this case, client/server) VPN solution. It is not suitable for LAN-to-LAN VPNs.

7.5 Quality of Service Protocols and VPNs

There are other Internet protocols that are applicable to VPNs, even though they are not VPN protocols themselves. They are important because they address an issue that the VPN protocols are not, themselves, equipped to deal with—quality of service.

The two that seem to have the best chance are the Resource Reservation Setup Protocol (RSVP) and Multi-Protocol Label Switching (MPLS). Both are under development by IETF working groups. They are an effort to prioritize Internet traffic. As we know, while they are all treated as equal, the urgency of IP packets is not equal. It doesn't matter a great deal if a packet carrying part of an email message is delayed a few seconds in reaching its destination. However, a packet carrying a bit of data from a videoconferencing session does need to reach its destination promptly if we're to avoid jerky video or mismatched audio and video.

One of the issues to be considered when planning a VPN is the quality of service the VPN requires. A VPN that will be used for videoconferencing requires a high degree of reliability and low latency. RSVP and MPLS are the

IETF's effort to address these problems. By attaching a priority to an IP packet and implementing in the routers some way of providing the appropriate level of service to each packet, it is hoped that the more time-critical packets will be routed more quickly and efficiently than packets that won't suffer from being delayed.

Both RSVP and MPLS require routers that are capable of handling them. Both types of routers are under development, so it will be some time before either protocol is ready for prime time. At this point it seems likely that MPLS will emerge as the protocol of choice, and VPN capabilities are being incorporated into it as it is being developed by the IETF.

7.6 Conclusion

In this chapter we've taken a look at how the many different protocols and algorithms fit together to create a VPN. However, we have not necessarily covered all the different VPN protocols; there are more ways than one to skin this virtual cat. The current trend is for standardization on IPSec, often in combination with L2TP. We hope this will provide the standardization the VPN industry requires.

However, it is going to be some time before full interoperability will be guaranteed, if it ever can be. Even if two vendors are both using the same protocol—L2TP, for example—their products may not interoperate well because they implement features such as encryption or authentication differently. Even though as of this writing IPSec offers the best chance of providing reliable interoperability, IPSec isn't quite soup yet. In short, interoperability is not guaranteed.

Now that we have some idea of all the different choices available, with regard to public vs. private networks, architectures, and the VPN protocols and how they work, we can begin to learn how to plan a VPN that best fits the environment it will operate in and that will best meet the requirements needed.

8

Architecture

As you'd expect, the architecture of a VPN is determined primarily by what you want the VPN to do. A VPN to serve road warriors will have one set of design requirements, while a VPN connecting two LANs will have another. A VPN extranet will have different requirements from a VPN intranet with respect to security. A VPN that is outsourced, with the work being done by a network service provider, mandates one type of design, while a LAN implemented in-house imposes different constraints.

In terms of physical architecture, the primary issue in all of these scenarios is *where* the VPN begins and ends; the tunneled, encrypted connection can terminate outside or inside the firewall, for example, or at the firewall itself. If the VPN is outsourced to a network service provider, it may terminate at the service provider's POP. While the most popular protocols are fairly flexible, even the choice of protocol can influence where the VPN terminates, as we've seen in our discussion of Secure SHell and SOCKS v.5.

VPN functions can be implemented in routers and switches; in firewalls; in dedicated boxes that do nothing but authentication, tunneling, and encryption/decryption for the VPN; and in workstations and laptops. A stand-alone box can be built specifically for that purpose, with the programming hardwired into the hardware and special chips handling encryption and decryption, or it can be a generic computer, with the VPN functions handled by software installed on the machine.

8.1 Software Versus Hardware Solutions

Setting aside the outsourcing option, with the exception of road warriors and their laptops virtually any of the scenarios can be implemented with a hardware package intended to support a VPN, with the tunneling and encryption and other VPN functions implemented in hardware, or they can be implemented by loading software on a more generic computer such as a Pentium II–based machine running Unix or Windows NT. Such a machine can be a box that is already functioning as a LAN server or perhaps being used as a firewall, or it can be a machine dedicated as a VPN server.

Taking the software solution first, simply loading VPN software on a system that is already functioning as a server or firewall is penny wise and pound foolish, because performance is going to suffer. Encryption is an important element in VPNs, and encryption is processor intensive, involving a series of complex mathematical operations. A software VPN solution that uses the relatively straightforward and fast DES algorithm can slow performance of a system by 40%. Using the more secure Triple-DES algorithm makes the performance hit even worse. Adding VPN functions to a machine that is already handling server or firewall chores is looking for trouble. Performance will not be acceptable, unless the system was vastly overengineered for its previous tasks.

If the computer is not doing anything else and is configured with a fast processor and RAM to handle VPN functions, a software-based VPN does have some advantages over a hardware-based VPN. Most important, it offers greater flexibility; as traffic on the VPN increases and outgrows the box handling it, it is relatively easy and inexpensive to install a faster computer using the same VPN software to cope with the increased load. The old computer can still be used for less demanding tasks.

There are chips available that are specifically designed to encrypt and decrypt traffic and to compress it. Hardware that is built for VPNs offers significant performance advantages over a software solution. Generally, in the VPN industry today the trend appears to be in the direction of hardware-based solutions. Major players such as Cisco, AT&T, and Lucent are integrating VPN capabilities right into their routers. However, it is more costly to upgrade a hardware box and, while VPN hardware prices are dropping and causing the gap to narrow, the question of what to do with the old box still remains.

Software VPN solutions will certainly continue to be available. The most obvious vendor is Microsoft, which currently bundles their PPTP VPN product with Windows NT Server and includes the client software in Windows NT Client and Windows 98. Microsoft also will be offering L2TP in future versions of Windows. That easy and inexpensive availability ensures Microsoft a prominent place in the VPN market.

PPTP and L2TP are logical choices for roving users to use for accessing a VPN through the Internet. However, on the server or LAN end, you should analyze your choices carefully before taking what appears to be a quick and easy route. As we've pointed out, serious questions have been raised about the security of Microsoft's implementation of PPTP. Even if Microsoft addresses those issues in Windows NT 5.0, the fact that PPTP or L2TP with IPSec encryption is likely to be loaded onto a system that is already burdened with other functions should make you ask yourself if it will really give you what you need in terms of performance. Every user joining the VPN through that server piles another load onto the processor. At the very least, it would be prudent to establish a dedicated VPN server to handle the load.

8.2 Hiding Your LAN

One of the factors you should consider as you plan your VPN is the opportunity to hide your LAN from the Internet. Remember from our discussion in Chapter 7 that most of the popular VPN protocols do offer this capability by concealing the original source and destination addresses of a packet within the VPN datagram. There are good reasons for doing it. One of the most valuable types of information that hackers seek out is the IP addresses of workstations or servers within a network. With those addresses, if they can somehow get through or around the firewall, they can mount assaults on each of those individual machines on the network. They can crash a server to get a core dump to read, or they can plant a keystroke logging program on a workstation to capture everything that user does. With such a program, they can capture log-in and password information that will give them access to other systems. The less that hackers know about your LAN, the safer you are. While hiding the source and destination IP addresses can impose some management challenges with regard to monitoring traffic on the LAN, the added security is worth it.

The protocol you choose will be one determining factor on this issue. With the most popular VPN protocols such as PPTP, L2TP, and IPSec, by encrypting your LAN's internal addresses with the data they can be hidden not only from the Internet's routers but from crackers looking for a way in to your system. It does depend on the way the protocols are implemented, of course. With Secure SHell, however, the source and destination addresses are not hidden from anyone running a packet sniffer to capture the traffic.

The architecture you select for your VPN can also determine if you can provide this protection. If, for example, you initiate the VPN tunnel at the workstation level on your LAN, it may be impossible to encrypt the original header within the payload.

8.3 User Authentication

In addition to the VPN itself, user authentication is another element to be considered in your VPN's architecture. Where the users are physically located can have a major impact on where the user database will be located, as can the size and scope of the VPN. For a small VPN that serves as an intranet, the problem is relatively simple; the local LAN's user database may suffice. A larger VPN, one that serves as an extranet, presents complications: a RADIUS server can be implemented, but should it be in-house or provided by a trusted third party? In very large VPNs, such as the automotive industry's ANX and the power industry's OASIS, a RADIUS server is probably the only viable solution.

If the VPN is outsourced, which we'll discuss specifically under the client/server VPN, there is the problem of providing the VPN service provider with a current user list. One of the simpler solutions for that might be to put a RADIUS server to use that you and the service provider both have access to. Don't neglect this aspect as you plan your VPN. It is crucial to the security of your network.

8.4 The Basic Scenarios

Essentially, while many if not most VPNs are a mix of the two, VPNs fall into one of two broad categories: client-to-server VPNs and VPNs that connect LAN to LAN across the Internet. The differences are not huge, although to further confuse the issue there are variations within the categories, such as an intranet versus an extranet on LAN-to-LAN VPNs. The primary issue is where the actual VPN work is done and where the secured tunnel terminates, particularly in relation to the firewall that is the common feature of virtually any attachment to the Internet.

8.4.1 The Client-to-LAN VPN

The most obvious example of the client-to-LAN VPN is a VPN established to serve a mobile workforce with remote access. In this situation, as we'll show you, on the client side there are really only two choices as to where the VPN tunnel can be implemented. We'll leave the LAN end of the VPN alone for now, because what applies to a LAN-to-LAN VPN pretty much applies to the LAN end of a remote access VPN, and the options are more complex.

But bear in mind, too, that "client-to-LAN VPN" can be a slippery term. In addition to the two remote access VPN scenarios, there are also two VPN protocols (SOCKS v.5 and Secure SHell) that dictate a client-to-LAN or client-to-server architecture for your VPN, although they are not typically used for remote access. As discussed in Chapter 7, these protocols operate at higher levels on the OSI model, specifically at the session layer in the case of SOCKS v.5 and at the application layer in the case of SSH. That mandates that at one end the VPN tunnel must originate at the workstation or client. On the LAN end, both protocols require the VPN to terminate at a server, either SOCKS or SSH enabled.

Voluntary or Client-Initiated Tunneling

The first type of remote access VPN architecture, with the VPN originating at a dial-in user's laptop, is illustrated in Figure 8-1. You may hear it referred to as *voluntary tunneling, client-initiated tunneling,* or *service-independent tunneling.* In this scenario, the remote user dials in to the Internet, connecting through a local ISP's network access server (NAS). VPN software runs on the user's laptop, tunneling and encrypting the data there for its passage through the Internet. Microsoft's PPTP is a prime example of this type of VPN, since it was designed to address the need for secured Internet connections to a LAN server.

For the sake of clarity, in all these illustrations we'll use thick shaded lines to represent protected VPN traffic, while unencrypted traffic will be indicated with thin black lines. For the sake of simplicity in this particular case, at the server end the VPN terminates at the LAN's security gateway; this is not the only option, as we'll see later.

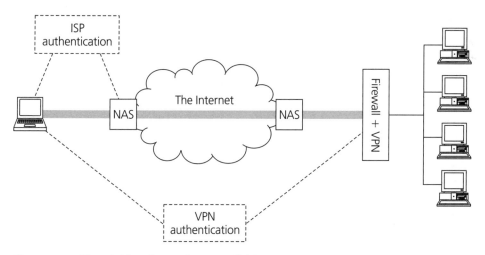

Figure 8-1   **Client-initiated tunneling on a dial-in VPN.**

In this architecture, as Figure 8-1 shows, and as we saw in our discussion of PPTP, user authentication is a two-step process. The ISP authenticates the user with regard to access to the Internet through their facility, perhaps using their own RADIUS server. Once that connection is made, the client next requests access to the VPN server. An exchange between the VPN server and the client authenticates the user for access to the network and the VPN is initiated. Software on the user's laptop encrypts the traffic and tunnels the packets.

The new Sun.NET VPN solution from Sun Microsystems, with its Java-based client application, uses the same architecture. There is a slight difference in the authentication process, however, because the Java applette has to be transferred before the tunnel can be established. With Sun.NET, the user is first authenticated by the ISP, similar to PPTP. When the user contacts the VPN server, he is asked for his log-on name and password. After authentication of the user, the Java code is downloaded to the client system. Once the Java application is up and running, it takes care of encryption and tunneling.

In this type of architecture, the ISP serves as nothing more than a courier to the data and does not even need to be aware that the VPN exists. The traffic reaching the NAS is already encrypted and encapsulated so that the true destination of the packet on the LAN beyond the VPN server may be concealed. Depending on what VPN protocol is being used—PPTP, for example—the contents of the packet need not even be an IP packet. There could be an Apple-Talk or IPX network at the other end.

However, the ISP does need to be able to transmit PPTP packets. Major providers such as AOL and Compuserve, as we've mentioned before, will not accept PPTP packets, making them unsuitable as VPN ISPs. Fortunately, most ISPs do not have this limitation.

The primary advantage to this architecture is flexibility. The user can connect through any ISP with whom he has an account to make his connection to the VPN. The user also has the ability to connect with any VPN on the Internet where he has authorized access. A sales rep who has access to the separate networks of several independent distributors, for example, would appreciate this capability. Naturally, the user does need to know how to make the connection to a specific VPN; he'll need to know the IP address of the server and, of course, need to have an assigned username and password with that VPN.

The primary disadvantage to the client-initiated architecture is that it puts a heavy burden on the client system, usually a user's laptop computer. Unless the client system is configured accordingly with a fast processor and plenty of RAM, performance will be unacceptably slow, particularly since the processor may have to wait for data coming in over a slow dial-up line before it can do the VPN processing. Even with a properly configured system, the performance will be noticeably slower than an unencrypted Internet connection.

This architecture also imposes some security issues that must be addressed. User authentication has to be accomplished by the VPN. Authentication over the Internet is hazardous. Exchanging a password over the Internet entails certain risks, unless provisions are made to encrypt the exchange. Then, too, there is the not-insignificant problem of secure key exchanges once the connection is established and before data transfer can actually begin.

Naturally, VPN vendors have solutions to these problems. With the potential for huge cost savings in going with a VPN for remote access causing strong demand, virtually all the major VPN products are equipped to handle the problem. IPSec, with its ISAKMP/Oakley key exchange, for example, offers a way to establish a secure tunnel and to exchange encryption keys. SKIP offers similar capabilities. RADIUS servers, certificate authorities, and other elements of a public key infrastructure will further improve the picture as they develop.

NAS-Initiated or Involuntary Tunneling

The second client/LAN architecture is referred to as *involuntary tunneling, NAS-initiated tunneling,* or *service-dependent tunneling.* Taking our road warrior example from above, Figure 8-2 illustrates a case in which the traffic between the client's laptop and the service provider's NAS is not tunneled. It could, however, be encrypted, but the need for this should be analyzed carefully before imposing that load on the laptop. One conceivable reason to do encryption is when the connection to the NAS is not considered secure for some reason. For example, perhaps the user is a consultant making

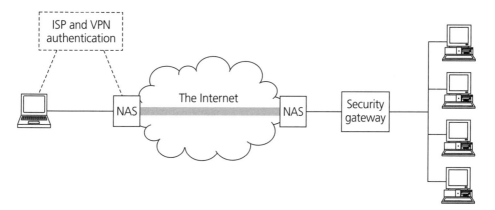

Figure 8-2   An involuntary tunneled VPN.

a connection through a client's office telephone system and is concerned about that client eavesdropping on communications that concern a different client. To spare the load on the client system, however, such a solution should be used only if absolutely necessary.

As Figure 8-2 shows, once the user makes the dial-in connection to the NAS, the ISP authenticates him not only for access to the Internet but to the VPN itself. This authentication is likely to be accomplished through the use of a RADIUS server, perhaps maintained by the ISP or even by a trusted third party. Notice that this does require the company that uses the VPN to somehow provide the ISP with a list of the VPN's users and to keep it constantly updated. Sharing a RADIUS server that also handles security for the LAN itself is one solution to the problem.

Another solution is for access to the actual LAN at the far end of the tunnel to be controlled by the LAN administrator, in much the same way it is done with voluntary tunneling. In such a case, the service provider authenticates the user for access to the Internet; then when the tunneled connection is established, the user enters a username and password for access to the network at the far end. It is obviously somewhat more cumbersome for the user, but it is simpler to establish and administer.

No matter how user authentication is handled, the involuntary tunneling scenario means that the termination point for the VPN is set by the service provider, giving the user no choice of networks to contact. The termination point of the tunnel will be the ISP's hardware at the POP where the server is connected. Decryption and encryption are likely to be handled there as well, although those chores can be passed along to the server. In a case where the client encrypts his traffic before it reaches the NAS, it's possible that the traffic through the Internet is double encrypted, first by the remote client, then by the ISP. The ISP's encryption is undone at the POP, and the client's encryption is decrypted by the VPN server.

In the involuntary tunneling scenario we're describing here, the VPN has essentially been outsourced to the ISP. The ISP has primary responsibility for security within the Internet, including encryption and decryption, along with its own key management. The advantage, in addition to lessening the work of the company that is using the VPN, is that encryption and tunneling are taken off the laptop, providing improved performance.

One disadvantage to this architecture is that the POP that the client calls has to know what to do and how to do it when the client calls in. The NAS *at that POP* must be able to authenticate the user, recognize him as a user of the particular VPN he is authorized to use, and be able to connect him to it in a secure fashion. In other words, it can't be just any POP on any ISP; it has to be the POP of an ISP that the company has outsourced the VPN to, a POP that knows that this VPN exists and how to manage the connection. If the ISP in question doesn't have a VPN-enabled POP where the user is, then the user will have to call long distance.

One solution to this problem is to permit access to the VPN by users who are calling in through unsecured ISPs, with the connection first being routed to the contracted ISP through a security gateway that can establish a tunnel to the endpoint. The drawback of this approach is that, until the caller's traffic reaches the security gateway, it is not protected.

It is in this type of VPN that you're likely to find the VPN functions being performed by a router or a switch. Cisco Systems developed the Layer 2 Forwarding protocol for their router products. This has since been replaced by L2TP. As Figure 8-3 illustrates, the LAN-to-LAN portion, for example, might originate at the ISP's NAS. As the illustration shows, however, road warriors with L2TP available on their laptops could dial in to any ISP, use L2TP to implement the tunnel from their laptop, and then connect to the ISP's POP that is running L2TP to serve the home office, where the tunnel would terminate and he'd connect to the LAN.

There is a large caveat that must go with this scenario, however. L2TP is still in development by the IETF and has not been finalized. Unless interoperability is ensured and the L2TP client and L2TP server are in total agreement on authentication and encryption, this process won't work. If the compatibility issue is to be resolved, the logical solution to the authentication/encryption problem is to employ IPSec; however, IPSec itself, as of this writing, has a ways to go before it is fully ready.

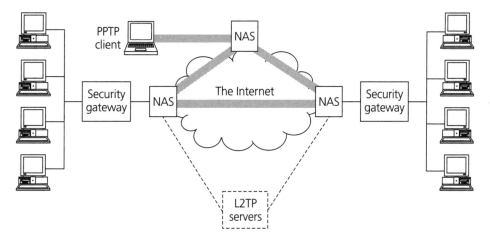

Figure 8-3   Combining PPTP and L2TP on a mixed VPN.

SOCKS v.5 Architecture

As we mentioned in Section 7.4.2, the SOCKS v.5 protocol requires both SOCKS-enabled client applications and a SOCKS server. SOCKS v.5 has actually been described as a firewall by some and a proxy server by others, and both descriptions are acceptable. SOCKS has an architecture of its own. It is a highly flexible protocol, and it can be used as either a client-to-LAN VPN or a LAN-to-LAN VPN, but even as the latter it behaves more like a client/server scenario than the LAN-to-LAN configurations we'll look at further on, because the applications on the clients have to be capable of working with the SOCKS server. One possible architecture for SOCKS v.5 is illustrated in Figure 8-4.

The client applications on the workstations that are to be on the VPN must be SOCKS enabled. At one time this required recompiling the source code of the applications to add the SOCKS capabilities. Now there are run-time modules to perform the SOCKS enabling and to eliminate the need to have the source code available for recompiling. The client connects with the SOCKS server, which authenticates it. The server then contacts the application server. A proxy circuit is established and the SOCKS server relays the data between the application client and the application server. The SOCKS server provides the security by controlling all transmissions between the client and the application server.

SOCKS v.5 offers a variety of architectures. While it can function as a firewall itself, one of its strengths is the way it can communicate through firewalls. This allows architectures such as the one shown in Figure 8-5,

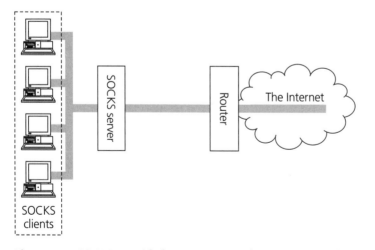

Figure 8-4   SOCKS v.5 with the SOCKS server between LAN and router.

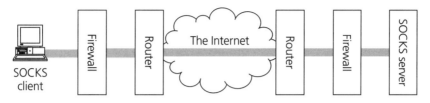

Figure 8-5   A SOCKS client connecting through firewalls and the Internet to an application server running SOCKS.

where the SOCKS client in one location is protected behind a firewall, as is the remote SOCKS application server. User authentication and encryption are handled between the SOCKS-running client and the SOCKS application server. However, this also means that encryption/decryption, with all its demands, is being performed on the client and on the application server, so they must be configured accordingly.

Obviously, there is nothing that precludes SOCKS v.5 from working as a remote access VPN. All that is needed is a SOCKS v.5 server at the LAN end and a SOCKS v.5–capable laptop connecting through the Internet. In fact, since SOCKS runs at the session level, it's entirely possible that a PPTP or L2TP tunnel—layer 2 protocols—can carry a SOCKS connection.

However, SOCKS v.5 is less than ideal as a remote access client VPN solution. It is not as easily implemented as L2TP, and it demands applications and networking that can be SOCKS enabled. For this reason, SOCKS v.5 VPNs are tending to be implemented as extranets rather than for remote access or as intranets.

Secure SHell

Secure SHell (SSH), as we mentioned, is an application level solution that allows a remote user to log on to a remote server and run programs. As we mentioned in Chapter 7, SSH offers security in the form of encryption and tunneling that programs such as rlogin do not provide. Because SSH runs on the client, as Figure 8-6 illustrates, and connects with an SSH-capable server, the VPN originates at the client system and terminates at the remote server.

This is a tightly constrained protocol: there is no other configuration possible for a Secure SHell VPN. The client connects directly with the server, logs in on it, and remotely runs programs on the server. Authentication and encryption are handled by client and server. To avoid poor performance, both ends must be configured so they can handle the process without bogging down. However, the actual application being run by the user is running on the server, not on the client.

While SSH has its limitations as a VPN protocol, it too can be used to create a remote access VPN. Since SSH runs at the application layer, it can connect

Figure 8-6   A VPN using Secure SHell.

to a server through a PPP connection. Since large amounts of data, such as graphics, are probably not going to be moved through the connection, it can be an efficient solution for use with a dial-up connection.

8.4.2 The LAN-to-LAN VPN

The architectural options for LAN-to-LAN VPNs are more varied because we're dealing with permanent connections that employ more elements than a simple dial-in hookup. While a road warrior simply dials in to the Internet through an ISP's POP, a LAN's permanent link to the Internet requires a connection that passes through defenses to protect it. Generally this involves some sort of security gateway or firewall, beyond which is a router to make the connection to the Internet. The question now becomes one of where the secured VPN connection terminates in relation to the router, the security gateway, and the LAN itself.

It is not necessary that the same architecture be used at both ends of the VPN. For the sake of clarity, however, we will zoom in on only one end of our LAN-to-LAN VPN and take a closer look to examine some of the scenarios available, bearing in mind that another LAN connected to the VPN might use a different design.

The Router as VPN Terminator

Use of the router as a VPN terminator shows signs of becoming one of the most popular architectures for VPNs. As Figure 8-7 shows, the configuration is simple and straightforward. From one router through the Internet to the terminating router, the traffic is tunneled and encrypted. Behind the router it is simply your usual LAN traffic, not tunneled and probably not encrypted unless your LAN requires it.

There are advantages to this configuration. The router performs all the functions required of the VPN: tunneling the packets and encrypting and decrypting the traffic. The main concern you should have for this choice is that the router must be properly configured to handle the load. With the router performing both routing and cryptosystem functions, it has to have the processor power to avoid performance problems. Encryption/decryption demands 50 to 100 times the processor power of simple routing. Bear in mind, too, that this

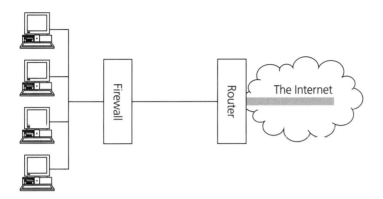

Figure 8-7   The router-terminated VPN.

one device is handling all the VPN traffic that passes through it. If there are a thousand users at the far end, all that traffic has to be encrypted, decrypted, and routed at your end. It can only be done without a noticeable penalty if the router is strong enough to handle it.

The Firewall as VPN Server

The usual connection to the Internet involves a firewall or security gateway on the LAN side and a router that connects to the Internet. The space between, referred to as the demilitarized zone (DMZ), is outside the firewall, hence accessible to the public and vulnerable. Aside from using the router for VPN tasks, the most obvious LAN-to-LAN VPN solution is to incorporate the termination point of the VPN right into the security gateway, as in Figure 8-8. Usually both tunneling and encryption/decryption of the VPN traffic are handled by the gateway itself. While encryption can be implemented on a LAN, perhaps at the workstation, it rarely is simply because it should not be necessary. A LAN protected by a firewall—and properly administered—should be secure enough. Behind the gateway, the data is handled just as all the other data on the LAN is handled.

This design, like the router-based VPN, is so obvious that many firewall vendors are incorporating VPN capabilities into their products. It should, in theory at least, provide a quick and relatively easy way to implement a VPN, both between two LANs and in a client/server VPN. Just how quick and easy it is, and how well it works, depends on the quality of the product, of course.

While this architecture relieves the router of the load, the drawback to combining the VPN terminator with the security gateway is the load it places on the security gateway. The firewall is already responsible for protecting your network; its responsibilities run from minimal packet filtering in some products all the way up to being an application level gateway capable of logging and controlling, even authenticating, all inbound and outbound traffic. It

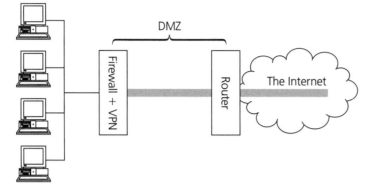

Figure 8-8   A LAN-to-LAN VPN with the security gateway handling the VPN process.

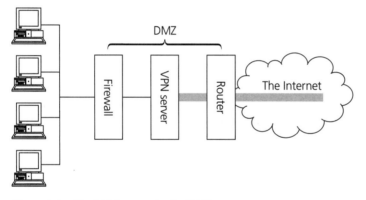

Figure 8-9   The VPN server in the DMZ.

might also be serving as a router. If a software VPN package is simply added to the existing gateway—for example, an already stressed Windows NT server—performance is certain to suffer. Even if the gateway is already configured to handle the existing burdens without laboring, performance will suffer if you add more tasks, affecting both VPN and non-VPN traffic.

Placing the VPN Server Between Firewall and Router

Obviously, separating the functions of the security gateway and the VPN eliminates the problem of the added burden on the security gateway, although it incurs the expense of adding an extra piece of hardware to your system. By using separate hardware, however, it is possible to locate the VPN server in any one of several other locations. The one illustrated in Figure 8-9 places it in the DMZ between the router and the security gateway. VPN traffic passes through the router, the data is extracted by the VPN server, and then it is passed on through the firewall to the LAN.

This appears to offer some added security, in that the VPN server is in a position to filter out attackers that have somehow penetrated the VPN tunnel and are trying to penetrate the LAN from that route. Non-VPN traffic, such as email or Web traffic, would bypass the VPN server to go straight to the firewall. On the downside, by placing the VPN server outside the firewall you are exposing it to direct attack from the Internet.

Placing the VPN Server Behind the Firewall

Placing the VPN server behind the firewall (Figure 8-10) protects it from direct assault unless the firewall is breached. At that point, the traffic is decrypted and passed on to the LAN by the VPN server.

A variation on this theme is to place the VPN server on a branch of the internal LAN. This scenario is illustrated in Figure 8-11. This design allows only the systems downstream on the branch interrupted by the VPN terminator to participate in the VPN. Naturally, their traffic with the LAN itself is not affected by passing through the terminator, which is configured to simply pass through non-VPN traffic. Workstations on the other branch of the LAN won't be able to understand the tunneled and encrypted VPN traffic on the line; they'll simply ignore it.

Terminating the VPN at the Workstation

The final possible scenario is to provide one or more workstations with VPN capabilities, as in Figure 8-12. This is very much like the client/LAN design we discussed in Section 8.4.1. The workstations are responsible for tunneling and encrypting the data. This configuration also suffers from the same drawback, placing an extra burden on the workstation. However, at least this

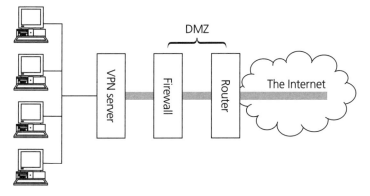

Figure 8-10 The VPN server behind the firewall.

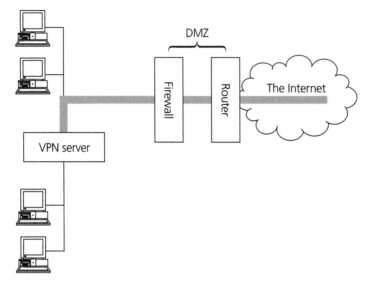

Figure 8-11   The VPN server on one branch of the LAN.

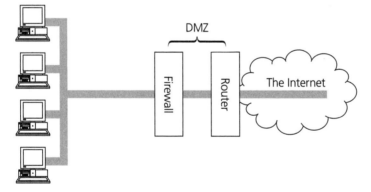

Figure 8-12   Terminating the VPN at the workstation.

arrangement does not slow down the network as a whole the way a firewall- or router-based VPN can. With this architecture, the performance hit is on the individual workstation, not on the LAN or the Internet connection itself. Bear in mind that it is not the VPN traffic itself that slows the Internet connection down but the *processing of VPN traffic* that creates the bottleneck.

This arrangement is a viable option for a LAN on which a comparatively small number of users need to have access to the VPN. For example, take the case of an extranet where a parts supplier is connected to a manufacturer's

VPN. Perhaps the only ones on the supplier's network who would need access to the manufacturer would be shipping, sales, and accounting, and within accounting only accounts receivable. This structure provides a fine degree of granularity. Only those who really need access to the VPN have it, without your network managers having to fret over the topology of your network while trying to implement a VPN terminator on one or more branches of the LAN. If someone in engineering needs to be added to the connection, it is simply a matter of installing VPN capabilities on her workstation and creating a user account on the VPN for her.

Naturally, even if the entire LAN is accessible on the VPN, that doesn't mean that every user on the VPN will have access. The filtering can also be accomplished by the user accounts that are established on the VPN. The CEO might have an account on the VPN, but the assistant vice president might not, simply because he doesn't need it. For security reasons, of course, the fewer people who have access to the VPN the better.

However, as we noted in Section 8.2, initiating the VPN at the workstation level sacrifices the ability to hide those addresses. Some of the internal architecture of your local network is exposed with this architecture.

8.5 Conclusion

This cursory examination of VPN architectures should give you an idea of the various options available to you. Every VPN will develop its own shape as it grows. The first connection, perhaps one LAN to another, sets the tone, but as remote users are added and as other LANs are attached, variations will develop. As you design that first link, you should have in mind what the future may hold, and you should allow for it. Otherwise you may find yourself at a dead end with no option but to tear everything out and start all over again just to add that next vital connection to a supplier, customer, or new branch office.

The primary issues to consider as you develop your VPN's architecture are functionality, security, ease of management, load balancing, and flexibility. Make sure that the architecture you settle on will do what you need to have done. Don't let the design you choose inadvertently open holes in your security. Bear in mind administrative tasks such as account management, system tracking, and logging as you design it. Make sure your VPN processing doesn't create a bottleneck that slows down all the traffic passing through it. And finally, consider the future so you don't box yourself in with an architecture that can't meet it.

9

Planning Your VPN

There's an old adage that says, "If you fail to plan then plan to fail." This is as true for putting together a VPN as it is for any other information system. If your VPN is not well thought out, you could see all those projected savings and efficiencies evaporate. You'll have spent a lot of time and money and you'll be left with something that doesn't do what you really need done or that doesn't work at all.

There is no way that we can design your VPN for you. The possibilities are endless, depending on the size of your organization, the geography of it, the technical skills you have to draw on, and—not least of all—what you want to do with your VPN. Then there's the fact that the technology is changing so rapidly that anything we describe now might be obsolete by the time you're reading this. However, there are certain logical steps to take when planning a VPN.

9.1 Analyze Your Needs

As we pointed out back in Chapter 3, one of the issues you must look at is whether you really need a VPN. If you have only a small mobile workforce that doesn't need regular contact with the network, then a VPN may well be more expensive, more trouble, and more risky than using your current remote access methods. On the other hand, if you have distributed offices, each with its own LAN, a VPN may provide an opportunity for collaborative computing that can show important benefits.

9.1.1 Consider the Possibilities

As you look at your needs, bear in mind that a VPN can function in three different capacities: as a remote access server, as a corporate intranet, and as an extranet. Looked at from those viewpoints, consider the following factors that may justify the implementation of a VPN.

1. A need for cost-effective remote access, such as
    *   For a large mobile workforce that will benefit from regular access to the company network. For example, you have a sales force that needs regular updates to the catalog, price lists, and product availability information and is making frequent, expensive long-distance calls for the information.
    *   For widely dispersed small facilities that need regular but not constant access to the company network. An overseas office may have daily reports to file that require only a few minutes of online time. To dial in long distance, however, is prohibitively expensive, compared to using a dial-up account with their local ISP.
    *   For overseas offices that are incurring costly long-distance charges with calls that could be handled using IP phone technology or remote access through the Internet.
2. A need for a company intranet connecting distributed facilities, a network that will provide
    *   Administrative efficiencies such as transfers or consolidation of accounting and timekeeping data from distributed facilities.
    *   Improved communications and coordination among geographically separated divisions, offices, warehouses, factories, sales outlets, etc. For example, a VPN can offer shipment tracking information.
    *   Collaborative projects among the dispersed workforce.
    *   Improved corporate communications such as email, message-based conferencing, and videoconferencing.
    *   Efficiencies gained through the sharing of corporate databases, either centralized or distributed among divisions.
3. A need for a corporate extranet, providing enhanced communications with suppliers and customers for
    *   Electronic data interchange to enhance business efficiency.
    *   Improved collaboration on design and engineering efforts.
    *   Enhanced customer relations through improved communications.

9.1.2 Look at What You Are Doing Now

It is very seductive to look at these opportunities and to immediately leap to the conclusion that a VPN will solve all your company's problems. Be wary.

Look at the work your organization is doing now and how it is doing it. Analyze your telephone traffic, for example. Are there regular, long, expensive long-distance calls being made between your home office and the factory in Singapore? Does it take days for engineering problems to be resolved using physical transfers of hard copy documents that could be moved electronically? Are sales representatives in Chicago, San Francisco, and Honolulu having to wait for deliveries from Federal Express of the latest product lists before they can call on customers, or are they running up astronomical bills calling your remote access server to download them? Do they need to clear contract details with the home office before they can close the deal?

Is the Los Angeles office using Federal Express to send stacks of timesheets to the accounting department in New York every Friday for processing? While you're looking at that traffic pattern, does it really matter if they don't get there until Monday, or would it speed things up to have them there on Friday so the home office computers can crunch the numbers over the weekend? And even more to the point, would it increase efficiencies (by eliminating rekeying) to have those time figures entered into the network at the local office level for consolidation through the VPN at headquarters?

If a look at your current operations doesn't show a clear need to improve existing operations such as these, proceed cautiously. This is not to say that a VPN would not benefit you, but make sure you can make a good case for it before you plunge in. If you are already running a leased-line WAN, do a cost comparison between what you are running nfpow and the possible VPN scenarios using PVCs through a frame relay service or going through the Internet. Perhaps you are running an X.25 network that has been engineered to meet a seasonally high bandwidth during the Christmas selling season and is then underutilized the rest of the year. Perhaps, too, you have developed a need for greater flexibility and scalability than is possible with your current WAN. However, don't forget to factor in the costs that a changeover will entail. VPNs can look misleadingly attractive if you don't ferret out hidden costs that may be lurking in the shadows, such as staff retraining or modifications to your existing infrastructure of cables, routers, switches, firewalls, and servers.

9.2 Take a *Detailed* Inventory of Your Resources

Before you set out, you need to know where you are now as well as where you are going. You need to know what you have, what you are connecting up, and what you are bringing to the project in terms of resources, both material and human.

9.2.1 Inventory Your Material Resources

You need to be certain you know how your current, enterprise-wide information system is composed. Take it from the top all the way down to the lowest level that is feasible. If you have mainframes or centralized data processing units, know where they are physically located, what platforms and operating systems they use, what applications they are running, and what data is maintained on them and how.

What networks are you running in every facility you intend to tie into the VPN? It may be that they are all running IP networks; however, if you've had LANs online for more than 2 or 3 years, chances are that somewhere in there you will find at least one Novell network, and you may find you have an AppleTalk network serving your engineering or graphics offices. This is important to know, because either you will have to convert them over to TCP/IP or they will be an important factor in determining the protocols and products that are available to you. There is also the likelihood that you are running a mixture of desktop operating systems as well. Can you standardize those, or will you have to satisfy a mixture of platforms?

Mixing both network operating systems (NOSs) and desktop operating systems on a VPN multiplies your problems. Glenn Botkin at Galaxy Scientific learned that as he was setting up Galaxy's own VPN. When they started they had networks running Novell 3.11, 3.12, and 4.01, as well as Windows NT 3.51, with one office about to move to Windows NT 4.0. There were also a couple of flavors of Unix to deal with. On the desktop he found a mix of Windows 3.1, 3.11, and Windows 95, plus a smattering of Mac users.

Early in the project they addressed the NOS issue by integrating all the different systems using IP. They were also of the opinion that while Windows NT offered a lot of good connectivity features and simpler administration, Novell was still the best system by far for LANs. It was early in the VPN industry, so things have changed a little since then, but it took them 3 months to find out that trying to get Novell and Windows NT to talk to each other was problematic. Although local connectivity and tunneling the IPX traffic met with some success, there were continual trans-site drive mapping and systems management problems. Finally the decision was made to go entirely to Windows NT. In a 2-week period they bought, configured, and installed new servers running Windows NT 4.0 for all seven locations they were connecting. Even today, with IP connectivity greatly improved both in Windows NT and in NetWare, it is not wise to assume that you'll be able to mix your networks on the VPN without encountering some challenges.

On the desktop, Galaxy migrated their Windows users to Windows 95. Some of the Mac users migrated to Windows 95, but a 100% shift there was not possible. Some of the artists still clung to their Macs, and there was a large volume of historical files that demanded a Mac presence. Eventually the Macs were linked into the VPN as well, but it took time.

If you already have connections to the Internet, what bandwidth does each one offer? How are they protected in terms of firewalls? What are they being used for? When you get to the actual planning stage, you'll need to know if they can serve as is or if they should be upgraded or modified.

How is user authentication on these LANs implemented? Do you have one centralized user database or, as is much more likely, are there scattered databases? As you'd expect, if the database is centralized in a way that a VPN can utilize it, your system for user authentication in a VPN might be simplified. But if the database is not centralized, and the chances are that unless you're already running a WAN, it isn't, you will have to develop some system to authenticate users from each LAN to the VPN. Users are not going to be overjoyed to have to maintain multiple passwords for access throughout the VPN, but it may be possible to limit the need to two passwords, one for access to their LAN and the second to the wider world of the VPN by way of the VPN server in the central data processing office.

Don't stop working on your inventory until you have drilled right down to the user level. You should have the best idea possible of the desktop hardware and operating systems they are using. You should also know what applications they are running—what they are doing with their machines—so the VPN can be designed to serve them properly. While you're there, try to ferret out any user-installed options, such as remote access software and modems, because these offer an entry point for someone trying to penetrate your network. By providing dial-in VPN access, you may be able to close these holes.

Part of the inventory should include how many users you are going to need to serve at each facility and how much bandwidth they will require. How many remote access users are you going to need to serve, and from where? What systems do your road warriors have, and are you going to have to upgrade them to handle the load a VPN imposes? Are you going to need to provide access to telecommuters who would benefit from an ISDN line to their home, or are you simply supporting workers who need to dial in from time to time to retrieve their email? Providing such a capability would reduce the likelihood of those illicit modems sneaking in the door and would improve your overall security.

Of course, this inventory is one you should already have, but how many of us can justify the time it takes to do it and to keep it up-to-date? If nothing else comes out of this possible project, you'll end up with a good inventory in hand.

9.2.2 Inventory Your Human Resources

Take a careful look at what your information systems (IS) offices bring to the project. Do you have the personnel and expertise to implement this project with your existing resources, or are you going to have to add staff? If you are going to implement an Internet-based VPN, you should take a hard look at their Internet experience. How much do they know about configuring security gateways? Can they configure and troubleshoot a router?

Consider, too, your entire information systems structure, not just what you have immediately around you. Do you have a centralized IS function? If so, it will greatly simplify the process. If, as is more likely, each location you want to tie into the VPN has its own administrator, you're going to have to plan on somehow bringing them all together so they are all on the same page. This is especially true if you are negotiating the NOS issue as you pull the system together. You should allow for this in your budget as well. You will almost certainly need to appoint one person to head up the project, in order to coordinate the efforts at all the locations you're bringing onto the VPN, and the earlier he or she is identified and brought aboard, the better off you'll be.

Glenn Botkin got the assignment at Galaxy Scientific, and he even managed to convince management to hold a 3-day meeting with all the LAN administrators to pull the project together. Botkin notes that the only reason this kind of coordination was possible at all was thanks to the support and sponsorship he had from the company's top-level management. At that time, the systems administrators still reported to their local vice presidents. This coalition that Botkin created is still known as the "TechHerd." Managing programmers has been compared to the challenge of herding cats: systems administrators in different shops show similar characteristics. Know your people. Make sure you know what you're dealing with at that level.

Don't neglect a look at your existing user support facilities. A change to a VPN is certain to increase the load on your user support staff. To best utilize the new VPN, for example, you may want to migrate users from cc:Mail to Exchange or to install Lotus Notes, which can be quite a jolt. Above all else, don't ignore the increased management burden that having a VPN is going to place on your own central management information systems (MIS) staff. As we'll discuss in Chapter 10, maintaining security on a VPN can be an order of magnitude greater than the chore of doing so on a LAN.

The results of this inventory are crucial to your next decision.

9.2.3 Outsourced Versus In-House

Based on the results of your human resources audit, you should next consider the option of outsourcing the project. One of the key justifications for outsourcing is the need for outside expertise and human resources both to build the VPN and to run it once it is up. On the implementation issue, although the picture has changed recently, with greater standardization on protocols such as IPSec, there is still virtually no plug and play in the VPN industry. Even the PPTP support built into Microsoft Windows NT requires setting up the Windows Remote Access Server. Microsoft solved the complexities of authentication and encryption key management in a way that, while appearing relatively easy to implement, raises serious security concerns. Bringing other, more secure VPN products online is even more demanding. Remember our discussions in Chapters 5 through 7 of the complexities of encryption, key management, and user authentication. Configuring these features is likely to be complex, and unless the clients and servers are all in agreement on all the little details, connections will fail to be made and you'll have dissatisfied users.

When we get into Chapter 10 on managing your VPN, you'll discover that there are complexities there as well. While it might seem reasonable to say that a VPN is like one big LAN, that does not mean that managing it is as simple as managing one small LAN. Size breeds complexity. There are more nodes, more users, and probably more applications to be dealt with. Each of these factors increases the number of potential interactions on the network. You might want to let someone else deal with these complexities, rather than try to manage them yourself.

If you come to the conclusion that you don't have the people to make this project work, don't panic. Vendors offer a variety of outsourcing options. You'll find a list of vendors in Appendix A, but bear in mind that this is anything but a comprehensive list. Many ISPs and networking consultants are offering VPN services to their customers. You'll have to decide whether you want to outsource some or all of the project or to implement it completely in-house.

As Table 9-1 from Cisco Systems indicates, there are a range of outsourcing options. It is possible, for example, to turn the entire project over to a provider such as your ISP. Along with providing the Internet connection, they will design the VPN, supply the hardware (which can be physically located on your premises), install and configure all the software, and handle external security, technical support, and management, including user authentication. This will cost, of course, but if your information management structure is already stressed the expense may be a bargain compared to implementing the project yourself.

Bear in mind, however, that the more of the project you outsource the more control you relinquish. At the most extreme point, you will have turned over everything but responsibility for your internal security to the provider. That means that you do not have control over much: For example, in such a case

Table 9-1 Chart showing the range of outsourcing options.

Sharing VPN Tasks with a Service Provider

HEAVY RESPONSIBILITY

◄ Retain In-House Control

Outsource to Service Provider ►

Network manager designs, installs, and manages VPNs	**Network manager** designs VPN, installs and manages central site equipment, and manages security services	**Network manager** provides application support and help desk service to all users and ongoing equipment support at central site	**Network manager** provides support to central site users and controls security functions	**Network manager** maintains in-house security service only
Service provider provides IP network access only	**Service provider** installs and manages remote site equipment	**Service provider** provides VPN equipment and guarantees performance levels	**Service provider** designs VPN solution and supports remote site users	**Service provider** provides complete VPN solution including training, service, and "24 by 7" support

HEAVY RESPONSIBILITY

you're yielding training of your people to the provider, something you may prefer to maintain in-house. Expanding or modifying the VPN is also in the hands of your provider. If you want to add a new feature, you'll have to negotiate it with them. Even something that you might expect to handle totally in-house, such as adding or upgrading an application, may not be in your hands. The more you outsource responsibility, the less control you retain.

A compromise is to go for a turnkey system, where the ISP or a VPN vendor handles the installation and then turns the management over to you once the system is up and running. You can take the route Galaxy Scientific did: they outsourced the actual connections through PSINet's backbone but handled the internal configuration of the VPN themselves. The one caution with any of these choices is to make sure you know *exactly* what the service provider will do for you—what their responsibilities are and what yours are.

To date, many if not a majority of companies implementing VPNs have taken one outsourcing option or another. Many go straight to an ISP for their VPN. Major ISPs such as Concentric Network offer a range of choices, with specialized VPN packages to provide intranet, extranet, or remote access networks. They will put the system together from end to end, relieving your shop of having to wrestle with getting all the pieces in place and working together. Once the VPN is online, they will even manage it for you, if that is what you want. Or you can go for a contract that has them turn the management of it over to you. Another outsourcing option is to go to a value-added reseller (VAR) for your VPN. The vendor comes in and sets up the servers and clients and makes sure everything is working smoothly before turning the operation over to you.

If you do outsource the project, in addition to deciding how much to outsource make sure to nail down what kind of support you will have from the provider once the system is up, and get it in writing. We'll discuss this further in Chapter 10.

9.3 Establish the Goals for Your VPN

The goals you spell out for your VPN will depend upon the needs you have identified. The more specific you can be in developing your goals, the better you will be able to define the shape of your VPN. "Saving $250,000 by providing remote access to 2,000 salespeople located in 14 countries by connecting them through the Internet" sounds better than "Saving a lot of money on phone bills."

Ask yourself who will be using the VPN. How many remote access users do we have now that are to be served by the VPN? How many branch offices are there? Will we extend the VPN to our customers and suppliers? Do we need international access and will that be limited to fixed offices or will it include our mobile workforce? Obviously, much of this information will come from the inventory you just completed.

Look for the benefits you can expect to enjoy. How much is your current system costing you, and what is the projected cost for the same services using a VPN? There are worksheets available on some VPN vendor Web sites for just this purpose. Among them are Bay Networks *(http://www.baynetworks.com)* and Shiva *(http://www.shiva.com/remote/vpnroi)*. Be conservative as you fill them in and cautiously skeptical of the numbers generated by any VPN vendor's calculations. The vendors are, after all, selling the technology. Even so, these worksheets should give you some idea of what you can hope for in the way of savings. Obviously you can't be highly specific, and it is prudent to be pessimistic rather than optimistic. If you wind up saving more than you projected when you made the presentation touting the VPN to the CEO, you look like a genius, but if you fail to reach those savings he'll want to know why.

How will the VPN be used by the people in your organization? What applications are they using that will benefit from the VPN, and what applications do you want to implement on the VPN that cannot be implemented now, such as Lotus Notes? These, too, are goals.

How will a VPN benefit your relations with your customers and suppliers? Will you be implementing EDI? Will you want to exchange engineering data with your suppliers?

Make sure you can do what you want to do over your VPN, verify what will be required of the VPN to do it, and make sure you're talking to genuinely knowledgeable people. Galaxy Scientific, for example, checked with their vendor to make sure that they would be able to run their electronic timesheets and accounting over the VPN using 56 Kbps connections; they got the OK, with some minor caveats. However, when they actually tried to do it, it failed. A talk with tech support at the vendor got a different answer from the first time. It took upgrading the connections, waiting for an upgrade from the vendor, and some other fancy footwork to make it work.

On the other hand, after they'd been running Microsoft Exchange over the remaining 56 Kbps lines for a year, Microsoft told Galaxy that that was impossible. In short, take everything you're told with a shaker of salt and be braced for surprises.

Developing these goals is a matter of looking at what you are doing now and seeing ways these tasks can be done using a VPN. Don't focus strictly on your primary mission (making and selling widgets, for example). Look at the support structure you have established that lets you sell widgets at a profit. This includes accounting, sales, engineering and design, research and development, marketing, purchasing, etc. While you're thinking of developing an extranet to connect with the contractor who is making your widgets, don't ignore a possible connection to your advertising agency to enhance cooperation in the development of new marketing campaigns.

Include in your goals such factors as security and performance. Again, the more specific you are, the better it will help define your VPN's design parameters. For example, if you can define the performance standards that are needed for something like videoconferencing, they will guide you in designing your connections with regard to bandwidth and also help you decide your need for service level agreements.

Write those goals down, because they are vital to the design of your VPN. You may even want to post them on the wall over your desk, so you can look at them every day. That way you'll know why you're putting in the long hours it will undoubtedly take to bring your VPN online.

9.4 Plan for the Evolution/Expansion of the Network

Any successful business is a growing business. At the very least it will be an evolving business. Envision how your VPN will have to evolve in accordance with your long-range plans. If acquisitions are in your future, you'll probably want a VPN that offers a great deal of flexibility with regard to connecting with other networks. If you are a fast food chain and are adding restaurants at a great clip, you'll want a VPN that is easily scalable. Make sure to look at what you are using now and how it meshes with possible future plans.

You may have to dig deeply to ferret out potential problems that may arise down the road. A medical software company, for example, implemented a VPN to serve their mobile workforce; while the VPN works, and they have enjoyed the savings they projected, they've also discovered that it is not as convenient as the dial-up connections they used in the past. In particular, some applications, such as Microsoft Networking, have connectivity problems, which the medical software company hopes will fade as the technology matures. Now they are also feeling pressure to provide telecommuting connections, which require Microsoft Networking. If they can't resolve these problems, they may have to rethink their strategy.

9.5 Begin to Sketch Out a Budget

You don't need to nail your budget down to the penny at this point, but you should be looking at some ballpark figures for the various aspects of the project. The items to be considered include Internet connections, hardware expenses, labor costs (be *very* conservative here . . . it is better to overestimate these costs than to underestimate them), and so on. If you have a rough sketch of your project and are exploring outsourcing, this might be the time to contact some providers for input. Get prices from ISPs and vendors.

9.6 Study *All* Your Options

Don't automatically assume that a VPN is the perfect solution to meet your goals. Certainly on the surface a VPN looks like a cost-effective solution to implementing almost any WAN, but take the time to study the other options. Perhaps you are currently using leased lines for your WAN. Will the cost savings of switching to a VPN justify the expense and inconvenience of making the switch? If you are not using leased lines, do you need the greater bandwidth, reliability, and security of leased lines in preference to a less expensive but riskier VPN?

If a VPN is the answer, will a VPN built on a private service, such as a frame relay service provider, be more suitable than an Internet-based VPN? Remember that the primary trade-off here is cost vs. reliability and security. A service level agreement from a frame relay provider will offer better guarantees than can be found on the Internet and may provide that extra peace of mind that you require. Take the time to contact a few frame relay providers to get information on services, availability, and pricing. Don't automatically assume that the savings of going the Internet route will justify taking that route.

Somewhere along the line, make sure that a VPN is feasible and that the connectivity is really available. Unless you are located in the wilderness, the chances are that this is not a problem, but don't assume anything. Check out the services in the areas where you will need to connect, and while you're at it get some ballpark cost figures.

9.7 Develop an Architecture

It is at this point that you can begin to develop an architecture for your VPN, based on your requirements and what you already have in place. Your existing LANs will have an influence on this as will your needs and goals. Your existing connections and the connections dictated by your requirements can be sketched in. The chances are good that your needs will actually define the architecture for you.

Don't skimp on bandwidth when you plan your connections. Glenn Botkin of Galaxy Scientific notes that one of the things he wished he had done differently was to start with higher-speed connections. Initially, the connection at their corporate headquarters in Egg Harbor, N.J., and their offices in Atlanta, GA, Warminster, PA, Crystal City, VA, and Falls Church, VA, were 56 Kbps.

They have since been upgraded to 256 Kbps. He notes that going from 56 Kbps to 256 Kbps was difficult, because it required new local telco connections and equipment as well as extensive network reconfiguration. From 256 Kbps up, he notes, is much easier because the connections and equipment remain unchanged.

This reinforces the idea of allowing room for the VPN to expand, both in capabilities and geographically. It is highly probable that once the VPN is in place to meet the goals you have already identified, other opportunities to put it to use will present themselves. Also, as users become comfortable with the VPN they will utilize it more and traffic will increase. All of these factors are likely to increase demand for bandwidth.

When you start selecting products, allow for this increasing traffic and expanded utilization as well. For example, it is wise to overengineer your servers right from the start, rather than face the cost and hassle of updating them 6 months down the line. The same is true of routers and firewalls.

Pay attention to compatibility issues. If you are running non-IP LANs, make sure your design will accommodate them or consider standardizing on one common platform. Similarly, you are likely to be facing a more complex situation than you realize if you are running different operating systems in different locations. While it is entirely possible to implement a PPTP VPN that will transport AppleTalk and IPX packets, how easy is it going to be to give users running the Mac OS the same services over the VPN that users running Windows will have? Some products are designed to handle these incompatibilities—FileMaker Pro, for example, uses the same file format for both its Windows and Macintosh database products and the files can be read by either version—but others are not.

If you are planning an extranet, make sure you are in contact with your partners in the project. Know what they are running, what their connections are, what compatibility issues may arise there, and plan accordingly. Obviously, you must work with them in the planning process. You'll need the skills of a diplomat to negotiate the process.

Remember the KISS principle—keep it simple, sucker. Standardize and simplify things as much as possible. If some of your options are at the leading (bleeding) edge of technology, consider delaying them until the technology has been proven.

9.8 A Review of the Protocols

At this point, since they have a major impact on the architectural options you have available to you, it's worth taking a look at the VPN protocols we discussed earlier. (For a more detailed understanding of how they work, you'll want to refer to Chapters 5–8.) To help you with your planning, Table 9-2

Table 9-2 VPN protocols.

	AltaVista	IPSec	L2TP	PPTP	SKIP	SOCKS v.5	SSH2	Sun.NET
Architectural Options	C/S, LAN/LAN	C/S, NAS/NAS, LAN/LAN	C/S, C/NAS, NAS/NAS, LAN/LAN	C/S, C/NAS, NAS/NAS, LAN/LAN	C/S, LAN/LAN	C/S (requires SOCKS server, SOCKS client)	C/S only	C/S only
Hides illegal IP addresses	Yes	Yes	Yes	Yes	Yes	Yes	No	No
Carries non-IP packets	No	Yes	Yes	Yes	No	No	No	No
Platform availability	DEC	Windows, Unix, probable industry standard	Windows NT (v.5), Unix	Windows NT/95, some Unix	SunOS, BSD, Linux, Windows NT/95	Windows, Windows NT	NetBSD, HP-UX, IBM AIX, Digital Unix, Solaris 2.6 (SSH v.1 available for most OSs)	Client any Java-capable appliance/ Sun server

	Col 1	Col 2	Col 3	Col 4	Col 5	Col 6	Col 7	Col 8
Remote access	Excellent	Fair	Fair	Good	Excellent	Excellent	Good	Good
Network to network	None	None	Good	Good	Good	Good	Good	Good
Scalability		None	Good	Good	Fair	Good	Excellent	Good
OSI layer		Application	Session	Between data link and network	Data link	Data link	Data link and network	Data link and network
Encryption specified		3DES	Not specified (supports GSS-API for negotiation)	RC2 and RC4 40 to 128 bit, DES 56 bit, 3DES 128 bit, Elvis+, SAFER	Not specified (Windows version uses DES, 40, 56, and 128 bit)	Not specified	DES-CBC 56 bit	RC4 128 bit domestic, 56 bit international
Supports IPSec for security		Yes	Yes	Yes	Yes	Yes	N/A	No
Supports X.509		Yes	Yes	Yes	Yes	Yes	Yes	Yes

summarizes the differences and similarities in terms of architectural options, security, remote access applicability, ability to transport foreign networking packets such as IPX, scalability, their chances of interoperability among products from competing vendors, etc. As you look over this table, keep in mind the points discussed in the rest of this section. They may help ease your confusion.

9.8.1 IPSec Is a Developing Industry Standard

IPSec is rapidly becoming the industry standard for VPN use. Although it is intended for much wider applicability as a secure protocol for all Internet solutions, it incorporates the features essential to VPNs: tunneling, encryption, and authentication. IPSec has the backing of major VPN vendors and of industries seeking broad-based VPN capabilities. Interoperability is improving thanks to the demands created by the automotive industry's ANX project. ICSA's certification program for interoperability offers some assurance that products from competing vendors will be able to communicate.

IPSec also offers the chance for standardization of other VPN protocols, specifically L2TP and PPTP, which do not themselves specify encryption standards. By implementing the authentication and encryption features specified in IPSec, vendors of these products provide at least some hope of consistency.

However, there are some caveats to using IPSec for your VPN if you are forced to build a VPN that encompasses products from competing vendors. First, IPSec's minimum encryption standards are just that; they should not be considered particularly strong. To provide greater security, stronger encryption algorithms should be implemented, and this does introduce the potential for incompatibility among competing products; these products will reduce security between them to the lowest common denominator required by IPSec, if they can even communicate at all.

Secondly, IPSec v.1 is still being refined by the IETF working group as of this writing. Among other things, for example, there are some obscure issues that are being addressed by the IPSec Working Group with regard to IPSec's use in remote access clients. Research the latest developments on IPSec before selecting your VPN products *(http://www.ietf.org/html.charters /ipsec-charter.html)*. There's enough slack in the current implementations of IPSec to warrant caution, particularly with regard to interoperability. Insist on ICSA certification (but be aware that some problems may still arise).

9.8.2 The Ready Availability of PPTP and L2TP

PPTP offers a quick and comparatively easy path to take in building your VPN. It is included with Windows NT 4.0 and Windows 98 and is planned for inclusion in Windows NT 5.0 (along with IPSec and L2TP). This ready availability makes implementation of either PPTP or L2TP in your VPN extremely tempting. Both appear to be particularly well suited for use in a VPN that is serving as a remote access server.

If you are willing to accept the security weaknesses inherent in Microsoft's implementation of PPTP, along with the potentially poor performance caused by the load that encryption imposes, you might consider implementing PPTP as a pilot project to explore the ways a VPN might benefit your organization. However, unless you want to encounter some potentially serious performance problems, it would be wise to plan on establishing a dedicated VPN server rather than implementing the protocol on a machine that is already serving another purpose.

L2TP is supposed to be backwardly compatible with PPTP and is to be included in Windows NT 5.0, making it a similarly useful product. Keep a close eye on how security is implemented in it, however. By using IPSec security (which should also be available in Windows NT 5.0) in combination with it, L2TP has the potential of being a viable VPN solution. Also, if you are running a pure Windows environment throughout your organization, PPTP and—when Windows NT 5.0 is released—L2TP are worth consideration.

9.8.3 SKIP Is Being Marginalized in the Market

While SKIP is an interesting product, it has not gained extremely wide support, even as a competitor of ISAKMP/Oakley in IPSec. The IPSec Working Group has settled on the latter for key management. This does not mean that SKIP will not find its uses. It has the advantage of not requiring the exchange of messages an ISAKMP/Oakley negotiation requires. It allows for one-way encryption and thus offers secure broadcast capabilities. (Whether this meets the definition of a VPN is open to question, of course.)

One big plus is that SKIP also provides crash protection that is not available in IPSec, since you can, in effect, mirror your VPN servers so that if one goes down the other picks up without missing a beat. If you demand an extremely high degree of reliability in your VPN, then SKIP is worth serious consideration.

9.8.4 AltaVista, SOCKS v.5, and Secure SHell Are Niche Products

AltaVista Tunnel is a proprietary offering from DEC, and there are other less-prominent proprietary VPN offerings on the market as well. There is nothing wrong with going that route, as long as interoperability with other VPN products is not an issue. If all you need (and ever will need) is an intranet, such products are viable choices. Otherwise, be wary.

AltaVista Tunnel is a well-defined VPN product. It is available for Digital Unix and Windows NT. For an intranet or extranet with partners who also use it, AltaVista is a viable solution. While it is likely to acquire IPSec, interoperability with products from other VPN vendors may be problematical in the near term and possibly beyond.

SOCKS v.5 is not likely to become a dominant force in the VPN marketplace. Its primary proponent, Aventail, has left the VPN market, switching its attention to ecommerce. Developed primarily as a proxy server, SOCKS is likely to continue in that role. If you already have need for a proxy server, a SOCKS server that can also serve as a VPN server is a viable option to consider. Otherwise SOCKS would not seem to be the best solution available. However, you do have to be alert to the applications you plan to use with SOCKS. They have to be compatible with SOCKS and able to work with the SOCKS engine that lets them connect with the SOCKS server.

Secure SHell is narrowly applicable as a client for gaining secure access to a remote server. It is basically a remote control product that includes encryption features that elevate it to VPN status. It is freely available for many operating systems but is seen primarily as a tool for the sophisticated computer user rather than the average employee.

9.8.5 Sun.NET Is an Unproven Product

Sun.NET came on the market almost too late for inclusion in this book. It is an intriguing concept, but it is obviously limited to client/server applications and is entirely Web based. It is intended for use by the general public and looks more like an ecommerce tool than an enterprise VPN. However, for a mobile workforce it has potential for use as a remote access tool.

9.9 Evaluate Products and Vendors

Begin by making a careful survey of the products that are out there. You should be able to eliminate a fair number that simply don't offer what you need to meet your goals. Don't ignore potential compatibility problems. Make sure that whatever VPN solution you settle on will get along with the networks you are running and the software you are using. IPSec, PPTP, and L2TP, which operate at the lower OSI layers, probably do not present a problem on this score.

Selecting a specific product will, at the very least, reduce the number of vendors to consider. From there, try to narrow the vendor list down to a manageable number to examine in greater detail. Dig into the vendors' backgrounds. Talk to those individuals you would routinely be working with (if possible) to find out if you feel comfortable that you're communicating clearly. Ask for company references and follow up on them. Don't forget to network with your peers to find others who have already implemented a VPN. Talk with them about their experiences with their vendors.

From your list of requirements, prepare a detailed Request for Proposal (RFP). That is the single best way to make sure that vendors you are considering know exactly what it is you want. It also provides a solid baseline for evaluating competing offerings from vendors. By making sure that everyone starts with the same premise, you can more easily compare their proposals. Don't expect this to produce uniform submissions from the vendors you approach, however. Every vendor, it seems, has to find ways to digress from the details included in your RFP. Don't let them blow smoke in your eyes. Make sure you understand exactly what it is they are proposing and how it differs from what you asked them for. If you don't like their suggestions, ask for a new proposal, discount them as you make your decision, or even drop them completely from consideration.

Make sure you find the best one that will give you what you are looking for; don't stop looking with the first product you find that seems to meet your requirements. There may be more than one, and some may work better than others. Don't ignore factors other than your VPN criteria. Research costs, security, and support as well. Find people who are already using the products that meet your needs and talk with them to get their experiences.

If you are going to outsource the project to an ISP or are implementing your VPN on a private backbone, in addition to what you'd do when looking for a product you should look for service guarantees. Convince yourself of the provider's security planning and continued support. Find out what sort of design and implementation assistance they offer. Learn about their systems and how they provide the reliability you need. What tech support do they offer? Is it available 24 hours a day, 7 days a week?

The same goes if you choose a turnkey system from a vendor. Make sure they will be there for you after the system is up and running should problems arise (and there will almost certainly be problems over the first few months). Make sure you are clear on just how much help they are going to give you after they turn the key over to you and for how long. If, for example, your server crashes after 6 months on the job, can you rely on them to help recover the system, to slot a new server into place, or are you on your own on that? What sort of extended service contracts are available, and how expensive are they?

Work to develop good contacts with your provider, whether you are outsourcing the whole project, buying a turnkey system, or building it yourself with a product you purchase from a vendor. Work with them as you develop the final details of the project. They should thoroughly know their product, and they may have suggestions on how you may want to alter the plan to take advantage of its strengths and avoid its weaknesses. If you are outsourcing the entire project, this is as much a partnership as a customer relationship. Interview the specific people you will be working with. Make sure you are comfortable with them, that they understand what you want, and that they can give it to you.

Get all agreements in writing. Doing business on a handshake may be a nice tradition, but it is easier to avoid confusion and conflicts later on if you put all the details down on paper and make sure that all parties know exactly what their responsibilities are. Include in these agreements such important matters as schedules, product specifications, and, of course, costs. As the project proceeds you should get status reports in writing. Verbal presentations with lots of flash and fury are no substitute for hard copy that sets out exactly where things stand.

9.10 Define a Pilot Project

Once you have settled on a product, an architecture, and a vendor or provider, don't plan on rolling out your VPN in one mighty wave. Set up a pilot project that does not replace or interfere with any existing systems. Keep it small and secure so you can test your concepts and the products you are considering without endangering any of your real data or systems.

Begin by testing the pilot thoroughly with your own IT staff before you inflict it upon other users. After you're satisfied that it works for you, test the concept thoroughly with a small, representative group of users. Do it in a way that will not interfere with their usual operations any more than necessary. Provide sufficient time for evaluation and stabilization before going "live."

9.11 Plan on a Phased Rollout

Once the pilot project has proven itself and you're convinced that you've solved the vast majority of the problems and eradicated every bug you've detected, you can start to move the project out into the real world. To the extent possible, try to roll it out in phases. This can be done by bringing one remote office or group of remote users online at a time and making sure that everything is working smoothly for them before beginning the next phase. Or it may be a matter of implementing one feature of the VPN at a time, beginning perhaps with email. It can even be highly granular, such as to implement email with one branch and then add email to the other branches. Implement the workgroup feature with one office, get it stable, then add the other offices one at a time. Save the most mission-critical functions for a time when you are confident that everything else on the system is stable, and then proceed just as cautiously with them.

As a real-world example of what we're talking about, one of the things that Glenn Botkin of Galaxy Scientific comments that he would change if he were doing his VPN project today would be to modularize the implementation of the VPN. He would begin with the infrastructure, i.e., the connections, routers, etc. Then he would add email and make sure that was stabilized before adding new applications. He notes that the first 6 months with their VPN were tumultuous, as users got hit with new capabilities and different ways of doing things. This was in addition to the glitches that are inevitable as any new system settles in. Much of this tumult, he notes, was not directly a result of implementing the VPN but was caused by the host of new applications they added on the intranet at the same time.

Get the VPN up and running first, then start adding features to it and wait for each to settle in before tackling the next one. Give your users time to adapt to each change. Make sure, too, that you keep them informed as to what you are doing and why. Nothing is more frustrating to an end user than the feeling of being yanked around and used as a guinea pig for no good reason and with no foreseeable end in sight. Remember, the user has a job to do, in addition to being your beta tester.

Be prepared to pull the plug at any time during the rollout process. Whatever you do, don't junk the old system the moment you get the VPN up and running. Make sure you have a good fallback position should things go wrong. Plan for things to go wrong; they will. If you're prepared for the worst, then it won't be the worst it could be.

Only after the whole system is up and running and has been running for a decent length of time should you get rid of the old system. Once you have total confidence in your VPN, you can mothball the old remote access server, for example. Just in case, however, you might want to keep it in the closet for a while longer.

9.12 Conclusion

Implementing a VPN requires careful planning, knowing exactly where you are, and knowing where you are going with it. It also can place some heavy demands on your IT staff and your users. Take your time and make sure you know exactly what you're doing before proceeding. Analyze your needs, inventory your resources exhaustively, define precise but expandable goals and plan your architecture, select your vendors carefully, and then proceed slowly and incrementally with a phased rollout. You should do just fine.

Administration and Management

Most VPN products come with their own management tools. They are not unlike the tools you'll already have for managing your LAN. You'll need to perform essentially the same tasks for a VPN that you do for any network. Obviously user authentication and access control are major concerns. You'll want to be able to track traffic and log any problems that arise so they can be located and remedied. You'll have to add or remove nodes and user accounts and manage files and servers. But managing a VPN is not exactly like managing a LAN or even a WAN. The nature and architecture of VPNs stretches some aspects far beyond the range found in the average LAN.

Security is one aspect of particular importance. Also, when you implement the VPN there is the sudden increase in the number of users you are responsible for. Instead of making sure just Joe down the hall, whom you have coffee with every morning, has access, you have to arrange access for a hundred or a thousand others across the country whom you've never met. Another management item to attend to is somehow guaranteeing that the VPN doesn't let you down—that the system stays up and that data moves smoothly through it. Since the major link that creates your VPN (the public backbone) is not under your direct control, there is only so much you can do about this, and one option may not even be available to you: a service level agreement with your provider.

There is also the fact that with a VPN you are unavoidably dealing with a larger, more complex system than your existing network, and such a change will be a sudden growth spurt, unlike simply adding a few workstations to your existing LAN. If all you have been dealing with until now is a LAN and you are suddenly faced with a VPN created by joining together multiple local networks and adding a few hundred remote users, you'll find that you are facing a much more complex situation. On the other hand, if you are replacing an existing WAN with a VPN you might actually discover some advantages to your VPN over what you had previously been dealing with. For example, you may be able to work with remote offices without investing in expensive new management tools, because once it is set up a VPN behaves much like one big LAN.

10.1 Security

We've stressed security before, and we're going to stress it again here as a major management concern: it cannot be stressed enough. In going from a single LAN to a VPN that connects to other LANs, you are expanding the resources that you are responsible for protecting to include those on remote facilities. And even worse from a management perspective, whether your VPN is on the Internet or using PVCs on a frame relay backbone, your exposure to intruders is greater than if you are running an in-house LAN or even a leased-line WAN. You're sharing that public network with other people, millions of other people in the case of the Internet, and some of those people are "ethically challenged." While the majority of hackers (talented, creative and intelligent, good at what they do) may simply be amusing themselves by playing with tools they pick up off the many hacker sites online, some of them are simply maliciously inclined and others are conceivably in the employ of your competitors. No matter what the motivation, if they penetrate your system they can do major damage.

Bear in mind, too, that the Internet is an international medium, and even if you go the route of using a private backbone to connect your VPN, it may serve the entire world as well. Even if the Internet-based VPN you are running only connects two LANs in the same town, the infrastructure that you are using stretches around the globe, and your traffic may take the long way around. Even if it takes the most direct route, you are still exposed not only to the hacker down the block to the industrial spy in Bulgaria or Beijing as well. Geography means nothing to the Internet.

If your VPN is being used for remote access, and the chances are that it is, you are adding to your concerns the leading hazard faced by the road warrior: theft of his laptop with its wealth of information, including the client software designed to access the heart of your network. How much damage can be done if that road warrior tapes his password to the bottom of that laptop, where any thief can find it, or perhaps uses the "save password" option in his Windows 95 networking, so the machine automatically logs on when he boots up?

All of this means that maintaining good security procedures is even more important with a VPN than it is with a LAN, which has no contact with the outside world. Even if your only contact with the Internet up to this point has been a Web server outside the firewall, when you implement a VPN you are creating a door through your firewall for the VPN traffic, a door that anyone can test to see if he or she can penetrate. Most of the measures we'll recommend are ones that should already be in place on a LAN but that frequently are not implemented at all or are not implemented properly.

The security features of most VPNs are good, but they must be implemented properly to do their job. Furthermore, don't assume that you are safe simply because you have a VPN that is running 128-bit encryption. Obviously you should implement the strongest encryption possible on your system, bearing in mind the export restrictions that the government imposes. But don't let the quality of your encryption software lull you into a false sense of security. Encryption only protects the traffic, not your system, and key length or algorithm strength means absolutely nothing if someone can get into your network by looking like a legitimate user. The theft of your traffic is not where you are most vulnerable; your front door is your most vulnerable point, and once that has been compromised *all of the data on your network* is vulnerable, not just what travels over your VPN.

10.1.1 The First Line of Defense

There isn't a burglar in the world who is going to bother with trying to pick the lock of your front door if he can find the key to it under the doormat. As the old cartoon character Pogo used to say, "We has met the enemy, and he is us." The weakest security link in virtually any network is where the rubber meets the road, that is, where it begins: with the end user. The vast majority of LANs, WANs, and VPNs rely on the simplest and inherently least secure of authentication methods: the username and password log-on. Virtually all the VPN products on the market today offer that as one of the default settings, or else they provide for authentication by an outside source such as a RADIUS server that itself may use nothing stronger than that.

This most common form of authentication is inherently vulnerable, because it relies on the diligence of users who are usually technically unsophisticated, absent-minded, easily bored by the whole topic of security, and, frequently, lazy. They'll leave the door unlocked or the key in plain sight for anyone to guess or steal. Once that first authentication process is penetrated, your network is exposed. If Igor in Bulgaria somehow acquires the password of Jake, the highly mobile sales rep for eastern Europe, and then logs on as Jake, he is going to be authenticated as Jake.

Won't the firewall catch him?

It may not necessarily catch him in this case. Jake is a road warrior. His IP address changes daily, so the firewall filter may not catch Igor's address as a bad one. Once Igor is in the door the entire system is going to assume that he is Jake, and anywhere Jake has access Igor will be admitted. The encryption keys that are supposed to be protecting your data will automatically be handed to Igor by systems that have no way of knowing that he is not who he is pretending to be, because the RADIUS server in St. Louis authenticated Igor on the basis of having gotten the right password when "Jake" logged on.

If this happens, your system administrator won't even have a clue that you have an intruder unless an alarm is tripped when the real Jake suddenly logs on from Romania (if the system is configured to catch it) or when an administrator watching your traffic closely sees someone from sales suddenly accessing the accounting department's server and issuing a large check to a bank account in Switzerland. If the intrusion is discovered by someone reading system logs, by the time the record of the break-in is noticed it is probably too late.

Chances are that you won't be that lucky anyway. If Igor is clever, the first thing he will do upon gaining access to the network is plant some software that opens a hidden account, or tap into one of your inactive accounts, or acquire a password to a new server by installing a key logging program to capture the real Jake's keystrokes the next time he comes online. Igor may be able to hide his tracks, set up a program to erase the logs that record his actions, and hack the firewall to ignore his IP address. Once he's done that he can operate with impunity and rob you blind, if he's so inclined.

Your first line of defense, your log-in process, is your weakest barrier, unless you manage it properly. If you are going to stick with a simple password log-on system, it is vital that you carefully train your end users in proper security procedures and perpetually keep training them. They must constantly be reminded that they should never, ever reveal their password to anyone. Using what is called "social engineering," hackers can too easily con that information out of a naive user simply by calling them on the telephone and pretending to be someone from the security office or the network management office and claiming to be checking the network for some mythical problem.

If users are allowed to choose their own password, they had better know not to make it something easy to guess. Any word in the dictionary is vulnerable to a program that uses a dictionary attack. Just as vulnerable as a password is any fact about themselves that is easy to determine or guess, such as a birthday, anniversary, spouse or child's name, or anagram of a name. In fact, just about any password that is easy to remember is probably vulnerable. A good password should be a mixed and meaningless combination of letters, numbers, and, if possible, symbols. But it is not easy to get users to come up with such complicated strings on their own. One approach is to issue end users their passwords and to change them regularly so that if one is compromised the door doesn't remain open for long.

Such methods, of course, bring up the problem of the user remembering his or her password. As soon as you insist on meaningless character strings for passwords, the users are going to have trouble remembering them. Changing the password on a regular basis compounds the problem. Users are going to write their passwords down to help remember them. If the password is written down somewhere, it can be seen and read by anyone who passes by. Even worse than sticking it inside the lid or on the bottom of his or her laptop, a moderately computer literate road warrior might cobble up a keyboard macro that automates the log-on process. In such a case, once Igor has stolen Jake's laptop all he has to do is punch one or two keys and he's into your system.

There are more secure authentication methods available, such as a token method, in which a user has something like a mag stripe card such as is used with an ATM machine, combined with a personal identification number to be entered. These are more secure, but they are also more expensive, because they require a card reader to be installed on every terminal. SecureID, on the other hand, requires the user to enter a number on his calculator-like SecureID card and then to enter the resulting number into his computer. It's a little less convenient, but it eliminates the expense of a card reader.

Even more secure technologies are appearing on the market. For example, a smartcard holding a record of a user's fingerprint can be compared with the one he inputs using a fingerprint reader attached to a terminal. There are even face recognition systems under development. None of these measures, at present, are particularly reliable, which means a legitimate user under scrutiny by a face recognition system may find himself locked out if he gets a haircut. None will be cheap when they finally do become reliable and widely available. However, they are much more secure than many current methods.

Encryption of passwords as they are moved through the network is certainly important, but bear in mind that it does not require technical sophistication to steal a password and gain access to a system. It doesn't require packet sniffers or demon dialers, skillful attacks that penetrate firewalls, or hacked routers or switches. It doesn't require sophisticated cryptanalysis or even a simple brute force attack on a cryptosystem. All it requires is carelessness on the part of your users. That means you must try to keep them alert to the threat, and you must also watch your traffic carefully for unusual activity, such as Jake suddenly showing a lot of interest in the accounting department.

Along the same lines, don't let inactive accounts remain alive. If a hacker penetrates your network, he is likely to look for just such an account, so that when you lock the door he first used to get in he can shift over to the unused account. If someone leaves the company, kill that account. If someone goes on a sabbatical or vacation, suspend it so it can't be used.

Is it a lot of work? Yes, even when all you are responsible for is your local LAN (as you probably already know). When you add to that all the accounts that the VPN generates, your problem mushrooms and your vulnerability mushrooms as well. Even if you have outsourced the project, you still have the responsibility to monitor your provider's work. You'll need to maintain a watchful eye on your internal network traffic to catch anyone who might have slipped through the provider's security measures. Depending on the contract you have with them, their responsibility may stop at your door. It is not possible for them to know your systems nearly as well as you do, and you're probably not going to give them that good a look into your workings anyway.

To coin a phrase, the price of good security is eternal vigilance. Security is a full-time job even on a modest LAN. On a VPN, it becomes even more important and a greater challenge.

10.1.2 Beware of Back Doors

There are also more ways into a network than through the front door. Most networking software comes with certain default accounts established. One, in fact, is unavoidable, and that is an account for a system administrator. It has to be there or you'd have no way to administer the system. It is usually protected by some obvious username and password such as "supervisor" until you change it. (You did change those, didn't you?) There may also be guest accounts, with the mindless password "guest" assigned to it. Hackers know this, and they look for just such accounts.

Then, too, as mentioned in Section 9.2.1 about inventorying your system, there is the danger of an unauthorized, unknown back door, such as a modem installed by a user who wants to be able to log on from home to check his or her email. If a hacker knows just one company telephone number, he can set up a demon dialer to test all the numbers that are likely to belong to you. When a modem answers, he's got his foot in the door.

If you are running a VPN, the problem is compounded by the number of networks that it ties together. If you have branch offices in Duquesne, Dubuque, and Detroit, and each of them has a LAN, any one of them might still have one of those default accounts, or someone might have sneaked in a modem. Once a hacker gets into the LAN, depending how authentication and access to the VPN are set up, he may already be into your VPN, or he can look around for ways to get into your VPN and have access to all three of your branch offices along with your headquarters in Pittsburgh and your data processing center in Omaha.

This means that if you have overall responsibility for the VPN, you have to extend your interest to the LANs and remote users connected to it. Even if you don't take personal responsibility for every LAN on the VPN, you'd better be sure you can trust the work of the people who do have that responsibility.

Similarly, you must remain current on all of your networking software, from the VPN software itself on down to your network operating system, your browser software, etc. Make sure you have the latest patches in place so that security holes that have been uncovered have been fixed.

10.1.3 Security Through Obscurity

One of the simplest security features you can implement is to remain obscure. Don't advertise the fact that you have a VPN or a presence on the Internet. If hackers don't know you are there, they won't be looking for you. Certainly there is always the chance that they will stumble across your connections to the Internet as they explore. They may take a pass or two at your firewall, run a "whois" to find out who is using that IP address, but then get bored simply because you don't seem very interesting. Who is going to waste time on an office in Fairbanks that goes by the name of Smith and Smith when they have a much more interesting target in San Francisco with the words "INTERNATIONAL BANK" in big, bold letters in its name?

10.2 Keeping the VPN Up

A VPN that isn't there when you need it is potentially worse than no VPN at all. Once you come to depend on that easy connectivity, if something happens to take it down you could find important parts of your operation dead in the water. Just as with security, by its very nature a VPN is going to present reliability challenges that a simple LAN does not. A major challenge is the network over which you have no control, the backbone your VPN is using, whether it is the Internet or a private backbone. You can provide yourself with some peace of mind with a service level agreement with your provider, if such an agreement is available.

The second aspect of a VPN that can make maintaining it a challenge is the added complexity. Keeping a VPN working involves more than simply making sure the cables are still connected. As you add connections by hooking into other LANs or signing on remote users, the complexity of the system increases. You are dealing with more workstations and more servers. Unexpected conflicts can arise that have to be resolved. Directory services become more intricate. Drive mappings can become problematic. Along with making sure that the connections can still be made, you need to make sure that files don't suddenly vanish because of a directory services clash. You must also make sure that you're keeping up with the traffic and that bottlenecks don't develop that slow things down by causing packet loss.

10.2.1 Service Level Agreements

How much a Service level agreement (SLA) can mean to you depends on what the SLA covers. If your VPN is established over a single private backbone, the service provider can and should be able to offer assurances not available to an Internet-based VPN. For example, if you are paying for 768 Kbps PVCs then that is what you should get. Private line service carriers have offered agreements of this type for years. With the growth of commercial use of the Internet, the pressure is now on ISPs to offer similar guarantees, and many of them—including MCI, AT&T, PSINet, GTE Internetworking, Sprint, and Digex, Inc.—have taken to offering service level agreements free of charge with their VPN and dial-up services, as well as with dedicated lines such as T1 or ISDN.

Obviously, a VPN is a vital tool for your business. If it fails for even a short time, it can represent lost time and money for you and possibly even some serious out-of-pocket losses if, for example, a contract's penalty clause kicks in because of it. If your VPN goes down for a significant length of time, it could bring work to a halt at some of your facilities. For example, what if the connection is lost when a crucial project is being finalized between your main engineering office and a remote production facility?

A good SLA can offer a way to recoup at least some of your losses, but it is not likely to go beyond a credit toward the fee you pay to the ISP for your connection. For example, it may be set up such that if your connection is down for more than 10 minutes you get a credit equal to the per-day fee you're paying your service provider.

That may not sound like much, but such an SLA builds a fire under your ISP to make sure they keep you satisfied. If an SLA exists, the ISP will be much more interested in your welfare than if they don't have a financial stake in the relationship. Good ISPs will keep a close eye on both their network and your connections to it; they might give you a call if you suddenly shift a router and it shows up on their board, because such a shift could have an impact on the quality of service they have guaranteed by changing the load on the connection.

Most SLAs only state that if Internet service is interrupted for more than 10 or 15 minutes the customer will receive a full day of credit for the outage. Some ISPs, however, such as GTE, are taking SLAs a step further to encompass packet loss, which shows up as sluggish performance and is usually caused by a jammed-up router or the like.

To allow you to find out what's going on and to see just how well things are working, some ISPs, such as MCI and Digex, offer free Web-based tools to allow the customer to view network traffic. Other tools are available at a price that allow you to get more detailed information about the service you are getting from your ISP and within your own network. These can cost up to thousands of dollars a month to implement, but if your operation is big enough and vital to your business, that may be a wise investment.

Another guarantee that can be included in your SLA covers dropped connections encountered by your dial-in users. Few things are more frustrating than getting three quarters of the way through a 3 MB download only to lose the connection and then to have to start all over again. (The ISP can only offer this guarantee for dial-in users connecting through one of their own POPs, of course.)

A question that goes to the root of this whole discussion is whether an ISP can even offer a meaningful SLA for an Internet-based VPN. Realistically, as we've noted before, an ISP can only guarantee traffic on their own backbone and their own facilities. How can they guarantee anything once a packet leaves their domain to wend its way to its destination via someone else's backbone? The answer is they can't, and chances are the SLA you sign with them will limit their exposure along those lines. This means that SLAs covering things like packet loss and even down time are more detailed and may be written in a way that protects the ISP as well as protecting you. The more detailed of an SLA you request, the greater the chance that it is going to start to cost you money rather than coming free with the service. As a result, it pays to read the fine print on any SLA you sign, and you'd be wise to have a knowledgeable lawyer by your side as you do, so you will know exactly what the SLA covers. You need to know if it is worth what you will be paying.

10.2.2 Managing Performance on Your Part

While having an SLA can offer some assurance of performance and reliability, just as with security you are not relieved of managing your own segments. Your people are the ones who will have to monitor traffic and balance loads to avoid bottlenecks. Adding six employees at a remote office may mean upgrading that office's router or even the connection to the Internet to keep up with demand. Just the growth that comes as users become comfortable with using the VPN must be watched. Traffic patterns are going to evolve and change as your business grows and changes. Seasonal variations may shift the load from sales in October to shipping in November to accounting in December.

Your design division may invent the next Hula Hoop or Beanie Baby and throw everything out of kilter, from the plastics extrusion factory in Taiwan to the marketing office in San Francisco. A shareholder lawsuit will send traffic through your legal office surging. On an extranet, an increase in orders for widgets will require more communications with the raw materials supplier as you ramp up production. Traffic analyzing tools should be employed to keep you appraised of these changes, to ferret out potential bottlenecks before they result in irate users coming down on you with questions about why their node is suddenly so sluggish. Another solution is to employ routers that offer dynamic load balancing. However you do it, you've got to stay on top of your traffic patterns.

10.3 Managing One Big Network

In chaos mathematics there is an effect known as the "butterfly effect" that states that the motion of a butterfly's wings in an Indonesian rain forest can create eddies in the air that result in a blizzard in Boston. It is not quite that bad on a VPN, but what seems to be a simple change to one aspect of your VPN may result in unexpected and unpleasant effects on some other part of the network.

While it does depend on your architecture and the system you implement, with a VPN it's possible and even likely that the entire company's network will look like one big LAN from any perspective. The more transparent you make it to the end user, the more likely it is to confuse your systems management, particularly if they have moved from a system they are familiar with, such as Novell, to one they are not, such as Windows NT. Operations such as network directory services become even more important in order to avoid having files misplaced or lost completely. Simply adding a new server to the Chicago LAN might conflict with something in the St. Louis office. Even usernames can cause confusion if the system isn't set up to watch for potential conflicts and to prevent them.

For example, when they went to a VPN, Galaxy Scientific's VPN management structure left their existing LAN administrators responsible for their sites once the VPN came online. There was a learning curve involved, because only 2 weeks previously the two main sites had been Novell sites. Novell has a number of cross-checks and safeguards that make it harder to make changes. Now they were using Windows NT, which is easier to manage and more transparent to users and managers alike. This transparency that made it so much easier also made it riskier. One of the site administrators decided that too many people had access to his LAN's master password and he dug in and changed it, usually a wise move. Unfortunately, the unanticipated result of the change was that it locked out *all the other administrators from their own sites.*

Something as simple as changing email aliases can have an impact. This is a change you might want to make so that you don't broadcast network user IDs every time you send out an email. However, if you're using Windows NT and you don't do it the right way, suddenly your users will stop receiving their email because the system won't be able to find them. Such a seemingly innocent change on one LAN might even percolate through the entire system. On the other hand, it might suddenly isolate that LAN, or even some other LAN, from the rest of the system.

Because systems affect each other, anyone who has the power to make changes even at a local level must be careful and must maintain a meticulous log of any changes made so the system can be restored to its original condition if something goes wrong. For example, an administrator might make a series of changes in an effort to correct a problem specific to her site. Perhaps the changes don't correct the problem, so she tries to go back to where she came from, only she forgets one step in the restoration process. Even though the original series of changes didn't cause a major problem, whatever is left undone might have consequences for all the other sites on the VPN. Then you have a major snarl to untangle to get things back the way they should be.

Conversely, when something on one LAN suddenly stops working, if the problem isn't obvious you must look beyond it to see if a change somewhere else is causing the problem. If your local email suddenly vanishes, it may be because of a change made on a system a thousand miles away. If a file server on your own LAN becomes inaccessible, the cause might be local or it might be remote. Somehow you have to determine where the problem is before you start making wholesale changes on the apparently troubled LAN. Otherwise you may only create more problems, instead of fixing the one you already have. How much of a problem this type of interactivity is for you will depend on the system you select in the first place.

Depending, too, on the connections you have with your service provider, the problem may not even reside on the systems you are managing, but on theirs, particularly if you've outsourced some or all of the VPN to them. If your provider changes a filter setting somewhere in their system, it may have an impact on your traffic. It may be a big and obvious effect, such as cutting the connection to one site completely, or it may be more subtle, perhaps having an impact on local traffic, making it look like a strictly local problem when it is not.

This means that while outsourcing can provide benefits by sharing the burden of maintaining the system with your provider, you should also work hard to maintain a good working relationship with them, because you will probably have to work together side by side at some point to resolve such a problem. When such a situation arises, your first concern should be to get the problem resolved promptly, instead of finding someone to blame. Next you both must take steps to ensure that it doesn't happen again. Only then should you consider bringing up compensation as spelled out in the SLA you have with the provider. And even then, unless the losses are severe, you might want to skip that completely in favor of maintaining a good relationship with them.

Most accident investigators will tell you that rarely is there one single cause behind an accident. One driver in a head-on collision might have been drunk, but the other was distracted by changing the CD in his player and didn't see the drunk weave over the center line. You might make a seemingly simple change on your VPN that causes no apparent problems. Then your provider makes a similar change on their system that just happens to conflict with what you did and you get bitten. Fix the problem first, clear the highway and get traffic flowing, then figure out who—if anyone—is at fault.

In short, everyone responsible for any part of the VPN must have the big picture in mind. Yes, there must be a czar overlooking the whole; however, the local dukes must also be cognizant of how a change they make within their realm might impact the whole kingdom.

10.4 Conclusion

While the entire subject of setting up and managing a VPN of this may seem intimidating, it shouldn't be. VPNs are not inherently less reliable or less secure than any other network. While the Internet certainly has challenging characteristics, it is amazingly robust. VPN software has ample security features (and it is important that they be properly and conscientiously implemented).

The management of a VPN is not that different from managing a LAN. It is essentially a matter of scale. The network is larger, the security exposures are greater, and the management challenges are correspondingly increased. The tools are essentially the same. They use graphical interfaces that are commonly Web based so that they can be manipulated with your browser. Naturally, some products will have better management tools than others. That is just one more factor to include in your evaluations.

Granted, the difference in scale may be a quantum leap from where you are now. You may suddenly go from being responsible for maintaining a user database of a few hundred to a user database of a thousand or thousands. You may have to migrate your distributed user databases from their local servers to a RADIUS server, either your own or a trusted third party's. From worrying about gigabytes of files on a dozen servers you may suddenly find yourself coping with terabytes of files on scores of servers. Although the scale changes, the basic tasks remain.

Can you delegate some of this responsibility? Yes and no. Regardless of your architecture, unless you are running a very small VPN, individual LANs must almost certainly have their own administrators to handle local issues. This will ease your responsibilities with regard to the local LANs, and it may even reduce your technical workload. On the other hand, it still means that if the mud hits the fan, you're the one who has to run for the hose: you are going to have to manage those administrators. One of the most important aspects of that management is making sure each of them knows that he or she is part of a team that has to work together for the sake of the entire VPN.

Just as with any network, virtually any VPN requires a centralized point of management. Within the headquarters, functions such as traffic flow and security can be delegated to different individuals and probably should be. However, there must be someone with an overview of the entire network. It need not be a highly technically oriented individual. He or she must have the ability to see the big picture and at the same time must be able to communicate knowledgeably with technicians. This individual should also have excellent people skills, because soothing upset users is going to be part of the job description, along with cajoling a distant LAN administrator into setting aside his own pet project in favor of the operation of the whole and telling a division head that what she wants can't be done exactly the way she wants it done within the time frame she's asking.

VPN Developers, Vendors, and Service Providers

These are not comprehensive lists and are offered only as a convenience. The presence of any company on these lists should not be regarded as an endorsement, nor should the absence of a company be construed as criticism. There are literally thousands of developers, resellers, Internet service providers, and consultants who offer a range of VPN services. Many of the estimated 4,000 local ISPs offer a range of VPN services and are a good place to begin your search.

VPN Solution Developers and Vendors

3COM CORPORATION
http://www.3com.com
5400 Bayfront Plaza
Santa Clara, CA 95052-8145
Tel: 800-NET-3COM (800-638-3266)
408-326-5000
Fax: 408-326-5001

ADVANCED COMPUTER COMMUNICATIONS (ACC)
http://www.acc.com
340 Storke Road
Santa Barbara, CA 93117
Tel: 805-685-4455
Fax: 805-685-4465

ASCEND COMMUNICATIONS, INC.
http://www.ascend.com
One Ascend Plaza
1701 Harbor Bay Parkway
Alameda, CA 94502
Tel: 510-769-6001
Fax: 510-814-2300

ASHLEY LAURENT, INC.
http://laurent.osgroup.com
707 West Avenue, Suite 201
Austin, TX 78701;
Tel: 512-322-0676
Fax: 512-322-0680

ASSURED DIGITAL, INC. (ADI)
http://www.assured-digital.com
P.O. Box 248
9-11 Goldsmith Street
Littleton, MA 01460
Tel: 978-486-0555
Fax: 978-486-3772

AVENTAIL CORPORATION
http://www.aventail.com
808 Howell Street, 2nd floor
Seattle, WA 98101
Tel: 877-AVENTAIL (877-283-6824)
206-215-1111

BAY NETWORKS
http://www.baynetworks.com
4401 Great America Parkway
Santa Clara, CA 95054
Tel: 408-988-2400

CHECK POINT SOFTWARE TECHNOLOGIES
http://www.checkpoint.com
http://www.checkpoint.com /products/vpn1
Three Lagoon Drive, Suite 400
Redwood City, CA 94065
Tel: 650-628-2000
Fax: 650-654-4233

3A Jabotinsky Street, Diamond Tower
Ramat Gan 52520
Israel
Tel: +972-3-753-4555
Fax: +972-3-575-9256

CISCO SYSTEMS
http://www.cisco.com/warp/public /779/servpro/solutions/vpn/about.htm
170 West Tasman Drive
San Jose, CA 95134
Tel: 800-553-NETS (800-553-6387)
408-526-4000

COMPATIBLE SYSTEMS CORPORATION
http://www.compatible.com
P.O. Box 17220
Boulder, CO 80308
Tel: 800-356-0283
303-444-9532
Fax: 303-444-9595

DATA FELLOWS, INC.
http://www.datafellows.com
675 N. First Street, 8th floor
San Jose, CA 95112
Tel: 408-938-6700
Fax: 408-938-6701

DOLFIN DEVELOPMENTS, LTD.
http://www.dolfin.com
610 South Service Road West
Oakville, Ontario L6K 2H4
Canada

Tel: 800-668-7434
905-339-2323
Fax: 905-339-2392

E-LOCK TECHNOLOGIES, INC.
http://www.e-lock.com
10777 Main Street, Suite 300
Fairfax, VA 22030
Tel: 800-929-3054

ELRON SOFTWARE
http://www.elronsoftware.com
One Cambridge Center, 11th floor
Cambridge, MA 02142
Tel: 800-767-6683
Fax: 617-914-5001

EXONETS
http://www.exonets.com
230 210th Avenue NE
Redmond, WA 98053
Tel: 425-868-7346

EXTENDED SYSTEMS, INC.
http://www.extendsys.com
5777 N. Meeker Avenue
Boise, ID 83713
Tel: 800-235-7576
208-322-7800
Fax: 406-587-9170

FIBERLINK COMMUNICATIONS
http://www.fiberlinkcc.com /index.cfm
488 Norristown Road, Suite 240
Blue Bell, PA 19422
Tel: 800-LINK-NOW (800-546-5669)
610-941-2050
Fax: 610-941-2069

FORTRESS TECHNOLOGIES, INC.
http://www.fortresstech.com
2701 N. Rocky Point Drive, Suite 650
Tampa, FL 33607
Tel: 813-288-7388
Fax: 813-288-7389

FREEGATE CORPORATION
http://www.freegate.com
1208 East Arques Avenue
Sunnyvale, CA 94086
Tel: 408-617-1000
Fax: 408-617-1261

FREELINK COMMUNICATIONS, INC.
http://www.freelink.net

GALAXY SCIENTIFIC CORPORATION
http://www.galaxyscientific.com
Corporate Headquarters
2500 English Creek Ave., Bldg. 11
Egg Harbor Twp., NJ 08234-5562
Tel: 609-645-0900
Fax: 609-645-3316

INDUS RIVER NETWORKS, INC.
http://www.indusriver.com
31 Nagog Park
Acton, MA 01720
Tel: 978-266-8100
Fax: 978-266-8111

INFORMATION RESOURCES ENGINEERING, INC. (IRE)
http://www.ire.com
8029 Corporate Drive
Baltimore, MD 21236
Tel: 410-931-7500
Fax: 410-931-7524

INTELISPAN
http://www.intelispan.com
8220 East Gelding Drive
Scottsdale, AZ 85260
Tel: 602-443-3999
Fax: 602-443-4702

LUCENT TECHNOLOGIES
http://www.lucent.com/security
http://www.lucentncg.com
/enterprise-security/virtual
_private_network.asp
Remote Access Business Unit
4464 Willow Road
Pleasanton, CA 94588
Tel: 800-458-9966

MATROX NETWORKS
http://www.matrox.com
1055 St. Regis Boulevard
Dorval, Quebec H9P 2T4
Canada
Tel: 800-837-3611
514-822-6080
Fax: 514-822-6272

MICROSOFT CORPORATION
http://www.microsoft.com/isn
/network/access/default.asp
One Microsoft Way
Redmond, WA 98052-6399
Tel: 425-882-8080

NETSCREEN TECHNOLOGIES, INC.
http://www.netscreen.com/I
2860 San Tomas Expressway
Santa Clara, CA 95051
Tel: 877-NETSCREEN (877-638-7273)
408-330-7800

NEW OAK COMMUNICATIONS, INC.
Merger: See BAY NETWORKS

NOVELL, INC.
http://www.novell.com
http://www.novell.com
/bordermanager
122 East 1700 South
Provo, UT 84606
Tel: 801-861-7000

NTS
http://www.nts.com
550 Del Rey Avenue
Sunnyvale, CA 94086
Tel: 408-523-8100
Fax: 408-523-8118

RADGUARD
http://www.radguard.com
575 Corporate Drive
Mahwah, NJ 07430
Tel: 201-828-9611
Fax: 201-828-9613

24 Raoul Wallenberg Street
Tcl Aviv 69719
Israel
Tel: +972-3-645-5444
Fax: +972-3-648-0859

REDCREEK COMMUNICATIONS, INC.
http://www.redcreek.com/index.html
3900 Newpark Mall Road
Newark, CA 94560
Tel: 510-745-3900
Fax: 510-745-3999

SECURITY DYNAMICS TECHNOLOGIES, INC.
http://www.securid.com
20 Crosby Drive
Bedford, MA 01730
Tel: 800-SECURID (800-732-8743)
781-687-7000

SHIVA
http://www.shiva.com
28 Crosby Drive
Bedford, MA 01730
Tel: 781-687-1000
Fax: 781-687-1001

SSH COMMUNICATIONS SECURITY, INC.
http://www.ssh.fi
4320 Stevens Creek Blvd., Suite 220
San Jose, CA 95129
Tel: 408-615-5750
Fax: 408-615-5757

SUN MICROSYSTEMS, INC.
http://www.sun.com
901 San Antonio Road
Palo Alto, CA 94303
Tel: 650-960-1300

TECHNOLOGIC, INC.
http://www.tlogic.com/home.html
2990 Gateway Drive, Suite 950
Norcross, GA 30067
Tel: 800-615-9911
770-448-0334
Fax: 770-448-4547

TIMESTEP
http://www.timestep.com
593 Herndon Parkway
Herndon, VA 20170
Tel: 703-834-3600
Fax: 703-736-6260

362 Terry Fox Drive
Kanata, Ontario K2K 2P5
Canada
Tel: 613-599-3610
Fax: 613-599-3617

TRADEWAVE
http://www.tradewave.com
3636 Executive Center Drive,
Suite 100
Austin, TX 78731
Tel: 512-433-5300
Fax: 512-433-5303

V-ONE CORPORATION
http://www.v-one.com
20250 Century Boulevard, Suite 300
Germantown, MD 20874
Tel: 800-495-8663
301-515-5200
Fax: 301-515-5280

VPNET TECHNOLOGIES, INC.
http://www.vpnet.com
1530 Meridian Avenue
San Jose, CA 95125
Tel: 888-VPNET-88 (888-876-3888)
408-445-6600
Fax: 408-445-6611

VPN SYSTEMS, LTD.
http://www.vpnsystems.com
280 Cheese Factory Road
Honeoye Falls, NY 14472-9231
Tel: 716-624-8365

WATCHGUARD TECHNOLOGIES, INC.
http://www.watchguard.com
316 Occidental Avenue, Suite 200
Seattle, WA 98104
Tel: 206-521-8340
Fax: 206-521-8341

THE WIZARD'S GATE
Wizards, Inc. Computer and Internet Services
http://www.wizardsinc.net
1532 W. 3rd Avenue
Williamson, West Virginia 25661
Tel: 304-235-4NET (304-235-4638)
Fax: 304-235-4643

International Internet Service Providers, Frame Relay Service Providers, and VPN Outsource Providers

AT&T WORLDNET VIRTUAL PRIVATE NETWORK SERVICES
http://www.ipservices.att.com /worldnet/vpns
32 Avenue of the Americas
New York, NY 10013-2412

CABLE & WIRELESS COMMUNICATIONS PUBLIC LIMITED COMPANY
http://www.cwcom.co.uk/main.html

CONCENTRIC NETWORK CORPORATION
http://www.concentric.net
http://www.concentric.net /products_services/vpn_services
1400 Parkmoor Avenue
San Jose, CA 95126
Tel: 800-539-0214
408-817-2800
Fax: 409-817-2810

GLOBAL ONE
http://www.globalone.com
12490 Sunrise Valley Drive
Reston, VA 20196

For the U.S. and selected countries:
Tel: 800-598-7572
Fax: 800-598-7583
For all other countries:
Tel: 703-689-5138
Fax: 703-689-2248

GRIC COMMUNICATIONS
http://www.gric.com
1421 McCarthy Boulevard
Milpitas, CA 95035
Tel: 408-955-1920
Fax: 408-955-1968

GTE FRAME RELAY SERVICE
http://www.gte.com/Products/Prods /frfinfo.html
Tel: 800-483-1848

IPASS, INC.
http://www.ipass.com
650 Castro Street, Suite 500
Mountain View, CA 94041
Tel: 650-237-7300
Fax: 650-237-7321

MAS NET
http://www.masnet.net
4045 NW 64th, Suite 200
Oklahoma City, OK 73116
Tel: 800-364-9655
405-840-5200
Fax: 405-879-4528

MCI WORLDCOM
http://www.mciworldcom.com
http://www.mciworldcom.com /products+services/on_net /data_frame.shtml

PSINET
http://www.psi.net/access /PSINetintranet.html

QUAD INTERNATIONAL COMMUNICATIONS CORPORATION
http://www.qicc.com
P.O. Box 338
Moorpark, CA 93020-0338
Tel: 805-532-1012

SPIN RX MANAGEMENT SYSTEMS, LLC
http://www.spinrx.com
3751 Northampton Street NW
Washington, DC 20015-2980
Tel: 800-579-8707

SPRINT COMMUNICATIONS COMPANY, LP
http://www.sprintbiz.com/data /othersolutions.html

VELOCET COMMUNICATIONS
http://www.velocet.ca/homepage.htm
26 Soho Street, Suite 350
Toronto, Ontario M5T 1Z7
Canada
Tel: 877-VELOCET (877-835-6238)
416-410-2822

Resources

The following listing gives sources of further information on VPNs. In addition to the general resources listed here, many vendor sites listed in Appendix A offer white papers that approach VPNs from the perspective of their product offerings. See also the bibliography.

CRYPTOGRAPHY A 2 Z

http://www.ssh.fi/tech/crypto

This Web page lists international sources of cryptographic software and information on cryptographic methods, algorithms, and protocols. The scope includes encryption, decryption, cryptanalysis, steganography (hiding information), cryptographic software and tools, and assessments of cryptographic methods.

DTOOL

http://www.dtool.com/index1.htm

A repository of links, articles, tips, and news related to general networking and Internet programming issues. Among the items covered are networking, VPNs, frame relay, Simple Network Management Protocol (SNMP), LAN/WAN design, Web site design, HTML, Perl, Javascript, Java, and Unix.

E-LOCK TECHNOLOGIES

http://www.e-lock.com/white-p/SITES.HTM

This site provides a list of VPN and cryptography links.

INTERNATIONAL COMPUTER SECURITY ASSOCIATION (ICSA)

http://www.icsa.net

An authority on computer network security, ICSA is currently certifying products for use in the ANX VPN (see Section 2.2.1).

INTERNET ASSIGNED NUMBERS AUTHORITY (IANA)

http://www.iana.org

The group given the responsibility of assigning Internet IP addresses, protocol numbers, etc.

INTERNET ENGINEERING TASK FORCE (IETF)

http://www.ietf.org

IPSec Working Group

http://www.ietf.org/html.charters/ipsec-charter.html

The IETF working group charged with development of the IPSec protocol. A description of their work can be found at *http://www.ietf.org/html.charters /ipsec-charter.html*. IETF Requests for Comments pertaining to VPNs (RFCs 1825–29, 2401, 2402, 2406) can be searched for by number at *http://info .internet.isi.edu:80/7c/in-notes/rfc/.cache*.

KERBEROS

The MIT Kerberos Site

http://web.mit.edu/kerberos/www/

The Kerberos Reference Page

http://www.contrib.andrew.cmu.edu/~shadow/kerberos.html

NIST COMPUTER SECURITY RESOURCE CLEARINGHOUSE

http://csrc.ncsl.nist.gov

The Computer Security Resource Clearinghouse collects and disseminates computer security information and resources to help users, systems administrators, managers, and security professionals better protect their data and systems.

RSA DATA SECURITY, INC.

http://www.rsa.com

http://www.securitydynamics.com

A provider of encryption technologies, RSA's Web site offers a wealth of information on encryption and security matters. A particularly valuable resource is the RSA Laboratories' Frequently Asked Questions (FAQ) About Today's Cryptography, which can be found at *http://www.rsa.com/rsalabs/faq/*.

SECURE SHELL USER PAGES

http://www.ssh.org

A Web site devoted to Secure SHell, with links to a number of sites containing information and resources about Secure SHell.

S/WAN INITIATIVE

http://www.rsa.com/rsa/SWAN

RSA's S/WAN initiative is a consortium of leading vendors that are working together to demonstrate IPSec interoperability, in order to enable customers to mix and match the best firewall and TCP/IP stack products for building VPNs.

TOM DUNIGAN'S VPN PAGE

http://www.epm.ornl.gov/~dunigan/vpn.html
This Web page has a large number of links to resources on VPNs, security, encryption, etc.

TSIN dot COM

TSIN NEWS *http://www.tsin.com/tsinnews.html*
The Web site devoted to the ongoing development and implementation of Open Access Same Time Information Systems (OASIS).

THE UNOFFICIAL L2TP WEB PAGE

http://www.masinter.net/~l2tp
This Web page has links to all IETF Working Group L2TP drafts.

VPN CONSORTIUM

http://www.vpnc.org
The VPN Consortium is the newly established international trade association for manufacturers in the VPN market. It offers archives of the IPSec mailing list, tracing the development of the IPSec protocol, for as far back as 1992.

Glossary

AH (authentication header) In the IPSec protocol, the optional header that contains information for authenticating the data in the packet.

asymmetric encryption A system of encryption, sometimes referred to as public key encryption, that uses a pair of keys, one of which is a private key, the other of which is a public key that can be distributed to another user. There are two types of asymmetric encryption in wide use today (see *Diffie-Hellman encryption* and *RSA encryption*).

ATM (asynchronous transfer mode) An information transfer standard that is one of a general class of packet technologies. It supports higher speeds than frame relay and is used by many different information systems, including local area networks, to deliver traffic at varying rates, permitting a mix of voice, data, and video (multimedia).

authentication The process of proving the identity of any device that is attempting to build or use a virtual private network.

backbone The part of a network that acts as the primary path for traffic moving between, rather than within, networks.

bandwidth The data-carrying capacity of a network connection, used as an indication of speed.

bridge A device that passes packets between multiple network segments that are using the same communications protocol.

brute force attack An attack on a cryptosystem that uses a large amount of computing power in an attempt to test every possible key to find the right one.

certificate authority (CA) A system that manages encryption keys, so called because when it issues a key it issues at the same time a certificate that guarantees the validity of the key.

Challenge Handshake Authentication Protocol (CHAP) A user authentication protocol more secure than the standard *Password Authentication Protocol* (PAP). The authentication server sends the client program a key to be used to encrypt the username and password. This enables the username and password to be transmitted in an encrypted form to protect them against eavesdroppers.

circuit-switched network A network where a dedicated connection—a circuit—is established between point of origin and destination and all traffic between those points follows that route. The telephone network is an example of a circuit-switched network.

cryptanalysis The process of analyzing encrypted data with the goal of cracking the encryption and reading all the data.

cryptosystem A system for securing data from prying eyes. It consists of the process of authentication of the users of the system, encryption and decryption of the data, and verification of the integrity of the data.

datagram See *packet*.

Diffie-Hellman (DH) encryption An asymmetric encryption algorithm in which two parties exchange public keys, which are then used in conjunction with their respective private keys to generate a shared secret key for encryption/decryption of traffic between them.

digital signature A digest of a message, made by using a hashing function, which can be used to verify the integrity of the message.

DS-0, DS-1, DS-3 Standard telecommunications industry signal formats, which are distinguishable by bit rate (the number of binary digits transmitted per second). DS-0 transmits at 64 Kbps; DS-1 at 1.544 Mbps; and DS-3 at 45 Mbps. See also *T1* and *T3*.

DSL (digital subscriber line) Often abbreviated xDSL, ADSL, or RDSL, a digital subscriber line is a digital connection to your local telephone provider that provides higher-speed access to a data service than *ISDN* over standard copper telephone connections.

EDI (electronic data interchange) The general process of transmitting data through computer networks.

encapsulation Also referred to as *tunneling*, encapsulation is a process in which a new header is applied to a data packet so it can be routed through a network even though the packet's original header may contain a header for a different network protocol or addresses not acceptable to the transporting network.

encryption The process of disguising information in such a way as to hide its content, using any of a number of different encryption algorithms such as *RSA*, RC4, DES, etc.

encryption algorithms The computer "recipes" used to encrypt and decrypt data. They include Blowfish, CAST-64, CAST-80, CAST-128, RC2, RC4, RC5, DES, Triple-DES, *Diffie-Hellman*, and *RSA*. For detailed explanations of the various algorithms, RSA Data Security's Web site offers an extensive FAQ at *http://www.rsa.com /rsalabs/faq/.*

ESP (encapsulated security payload) In the IPSec protocol, the section of the packet that contains the payload, or data, usually, but not necessarily, in encrypted form.

extranet A network that permits access to information by outside organizations such as suppliers or customers.

firewall A system designed to prevent unauthorized access to or from a private network.

frame relay A high-speed, data packet switching service used to transmit data between computers. Frame relay supports data units of variable lengths at access speeds ranging from 56 Kbps to 1.5 Mbps.

FTP (File Transfer Protocol) A protocol used to transfer files over the Internet or IP-based networks.

GRE (Generic Routing Encapsulation) A protocol for performing encapsulation of one network protocol over another network protocol.

hash function A mathematical process that creates a digest of defined length of a message but that cannot easily be reversed to re-create the message.

hashing See *hash function.*

HTML (HyperText Markup Language) The document formatting language used for preparing documents to be viewed by a Web browser.

HTTP (HyperText Transport Protocol) The protocol that governs transmission of formatted documents such as Web pages over the Internet.

IANA (Internet Assigned Number Authority) The authority given the responsibility for assigning, among other things, IP addresses to those needing them on the Internet. Generally, blocks of numbers are assigned to ISPs, which then assign numbers within their blocks to their customers.

ICSA (International Computer Security Association) An independent company that provides security assurance services including suites for testing network security and certification of computer security products by testing them for effectiveness and interoperability.

IETF (Internet Engineering Task Force) The main standards organization for the Internet, open to any interested individual. The IETF is a large open international community of network designers, operators, vendors, and researchers concerned with the evolution of the Internet architecture and the smooth operation of the Internet.

IKE (Internet Key Exchange) See *ISAKMP/Oakley.*

intranet A company network in which access is restricted to users from within the organization.

IP (Internet Protocol) An Internet protocol that specifies the format of packets (datagrams) and the addressing scheme. Usually it is combined with *TCP* as TCP/IP.

IPSec (IP Security) An International Engineering Task Force (IETF) extension to the Internet Protocol (IP). It defines a suite of security protocols that authenticate TCP/IP connections, add data confidentiality and integrity to TCP/IP packets, and are transparent to the application. The IETF is in the process of developing this standard, which is detailed in IETF Requests for Comments (RFCs) 1825–1829.

ISAKMP/Oakley (Internet Security Association and Key Management Protocol/ Oakley) Now known as IKE, this public key management scheme is actually a hybrid protocol, integrating ISAKMP with the Oakley key exchange scheme. ISAKMP/ Oakley builds secure associations in multiprotocol environments and has very low overhead.

ISDN (Integrated Services Digital Network) An international communications standard for sending voice, video, and data over digital telephone lines. ISDN requires special metal wires and supports data transfer rates of 64 Kbps. Most ISDN lines offered by telephone companies give you two lines at once, called B channels. You can use one line for voice and the other for data, or you can use both lines for data to give you data rates of 128 Kbps.

ISP (Internet service provider) A company that provides access to the Internet. There are large ISPs, such as MCI, which offer Internet access all over the world, and there are small ISPs that may serve only a small town.

Kerberos An authentication system developed at the Massachusetts Institute of Technology (MIT). Kerberos is designed to enable two parties to exchange private information across an otherwise open network. It combines user authentication with key management on a session-by-session basis.

L2F (Layer 2 Forwarding) A tunneling protocol that Cisco Systems has submitted to the IETF as a proposed standard.

L2TP (Layer 2 Tunneling Protocol) A combination of L2F and Point-to-Point Tunneling Protocol (PPTP). Specifically, L2TP is designed to tunnel Point-to-Point Protocol (PPP) and Serial Line IP (SLIP) sessions over the Internet, operating at the data link layer of the OSI model. Similar to L2F, L2TP is targeted at the ISP market.

LAN (local area network) A network or group of network segments limited to one building or a campus.

LDAP (Lightweight Directory Access Protocol) A set of protocols for accessing information directories. LDAP is based on the standards contained within the X.500 standard but is significantly simpler and, unlike X.500, LDAP supports TCP/IP.

leased line A permanent telephone connection between two points, often used for data communications in a WAN.

local loop The connection between an end user and the local telephone exchange or point of presence *(POP)*.

MACs (message authentication codes) A method of verifying the integrity of data, similar to digital signatures.

man-in-the-middle attack An attack on a cryptosystem in which an unauthorized user impersonates a legitimate member of a cryptosystem to get in.

MPLS (Multi-Protocol Label Switching) A protocol under development by the IETF that is designed to provide a way of prioritizing Internet traffic in order to provide varying levels of quality of service. MPLS embodies some VPN features.

NAS (network access server) The computer that provides access to a network such as the Internet.

NIST (National Institute of Standards and Technology) A division of the U.S. Department of Commerce. NIST issues standards and guidelines that it hopes will be adopted by all computer systems in the United States. Official standards are published as FIPS (Federal Information Processing Standards) publications.

node The general term for devices that access a network.

NOS (network operating system)   An operating system that includes special functions for connecting computers and devices into a local area network (LAN). Novell's NetWare is a NOS, for example.

OEM (original equipment manufacturer)   A misleading term for a company that has a special relationship with computer producers. OEMs buy computers in bulk and customize them for a particular application. They then sell the customized computer under their own name. The term is really a misnomer because OEMs are not the original manufacturers—they are the customizers.

OSI (Open System Interconnection)   A framework used to describe the order in which protocols are implemented on networked systems.

OSPF (Open Shortest Path First)   A protocol that defines how routers share routing information. OSPF v.2 is defined in IETF RFC 1583. It is rapidly replacing the Routing Information Protocol *(RIP)* on the Internet.

packet   A block of electronic data with a header attached. The header indicates what the packet contains and, usually, where it originated and its destination.

packet-switched network   A communications network in which the information is broken down into packets and each packet is routed from point of origin to destination by switches or routers. The packets comprising a single message may take different routes to the destination. The Internet is a packet-switched network.

PAP (Password Authentication Protocol)   The most common form of user authentication, requiring the user to enter a username and password to gain access to a system.

peering   A relationship between two or more ISPs in which they create a link and agree to forward each other's packets directly across this link instead of using an Internet backbone.

perfect forward secrecy   A property of some cryptosystems in which keys are generated in such a way that they cannot easily be recovered or escrowed.

permanent virtual circuits   See *PVCs.*

PKCS (Public Key Cryptography Standards)   A set of standards, proposed in 1991, that were developed by RSA Data Security, Inc., to provide interoperability among encryption products as implemented by different vendors.

PKI   See *public key infrastructure.*

POP (point of presence)   A physical location where a network, usually the Internet, can be accessed.

PPP (Point-to-Point Protocol)   A data link protocol that provides dial-up access over serial lines. It is the protocol most commonly used for dial-up access to the Internet.

PPTP (Point-to-Point Tunneling Protocol)   A proposed VPN standard developed by Microsoft, 3Com, Ascend Communications, and several other vendors. PPTP encapsulates dial-up PPP traffic and is currently available for Windows NT servers and workstations, Windows 98, and also for Windows 95 workstations through an upgrade.

private key encryption   See *symmetric encryption.*

public key   An encryption key used in a public key or *asymmetric encryption* system, which can be exchanged with another user in an unprotected fashion.

public key encryption   See *asymmetric encryption.*

public key infrastructure (PKI)   A system of digital certificates, certificate authorities, and other registration authorities that verify and authenticate the validity of each party involved in an Internet transaction. Although various smaller PKIs exist, an overall PKI is under development at this time, with no single set of standards agreed upon as yet.

PVCs (permanent virtual circuits)   On frame relay networks, these are reserved connections that provide a guaranteed level of service between points.

RADIUS (Remote Authentication Dial-In User Service)   An authentication and accounting system used by many Internet service providers. When you enter your username and password, the information is passed to a RADIUS server, which checks that the information is correct and then authorizes access to the network, system, or VPN. Although not an official standard, the RADIUS specification is maintained by a working group of the IETF.

RAS   See *remote access server.*

rekeying   The process of issuing new encryption keys during a communication session, done to limit the amount of data encrypted by a given key.

remote access server (RAS)   A device that handles multiple incoming calls from remote users who need access to central network resources.

RIP (Routing Information Protocol)   A protocol that specifies how routers exchange routing table information. With RIP, routers periodically exchange entire tables. RIP is being replaced by a newer protocol called Open Shortest Path First *(OSPF).*

router   A device that connects two networks, similar to a *bridge*, that is able to filter and direct messages by various criteria—usually by IP address—in accordance with its routing tables.

RSA (Rivest Shamir Adleman) encryption   Along with *Diffie-Hellman* (DH), one of the two leading asymmetric encryption systems.

RSVP (Resource Reservation Setup Protocol)   A new Internet protocol that is being developed to enable the Internet to support specified levels of quality of service (QoS). See also *MPLS.*

SA (security association)   Under *IKE,* a security association is an agreement reached between two parties on encryption and authentication algorithms and keys so that those two parties can exchange information securely.

Secure SHell (SSH)   A replacement for programs such as rlogin that provides VPN features for secure connections with a remote server.

server   A computer or software program that provides services to clients such as file storage (file server), programs (application server), printer sharing (print server), fax (fax server), or modem sharing (modem server).

SHA (Secure Hash Algorithm)   A hash function developed by the federal government. SHA-1 is an upgrade that addressed the original algorithm's weaknesses. It is part of the NIST's Secure Hash Standard (SHS).

shared secret key   Usually used in reference to *Diffie-Hellman* encryption, this is an encryption key shared by both users for encrypting and decrypting their messages.

SKIP (Simple Key Management for Internet Protocol)   A public key management scheme, SKIP is optimized for client connections to a remote network and does not require the exchange of messages used by *IKE*.

SLIP (Serial Line IP)   A data link protocol for dial-up access to TCP/IP networks. It is commonly used to gain access to the Internet as well as to provide dial-up access between two LANs. PPP is more commonly used today for Internet access than is SLIP.

sniffer   A program and/or device that monitors data traveling over a network.

SNMP (Simple Network Management Protocol)   A set of protocols for managing complex networks.

SOCKS v.5   A protocol for handling *TCP* traffic through a proxy server. Version 5 adds authentication features, which allows it to offer VPN services not available in v.4.

Sun.NET   A Java-based VPN protocol from Sun Microsystems.

switch   A device that forwards packets to the appropriate port for the intended recipient.

symmetric encryption   An encryption scheme that uses the same secret key both to encrypt and decrypt the data.

T1   A 1.544 Mbps connection to the Internet. A T1 line actually consists of 24 individual channels, each of which supports 64 Kbps. Each 64 Kbps channel can be configured to carry voice or data traffic. Most telephone companies allow you to buy just some of these individual channels, known as fractional T1 access.

T3   The same as a DS-3 line, this is a dedicated phone connection supporting data rates of about 45 Mbps. A T3 line actually consists of 672 individual channels, each of which supports 64 Kbps. T3 lines are used mainly by Internet service providers that are connecting to the Internet backbone and for the backbone itself.

TACACS (Terminal Access Controller Access Control System)   A remote authentication and accounting communications protocol similar to RADIUS.

TCP (Transmission Control Protocol)   This protocol lets two hosts establish a connection and exchange streams of data. TCP guarantees delivery of data and also guarantees that packets will be delivered in the same order in which they were sent.

Tunneling   A method by which packets are encapsulated within a protocol by means of the addition of a header that is understood by the transporting network's routers and switches. For example, an IPX packet is encapsulated for transport over the Internet by adding an IP header that is read by the Internet's routers.

UDP (User Datagram Protocol)   UDP, like TCP, runs on top of IP networks. UDP provides very few error recovery services, offering instead a direct way to send and receive datagrams over an IP network. It's used primarily for broadcasting messages over a network.

verification   A process by which data that has been received is checked to make sure it is the same as the data that was sent.

VPN (virtual private network) A private network that uses a public network's infrastructure.

WAN (wide area network) A network that connects dispersed buildings or campuses, usually over a large distance.

World Wide Web Consortium (W3C) An international consortium of companies involved with the Internet and the Web. The organization's purpose is to develop open standards so that the Web evolves in a single direction rather than being splintered among competing factions. The W3C is the chief standards body for *HTTP* and *HTML*.

X.500 An ISO and ITU standard that defines how global directories should be structured. X.500 directories are hierarchical with different levels for each category of information, such as country, state, and city. See also *LDAP*.

X.509 The most widely used standard for defining digital certificates. X.509 is actually an International Telecommunications Union (ITU) recommendation, which means that it has not yet been officially defined or approved. As a result, the standard has been implemented in different ways. For example, both Netscape and Microsoft use X.509 certificates to implement Secure Sockets Layer (SSL) in their Web servers and browsers. But an X.509 certificate generated by Netscape may not be readable by Microsoft products and vice versa.

Bibliography

Ascend Communications, Inc. "Ascend Resource Guide VPN Cost Savings Analysis for the Enterprise" (white paper). Alameda, CA: 1997.

Automotive Industry Action Group. "The Business Case for ANX Service" (white paper). Southfield, MI: 1998.

Aventail Corporation. "SOCKS v.5" (white paper). Seattle: 1997–1998.

Cavanagh, James P. *Frame Relay Applications.* San Francisco: Morgan Kaufmann; 1998.

Check Point Software Technologies. "Virtual Private Network Security Components" (technical white paper). Redwood City, CA: 1998.

Cisco Systems. "Access VPN: Making a Case for Access VPNs" (white paper). San Jose, CA: August 17, 1998.
http://www.cisco.com/warp/public/779/servpro/solutions/vpn/avpn_bc.htm

Cisco Systems. "IP VPN Frequently Asked Questions" (white paper). San Jose, CA: August 11, 1998.
http://www.cisco.com/warp/public/779/servpro/solutions/vpn/ipvpn_qp.htm

Cisco Systems. "Layer 2 Tunneling Protocol: A Feature in Cisco IOS Software" (white paper). San Jose, CA: August 17, 1998.
http://www.cisco.com/warp/public/732/l2tp/l2tun_ds.htm

Cisco Systems. "L2TP Questions and Answers" (white paper). San Jose, CA: August 29, 1998.
http://www.cisco.com/warp/public/732/l2tp/l2tp_qp.htm

Compaq Digital Products and Services. "Digital AltaVista Tunnel 98" (white paper). Maynard, MA: March 31, 1998.
http://www.digital.com/info/CU7403/CU7403HM.HTM

Dutcher, William. "Reining in Remote Access: RADIUS and TACACS Compete to Bring Better Control Over Dial-up Access." *PC Week:* August 13, 1997.

Feldman, Jonathan. "SOCKS v.5: The UnFirewall." *Network Computing Online:* March 15, 1998.
http://www.nwc.com/905/905ws13.html

Frame Relay Forum. "The Basic Guide to Frame Relay Networking" (white paper). Fremont, CA: January 4, 1999.
http://www.frforum.com

IBM International Technical Support Organization. *A Comprehensive Guide to Virtual Private Networks. Volume I: IBM Firewall, Server, and Client Solutions.* Poughkeepsie, NY: IBM; 1998.
http://www.redbooks.ibm.com/SG245201/sg240002.html#HDRFIGLIST_START

IBM. "Prudential Implements $100 Million Networking Initiative: 12,000 Field Associates Will Access E-Business System Using IBM ThinkPads and IBM Consulting Assistance" (press release). Poughkeepsie, NY: 1998.
http://domino.www.ibm.com/Press/prnews.nsf/Contacts
/DB4F0A8F3FFA29A585256616006B996B?OpenDocument

Infonetics Research, Inc. "Virtual Private Networks: A Partnership Between Service Providers and Network Managers" (white paper). San Jose, CA: 1997.

Karvé, Anita. "Tutorials: Network Management. Lesson 115: IP Security: Security Extensions to IP Bring Authentication and Privacy to the Internet." *Network Magazine:* February 1998.

King, Christopher. "Web-Access Authentication Using RADIUS: An Intermediate Method for Secure Exchanges on the Web." *Web Techniques:* June 1996.

Masica, Ken. "SKIP Your Way to Security." *SunWorld:* June 1997.

NEC Laboratory Systems, Inc. "SOCKS v.5 Border Control Framework" (white paper). Melville, NY: 1998.

Neil, Stephanie. "Deciphering SLAs: Service Level Guarantees Can Differentiate a Good ISP, but Read the Fine Print." *PC Week Online:* July 13, 1998.

Neuman, B. Clifford, and Ts'o, Theodore. "Kerberos: An Authentication Service for Computer Networks" (USC/ISI Technical Report number ISI/RS-94-399). *IEEE Communications Magazine:* September 1994.

Pang, Albert. "Performance Guarantees Keep ISPs Competitive: Service Level Agreements Buttress Performance." *Internet Computing:* June 1, 1998.

Rickard, Jack. "Backbone Performance Measurements Measuring the Internet." *Boardwatch:* September 1998.

Schneier, Bruce. *Applied Cryptography, 2nd ed.* New York: John Wiley & Sons; 1996.

Schneier, Bruce. "Frequently Asked Questions: Microsoft's PPTP Implementation" (white paper). Minneapolis, MN: Counterpane Systems; 1998.
http://www.counterpane.com/pptp-faq.html

Schneier, Bruce, and Mudge, P. "Cryptanalysis of Microsoft's Point-to-Point Tunneling Protocol (PPTP)" (white paper). Minneapolis, MN: Counterpane Systems; 1998.
http://www.counterpane.com/pptp.html

Sullebarger, Bob. "Frame Relay: The LAN in the WAN. Part I." *Communications News:* May 1998.

Sullebarger, Bob. "Frame Relay: The LAN in the WAN. Part II." *Communications News:* June 1998.

TimeStep Corporation. "The Business Case for Secure VPNs" (white paper). Herndon, VA: 1997.

TimeStep Corporation. "Understanding the IPSec Protocol Suite" (white paper). Herndon, VA: 1997.

Tolles, Chris. "SKIP Encryption." *UNIX Review:* August 1998.

Windows NT Server Product Team. "PPTP Security: An Update." *Microsoft Windows NT Server Market Bulletin:* June 1998.

Index